THOMAS MERTON'S
Paradise Journey

—

Writings on CONTEMPLATION

—

William H. Shannon

BURNS & OATES

ST. ANTHONY MESSENGER PRESS

Cincinnati, Ohio

This book is a substantial revision of *Thomas Merton's Dark Path: The Inner Experience of a Contemplative* by William H. Shannon, ©1981.

First published in Great Britain in 2000 by Burns & Oates, Wellwood, North Farm Road, Tunbridge Wells, Kent TN2 3DR

ISBN (Burns & Oates) 0 86012 309 X

Cover design by Mary Alfieri
Cover photo by Sibylle Akers, reprinted with permission of the Abbey of Gethsemani. Colorization by Constance Wolfer.
Photo on page iv by John Howard Griffin, reprinted with permission of Robert Bonazzi and Elizabeth Griffin-Bonazzi.

Book design by Sandy L. Digman
Electronic pagination and format by Sandy L. Digman

ISBN 0-86716-348-8

Published by St. Anthony Messenger Press
Printed in the U.S.A.

Contents

Introduction   1

PART ONE

Early Writings on Contemplation

Chapter 1: What Is Contemplation?   25

Chapter 2: Seeds of Contemplation   43

Chapter 3: The Ascent to Truth   65

PART TWO

The Inner Landscape of Contemplation: Solitude

Chapter 4: Thoughts in Solitude *and "Notes for*   89
              a Philosophy of Solitude"

PART THREE

Later Writings on Contemplation

Chapter 5: The Inner Experience   113

Chapter 6: New Seeds of Contemplation   153

Chapter 7: The Climate of Monastic Prayer   183
              (*a.k.a.* Contemplative Prayer)

Chapter 8: Zen and the Birds of Appetite   209
              (With Some Reflections on
              Merton's Asian Journey)

PART FOUR

The Outer Landscape of Contemplation: The World

Chapter 9: Is the World a Problem?   245

Conclusion   277

Appendix   287

Works Cited   293

Index   297

> "**O**ur real journey in life is interior: it is a matter of growth, deepening and an ever greater surrender to the creative action of love and grace in our hearts."
>
> —Thomas Merton,
> *The Road to Joy*

Introduction

There is in us an instinct for newness, for renewal, for a liberation of creative power. We seek to awaken in ourselves a force which really changes our lives from within. And yet the same instinct tells us that this change is a recovery of that which is deepest, most original, most personal in ourselves.[1]

"America is discovering the contemplative life." Thus wrote Thomas Merton toward the end of his best-seller autobiography, *The Seven Storey Mountain*. I believe it is fair to say that these words proved to be prophetic: They represent one way of describing America (and perhaps other parts of the world, too) in the last half of the twentieth century. But the first half of the century was a different story. Contemplation was not then a familiar word nor had it been for several centuries in the Christian world.

I remember the year *The Seven Storey Mountain* was published. It was 1948. I was a young Roman Catholic priest, ordained five years. Contemplation, I can assure you, was not a word in my working vocabulary. I certainly had read about it. I knew about Saint John of the Cross and his lofty climb up Mount Carmel. I had also read about Saint Teresa of Avila and her glorious interior castle; but it never really dawned on me that that castle was a place for me to enter or the climb up Mount Carmel a journey that I could make. It was *The Seven Storey Mountain* and other Merton works that would follow that convinced me that contemplation might just be a possibility for me and for the people to whom I ministered as a priest. For me this was a wonderful awakening to a new dimension of human existence. It brought me a totally new perspective on how I was to live my life. It also enabled me to see that I might introduce others to a similar awakening that would offer them new insights—insights they had never dreamed of before—into the way they were called to live their lives. I don't for a minute mean to imply that contemplation became for me (or could become for anyone else) a solution to all the problems life brings. In fact, Merton would want to tell us that contemplation is not a solution to anything. It is something much more significant: It offers us a way of life, which may help us to see that most of the problems we wrestle with are pseudo-problems. Contemplation brings depth to a life that, without it, can only be shallow and superficial. It offers a sense of the authentically real to a human existence that otherwise would be lived only on the level of the artificial. It introduces an intuition of unity and simplicity into human lives that, without the contemplative dimension, are bound to be complex and fragmented.

Yet contemplation is not a self-induced experience. It is a gift of God that we have to be open to receive. If we seek contemplation, Merton would tell us, we will probably never find it; but if we dare open our heart to our own inner truth and to God's grace, contemplation may enter our lives unobserved. Then, perhaps for the first time, we will know who we are and in knowing ourselves we will know God; for it is God, Merton would say, who holds within the divine Self the secret of our own identity.

This book is written with the conviction that contemporary men and women in large numbers are searching for a greater interiority in their lives. Unhappy with an existence of "bread and circuses" lived merely on the surface of reality, they are increasingly looking inward to their own depths to find purpose and direction in their lives. Such people are ready for the contemplative experience, and Thomas Merton's writings on contemplation can help them move in that direction.

This is my second time around in tracing the development of Merton's understanding of contemplation. This book is an extensive revision of my very first book about Thomas Merton which was entitled *Thomas Merton's Dark Path*. It is a completely new edition of a book which I wrote in the first flush of a budding friendship with Merton: a friendship built solely through reading his works, as I never had the opportunity of meeting him. By the time I came to study his writings in earnest and reached a point where I felt able and eager to write a book about him, he was no longer writing about contemplation. He was experiencing it in its fullness. My book appeared in 1981; he had already disappeared into God in his strange accidental death in Bangkok on December 10, 1968.

Because this book is an extensive revision of my earlier work (with numerous changes and additions), I decided to give it a new title: *Thomas Merton's Paradise Journey*. It is an appropriate title, as "paradise" is a favorite theme in Merton's writings about contemplation. The original blessing God gave to his human creatures was the gift of paradise: a place of unity, harmony and contemplative joy. In paradise, God's human creatures were exactly what God intended them to be. There was perfect communication between them and God. They looked out upon the world of creation and saw reality as it truly was. The fall was a fall from unity and harmony into a condition of separateness and alienation. But, more than that, it involved a willful acceptance of unreality. Illusion entered into the picture to disrupt human communion with God. As Merton writes in *The New Man*: "Adam, stripped of his sincerity, ashamed to be what in fact he was, determined to fly from God and from reality, which he could no longer face without a disguise."[2]

The human story after the fall is the long arduous journey back to paradise. The way of that journey is contemplation. It is an interior journey, whereby we journey into our own depths and discover our true self and discover it in God. Just before he set out for Asia, Merton wrote to his friends: "Our real journey in life is interior: it is a matter of growth, deepening and an ever greater surrender to the creative action of love and grace in our hearts."[3] We journey toward paradise; yet in a sense we are already in paradise, because we are always in God. It is not enough, however, simply to state that we are in God. This is what we have to experience and can only experience in God's gift of contemplation. As Merton puts it:

> Paradise has been lost insofar as we have become involved in complexity and wound up in ourselves so that we are estranged from our own freedom and our own simplicity. Paradise cannot be opened to us except by a free gift of the divine mercy. *Yet it is true to say that Paradise is always present within us, since God Himself is present, though perhaps inaccessible.*[4]

The deep anguish in the human heart is its need to experience this union with God. For we never quite lose the divine image in which we were made. In Merton's words:

> The human soul is still the image of God, and no matter how far it travels away from Him into the regions of unreality, it never becomes so completely unreal that its original destiny can cease to torment it with a need to return to itself in God, and become, once again, real.[5]

One of the goals I hope to achieve in this book is to track Merton's discovery of contemplation. I want to show how coming to understand contemplation was an ongoing endeavor in his life: from his early eager desire to share with others all he had learned about contemplation to the point much later in his life when he began to feel that he ought to stop "spinning a lot of words about life or God or prayer," as he wrote to Mother Angela Collins in December of 1966. He went on to tell her: "I feel in fact immensely poor and fallible...I don't really want to write much about 'spiritual things'...I have gradually developed a sort of nausea for talking about it. Except when I really have to."[6] Notice how he left himself a loophole: the times he *had* to write about contemplation. Actually he could not keep away from the topic. He kept writing about it to the very end. In fact, at the very time he wrote these words to Mother Angela, he was in process of preparing *The Climate of Monastic Prayer* for publication!

In his autobiography, Thomas Merton tells the story of his own discovery of the contemplative life. How clearly he understood the meaning of contemplation in 1948 when *The Seven Storey Mountain* was published is not easy to judge. Speaking of his days at Columbia just before his reception into the Catholic Church, he remembers how he was able to talk learnedly about the experiential knowledge of God, "and all the while I was stoking the fires of the argument with Scotch and soda."[7] He writes amusedly about his first reading of the *Spiritual Directory*. It was the book that was to tell him about the meaning of Trappist life. He read it while he was still in the guesthouse at Gethsemani Abbey, waiting to be admitted to the novitiate.

> [T]here were some cautious words about mystical contemplation which, I was told, was "not required" but which God sometimes "vouchsafed." That word "vouchsafe"! It almost sounded as if the grace came to you dressed up in a crinoline. In fact, to my way of interpreting it, when a spiritual book tells you that "infused contemplation is sometimes vouchsafed," the idea you are supposed to get is this: "infused contemplation is all right for the saints, but as for *you*: hands off!" ...If God wanted to do any of this "vouchsafing," He could go ahead and "vouchsafe."[8]

Writing in 1942, when he was but a short time in the monastery, Merton ventured the opinion: "Our [Cistercian] monasteries produce very few pure contemplatives. The life is too active.... [At Gethsemani] there is an almost exaggerated reverence for work.... It goes by the name of "active contemplation."[9] He wonders whether this is really contemplation at all.

The most extensive references to "contemplation" in *The Seven Storey Mountain* come in a section near the end of the book (pages 414-419) which was originally an article written for *Commonweal* that got inserted into the book at the last moment. The article was entitled "Active and Contemplative Orders."[10] It deals with the difference between religious communities which engage in ministries outside the community and those who lead a cloistered life. It seems to conclude that the life of pure contemplation is *per se* the highest vocation, though agreeing with Thomas Aquinas that the "mixed life" (which includes contemplation overflowing into acts of love that communicate what it knows about God to other people) is, in the practical order, actually superior to one or the other considered separately. This entire matter, so seriously discussed in spiritual literature at the time, seems today a rather sterile and impractical topic, based as it is on a dualism that separates God from God's creation. Such a dualism Merton gradually moved away from, as his understanding of contemplation developed and deepened.

After all, when *The Seven Storey Mountain* was published, he was a young monk, with only seven monastic years behind him and twenty more years to come. Those ensuing years would witness a maturing of his understanding of contemplation, as well as of a number of other things. Understanding would grow out of experience and experience would be articulated in writing. During the twenty years following *The Seven Storey Mountain*, he poured out many words about contemplation without ever feeling that what he said was adequate to describe the reality. The experience of contemplation, as he realized more and more, cannot be captured in words.

Yet words were his "trade." He had to write. He was a born writer. In the first volume of the Merton journals, *Run to the Mountain*, he asks himself: "Why do I write so much about things about which I know so little?"[11] Setting aside the modesty implicit in the question (he often did know what he was talking about), one is tempted to answer: "Because you can't control your pen! Once it gets on a roll you simply cannot stop it. You have ink in your veins."

A versatile writer interested in many areas of the human condition, Merton felt compelled to write on a wide variety of subjects, as his reading, reflection and dialogue continually expanded the horizons of his interests and concerns. He was a generalist rather than a specialist, his ready pen moving easily from one subject to another. He could write apocalyptic poems about the catastrophic state of world affairs (like the "Original Child Bomb"[12]) or a simple reflective poem about a little girl's drawing ("Grace's House"[13]). He could discourse on the renewal of monastic life in the twentieth century[14] and on the threats of civil strife and international warfare in an age of unrest and social upheaval.[15] He could correspond happily with a young high school girl in California[16] and as easily with the German psychoanalyst Erich Fromm[17] or the Polish poet Czeslaw Milosz.[18] He was in no sense a narrow man; and as his reading fed his inquisitive mind, his writing struck off in many directions. He was an enthusiast who would take up a subject, read all he could find about it, filter it through his rich background, get to the heart of an issue (often at least) and then offer his readers the fruits of his reading and reflection. Yet, if one takes a broad look at his writings, it can be said, I think, that contemplation was the explicit theme, or at least the implied background, of most everything that Merton wrote. It was the cloud by day and the fire by night.

To use a helpful analogy from the photographic art of which he was so fond, Merton viewed the world through a wide-angle lens, encompassing a wide field of vision. Yet it is the intent of this book to suggest that frequently on the camera through which he viewed reality there was a telephoto lens that focused sharply on a single subject— contemplation. Contemplation was not one of many topics in Merton's field of vision, it was the focal point: the point he frequently and regularly "zoomed in" on. It was the *point vierge*[19] he speaks of in *Conjectures of a Guilty Bystander*, the center from which his reflections on the human condition came forth and the goal to which they returned.

Contemplation was at the center of his thinking about God and about prayer. It was also the starting point of his anthropology. Merton sees the story of the fall from paradise in Genesis as mythologizing the alienation we all experience in our existence. For Merton it is a fall from the contemplative state:[20] women and men experience a fragmentation of the human spirit and the loss of their original unity with God, with one another, with all humanity and indeed with all the cosmos.

Contemplation is also the key to Merton's understanding of redemption. Redemption is the return to the paradisal state. It is the recovery of the original unity that characterized the human condition as God intended and intends us to be. It is the overcoming of all that alienates us from God, from our own true selves and from our fellow human beings. The way back to paradise and to original unity is the road of contemplation.

In all his writings, whether he speaks explicitly of contemplation or not, Merton never forgot the primacy of what Mircea Eliade calls "the eternal return": the return to God and to integral unity, a return effected in this life by contemplation. In his poem "The Captives—A Psalm," which appears in *The Tears of the Blind Lions*, Merton writes:

> May my bones burn and ravens eat my flesh
> If I forget thee, contemplation.[21]

The Tears of the Blind Lions was published in 1949, the year which also saw the publication of *Seeds of Contemplation*—a series of *pensées* on contemplation that achieved instant popularity. (Merton would revise it extensively in 1962 as *New Seeds of Contemplation*.) A year earlier, Merton had written a booklet called *What Is Contemplation?*, which was later to be considerably expanded as *The Inner Experience*. One of his last books, prepared for publication before he left for his trip to the East, but published after his death, was *The Climate of Monastic Prayer*, also published under the title *Contemplative Prayer*. The twenty years that elapsed between the publication of *What Is Contemplation?* and *Contemplative Prayer* witnessed an abundance of books and articles that dealt in one way or another with the contemplative experience. He did indeed remain faithful to the promise he made in his poem: to never forget contemplation.

Though in his earlier writings Merton links contemplation with Baptism and always remained, in a Christian context, faithful to this intuition, nonetheless, his growing appreciation of Eastern religions, especially Zen, opened his mind to the realization that true contemplation does exist outside the Christian setting. Contemplation, he came to see, was a way of life to which human persons are called by virtue of their humanity. It is not a uniquely Christian phenomenon. Whether the Christian contemplative experience is the same as the Zen satori experience is another matter, and a question that Merton never completely resolved. At times he seems to distinguish them; at other times he seems to identify them as experiences, though his articulation of the experience as a Christian theologian would differ from, say, D. T. Suzuki's articulation of the experience as a Zen master. Each would describe the experience in terms consonant with the religious tradition to which he subscribed. But whether the experiences are identical or not and however they are to be described, Merton certainly came to believe that the contemplative experience existed outside the parameters of the Christian community.

If he believed that the Christian call to contemplation is an invitation extended to all, he was equally convinced that acceptance of that invitation called for a willingness to undergo the necessary discipline that it requires. For this reason, he sees the monastic environment as the ideal locus for developing and living the contemplative experience. For the monastic life is the experience of the desert where one goes to seek God alone and finds sufficiency only in God. This sense of total dependence on God, a necessary prerequisite for contemplation, is more easily achieved in a monastic setting. The monastic life more easily provides the solitude, without which the contemplative spirit cannot flourish. Merton's ongoing struggle to achieve deeper solitude even in the monastic life indicates the importance he attached to solitude as the atmosphere in which contemplation can flower.

In fact, the early Merton (say up to the mid-1950's) seems to come very close to an elitist view of the contemplative life. For while he believed that God manifests himself to all who love him, he seemed to feel that the discipline and solitude essential to contemplation simply could not be achieved "in the world." People who live in the world and unite themselves to God in the activities of their lives may very well have an extremely simple prayer life that brings them to the "threshold of contemplation."[22] But it is difficult, if not very nearly impossible, for them to cross that threshold into the realms of true contemplation. Merton describes such persons as "quasi-contemplatives" or "hidden contemplatives."[23] Their sanctity may well surpass that of the cloistered monk; nonetheless, the doors of contemplation open to them only with the greatest difficulty.[24]

This distinction between "real" contemplatives and "hidden contemplatives" betrays, I believe, a certain inconsistency in Merton. At any rate it is a distinction that he does not stress: It occurs only in *What Is Contemplation?* and in the rewrite of that work, *The Inner Experience*. Perhaps truer to his understanding of contemplation is the distinction he draws between those who are *juridically* contemplatives (namely, contemplatives by their vocation, i.e., monastics[25]) and those who are contemplatives in the world.

In the long run, neither of these distinctions, it seems to me, matters a great deal. For people who are not monastics take what Merton said (whether he was speaking to them or to monks) and quite comfortably adapt it to their lives. This is a part—and a healthy part, I believe—of the Merton phenomenon: people whose lives are far removed from the cloister are convinced that he is writing to them. What he says strikes a responsive chord in them and in their lives. In fact, it is probably true to say that Merton's largest reading public is made up of non-monastics rather than people who live in monasteries.

Merton sees the contemplative experience as an experience of oneness and transcendent unity. The quaint translation of Julian of Norwich puts it this way: "Prayer oneth the soul to God." But, at the same time, it "oneth" the soul to itself. Contemplation brings together the scattered bits of one's person and unifies them in the intuition of the real self. This inner unity makes possible a simultaneous intuition of one's unity with God and with all the creatures he has made. Achieving such unity in the midst of an alienated world calls for much solitude and detachment. Silence and self-discipline, therefore, are necessary preliminaries to opening oneself to the unifying forces that the Spirit of God exercises on the human spirit.

The unity achieved in the contemplative way of life transcends all philosophical and theological systems, even creedal statements, that may attempt to express that unity. To use William James's terms, the experience is noetic (the contemplative knows something he or she did not know before), yet ineffable (she or he cannot articulate in any satisfactory way what has been experienced). "The one who knows does not speak; the one who speaks, (often) does not know." As Merton puts it:

> The God who in a certain sense is "known" in the articles of faith is "known as unknown" beyond those articles. One might even say, with some of the Fathers of the Church, that while our concepts may tell us that "God is," our knowledge of God beyond those concepts is a knowledge of Him "as though He were not," since His being is not accessible to us in direct experience.[26]

The Kataphatic and Apophatic Traditions

Knowing God through concepts (knowing that "God is") and knowing God beyond concepts (knowing God "as though he were not") suggest the two theological traditions that have attempted to express the contemplative experience: the kataphatic tradition and the apophatic. Both these traditions help us to realize the utter inadequacy of human words to speak about God. For God is mystery. All the knowledge we have about God comes from some *human* experience of that mystery. We have no divine language, only a human language. This means that *the words we possess are only able to express the human experience, not the divine reality experienced*. It is for this reason that all our language about God is metaphorical. We use words as much and as well as we can. This is the way of the kataphatic tradition. But after we have used all the words we can, we have to say: but they are so feeble and inadequate. They hardly express the divine reality at all. At this point we are beginning to move toward the apophatic way.

Thus, the kataphatic tradition is the tradition of light; it arrives at an understanding of God through affirmation (the Greek word *kataphasis* means "affirmation"). We come to know about God by affirming that he possesses all the perfections we find in creatures, and, more than that, that she[27] possesses them to the highest possible degree. Kataphatic articulation of the contemplative experience makes use of symbols drawn from the created order to describe the reality of God. The goodness and beauty of what is finite help us to affirm the goodness and the beauty of what is infinite. Kataphatic theology proceeds by way of analogy. The experiences of fatherhood, of motherhood, of goodness, of justice, of compassion in a human context— which are our experiences of created being—serve as windows whereby we look out through the created world to the reality of God. These experiences are used analogically to tell us something about God. Analogy is at the heart of all our theological language. When we use analogy we apply a term to two realities, expressing something that exists in both realities, but in different ways. In other words, the two realities are similar with regard to this term, but also dissimilar. Let me use an example of analogy that appeared in my book *Silence on Fire*:

> Suppose you have a friend whose name is Bertha. She is married, has several children. Nothing seems too much for her to do for her husband and children. As a matter of fact, you might feel that she carries her devotion too far. You might even say: "Bertha is a slave to her family." Now

when you say that you are using analogy. You are saying that there is something about Bertha that is similar to what you think is true of a slave. Slaves belong to their masters in the totality of their lives: their actions, their time, their movements are all in the master's control. Bertha appears to be similar to the slave in that she seems to belong so totally to her family.... But there are significant differences between Bertha and the slave. The slave belongs totally to the master, not by choice but by a necessity imposed upon the slave. Bertha's total gift of herself to her family, on the other hand, is a free decision that she makes herself. It is not necessity but love and unselfish dedication that move her to spend herself for her husband and children.[28]

I think you can see the point of this analogy. Bertha in some ways is like a slave (there is some similarity), but in many more important ways she is not like a slave (there is dissimilarity). Analogy is the only way we can speak about God. Hence every similarity between God and creatures (as when we say: God is wise, compassionate, just, merciful) must be understood to include an even greater dissimilarity (for example, the wisdom of God is unlike human wisdom, for it infinitely surpasses human wisdom). The Fourth Lateran Council expressed this truth very concisely: "Between creator and creature no similarity can be found so great but that the dissimilarity is not even greater."[29]

Thus kataphatic theology, which proceeds by way of analogy, can only tell us *about God or about what God does*. It cannot penetrate to God's deepest essence, the divine life itself. For no created symbol, however deeply experienced, can adequately mirror the reality of God. They tell us so little about God. It's like looking at the universe through the windows of your home. No matter how many windows you may have in your home, the view of the universe you get through them is pretty skimpy. There is too much of the universe that we simply do not know: What we don't know is much greater than what we do know. This applies in an infinitely greater sense to God. Our knowledge of God is so meager that we could appropriately say we simply do not know God.

Some readers may remember a television show of some years ago, called, if I remember correctly, *The Millionaire*. It had to do with the Beresford-Tipton estate and its philanthropist who each week gave a million dollars to someone in need. His representative would come to him at the proper time. The millionaire would tell him about the person who was to be the beneficiary that week and then direct him to give that person a million dollars. The rest of the story told how the million dollars was used. One of the fascinating elements of the story was that, while you saw what he did for others, you never saw the millionaire face to face. You got to see only his back. In the Bible seeing the face of God is a synonym for experiencing the divine presence. It is an appropriate symbol. For when we meet someone it is the person's face that makes him or her most immediately present to us. The psalms express a longing to see the face of God. Yet it is a biblical dictum that no one can see the face of God. There is a dramatic scene in Chapter 33 of Exodus. Moses asks to see "the glory of God." But he is told he cannot see God's face. God says to him: "[W]hile my glory passes by, I will put you in a cleft of the rock, and I will cover you with my hand until I have passed by; then I will take away my hand, and you shall see my back; but my face shall not be seen" (Exodus 33:22-23). To see God's face would be to know God in God's divine being. This we cannot do. We can see the things God has done. But at best we can only see God's back. That is why there has always been in the Christian mystical tradition a strong apophatic element.

Apophaticism is the contemplative tradition of darkness and negation (the Greek word *apophasis* means "negation" or "denial"). Apophaticism is an essential step in the truly contemplative experience. For there comes a point in the life of the would-be contemplative when concepts and images will no longer do; indeed, they become a hindrance to the deep experience of God. While it is true that all creatures bear in themselves the imprint of God, there is, nonetheless, an infinite distance between God and created things. One simply cannot enter through creatures into the presence of God in

God's own being. Hence, sooner or later, the contemplative must renounce the mind's activity, put out the light of the intellect, and enter into the darkness, wherein there is an "experience" of the ineffable reality of what is beyond experience. The presence of God is "known," not in clear vision, but as "unknown." (Lest the reader get discouraged and doubt the use of God-talk at all, I wish at this point to offer, by way of encouragement, an insight—to be developed later—that the bridge between the kataphatic way and the apophatic is love. The God our minds cannot grasp can be "known" by the human heart, which, as Pascal has said "has its reasons which reason cannot know." But this is to anticipate.)

The apophatic way has a long history in the Christian mystical tradition. It is the way of Gregory of Nyssa, Pseudo-Dionysius, Meister Eckhart, John of the Cross, and many others. It is also the way of Thomas Merton. He writes in *Contemplation in a World of Action*:

> The Christian contemplative is aware that in the mystical tradition both of the Eastern and Western Churches there is a strong element of what has been called "apophatic theology." This apophatic tradition concerns itself with the most fundamental datum of all faith—and one which is often forgotten; the God who has revealed Himself to us in His Word has revealed himself as unknown in His ultimate essence, for He is beyond all mere human vision. "You cannot see my face; no man shall see me and live" (Exodus 33:20).[30]

Merton never denied the value of the kataphatic approach to God, but he was strongly convinced that ultimately it must yield place to apophaticism. Thus he writes:

> Now, while the Christian contemplative must certainly develop by study, the theological understanding of concepts about God, he is called mainly to penetrate the wordless darkness and apophatic light of an experience beyond concepts, and here he gradually becomes familiar with a God who is "absent" and as it were "non-existent" to all human experience.[31]

Apophaticism thrives on paradoxical expressions. Thus Merton, in the above quotation, speaks of the "wordless darkness" that is "apophatic light." In apophatic contemplation, God is "experienced" as "a dazzling darkness" or as "the brightness of a most lucid darkness." The author of the *Cloud of Unknowing*, who ardently espoused the apophatic way, speaks of two clouds: "the cloud of forgetfulness" that one must put between himself and creatures (and creatures would include concepts and images) and "the cloud of unknowing" that one must enter into to find God in a totally ineffable experience. In contemplation, God is known in darkness, that is, by not knowing him. God is sought and is found through not finding him. In a taped lecture given in one of his Sunday sessions with the novices of Gethsemani, Merton quotes Meister Eckhart (another enthusiastic exponent of the dark way): "Seek God, so as never to find him."[32] The point Eckhart is making is that, once you seem to have found God, it is not God whom you have found. Once you seem to grasp God, God eludes you. When you seem to have found God, what you have found is not God. For God is not an object or a thing alongside of other objects and things: God is the All whom we can discover only in the experience of not discovering. This is the paradoxical language of the apophatic tradition. It is a way of struggling with words to express that which is beyond all words.

Apophaticism and Human Identity

A distinctive feature of Merton's apophatic approach to contemplation is his application of the way of darkness and negation to the discovery of our real self. His anthropology is as apophatic as his theology. For the real self, being our own subjectivity, cannot be known, because it cannot be objectified. For as soon as you attempt to objectify it in images and concepts, you have lost sight of it. You have turned it into an object distinct from your real self, the subject. Perhaps this analogy will help: You see with your eyes, but you cannot see your eyes. This is to say that you cannot turn your eyes into an object that you see. Of course you can look at your eyes in a mirror, but what you see is not your eyes but their reflection. So we can see the real self reflected in what we do, but the real self as it truly is can only be grasped in an intuitive darkness that coincides in some mysterious way with the intuition of the reality of God.

An Overview of the Contents

This book will be divided into four parts. Part One will attempt to sum up Merton's understanding of contemplation in his earliest writings on the subject, namely, *What Is Contemplation?*, *Seeds of Contemplation* and *The Ascent to Truth*.

Part Two, which I have called "The Inner Landscape of Contemplation: Solitude," discusses the necessity of some kind of inner silence and solitude without which contemplation simply cannot exist. The problem of living one's life in such a way as not to allow the demands life makes and the turmoil it often brings to suffocate our inner peace is one of the principal challenges we must deal with if we are serious in our desire to be contemplative. This inner discipline is a topic Merton discusses in a number of places. I have chosen to summarize his thinking in one book, *Thoughts in Solitude,* and one essay, "Notes for a Philosophy of Solitude" from *Disputed Questions.*

Part Three is an effort to explore some of Merton's more mature writings on contemplation. *The Inner Experience* serves as something of a transitional work between the earlier and later writings. I will discuss also *New Seeds of Contemplation, Contemplative Prayer* (originally published as *The Climate of Monastic Prayer*) and *Zen and the Birds of Appetite.*

Part Four is entitled "The Outer Landscape of Contemplation: The World." In the revised edition of *Thomas Merton's Dark Path* (1987), I wrote a new preface in which I attempted to deal with the contemplative's relationship to the world. But merely adding a new preface is hardly a satisfactory way of revising a book. I am grateful that developing technology and the generosity of St. Anthony Messenger Press have made it possible for me to do the extensive revision of this book which I have long wanted to do. In Part Four I will make use of sections from *Conjectures of a Guilty Bystander*, some essays in *Contemplation in a World of Action*, as well as some brief selections from Merton's letters and journals. Please note that the parenthetical citations within each chapter refer to the primary source under discussion.

I am attempting in this book to offer reflections on much of what Thomas Merton wrote about contemplation. I am dealing with his major writings on this subject. It is important to say, however, that in writings not specifically about contemplation Merton does offer, almost in passing, important insights on the contemplative dimension of life. Thus, in the five volumes of his letters and in the seven volumes of his journals, such reflections—some brief, some fairly lengthy—make frequent appearances. I have made occasional references to these reflections, but have made no detailed attempt to incorporate such material into this book. The temptation to do so was strong but I resisted it, realizing that doing so would extend this book beyond reasonable limits. I also feel that a good grasp of what Merton explicitly wrote about contemplation is an indispensable help toward understanding what he said about it in other contexts.

In sending this completely new edition of an earlier book on its way, I want to thank the many reviewers who spoke so graciously about the first edition. I want also to acknowledge the many correspondents who wrote to me about it and to say that I cherish the friendships it has brought into being. I offer this edition to them and to all who search for a deeper interiority in their lives. I hope we can search together.

Notes

[1] Thomas Merton, *Honorable Reader: Reflections on My Work*, Robert E. Daggy, ed. (New York: Crossroad, 1989), p. 131.

[2] Thomas Merton, *The New Man* (New York: Farrar, Straus, Giroux, 1961), p. 77.

[3] Thomas Merton, *The Road to Joy: The Letters of Thomas Merton to New and Old Friends*, Robert E. Daggy, ed. (New York: Farrar, Straus, Giroux, 1989), p. 118.

[4] Thomas Merton, *Zen and the Birds of Appetite* (New York: New Directions, 1968), p. 137 (emphasis added).

[5] *New Man*, p. 112. In *The New Man*, Merton offers a splendid presentation of the original blessing given to Adam and Eve by God and their tragic fall from that state of blessedness.

[6] *The Letters of Thomas Merton: The School of Charity: The Letters of Thomas Merton on Religious Renewal*, Patrick Hart, ed. (San Diego: Harcourt Brace Jovanovich, 1993), p. 323.

[7] Thomas Merton, *The Seven Storey Mountain* (New York: Harcourt Brace Jovanovich, 1948), p. 205.

[8] *Seven Storey Mountain*, p. 375.

[9] *Seven Storey Mountain*, p. 389.

[10] *Commonweal*, 5 December 1947.

[11] *Run to the Mountain: The Story of a Vocation: The Journals of Thomas Merton, Vol. I*, Patrick Hart, ed. (San Francisco: HarperSanFrancisco, 1995), p. 144.

[12] Thomas Merton, *The Collected Poems of Thomas Merton* (New York: New Directions, 1980), pp. 291-302.

[13] *Collected Poems*, pp. 330-331.

[14] See, for example, Thomas Merton, *Contemplation in a World of Action* (Garden City, N.Y.: Doubleday, 1971).

[15] See Thomas Merton, *Passion for Peace: The Social Essays*, William H. Shannon, ed. and intro. (New York: Crossroad, 1995); Thomas Merton, *Conjectures of a Guilty Bystander* (Garden City, N.Y.: Doubleday, 1966); Thomas Merton, *Faith and Violence: Christian*

Teaching and Christian Practice (Notre Dame, Ind.: University of Notre Dame Press, 1968).

[16] Suzane Butorovich: see *Road to Joy*, pp. 308-309.

[17] Thomas Merton, *The Hidden Ground of Love: The Letters of Thomas Merton on Religious Experience and Social Concerns*, William H. Shannon, ed. (New York: Farrar, Straus, Giroux, 1985), pp. 308-324.

[18] Thomas Merton, *The Courage for Truth: The Letters of Thomas Merton to Writers*, Christine M. Bochen, ed. (New York: Farrar, Straus, Giroux, 1993), pp. 53-86.

[19] See Thomas Merton, *Conjectures of a Guilty Bystander* (New York: Image, 1968), pp. 131, 158.

[20] See Thomas Merton, *The New Man* (New York: Farrar, Straus, Giroux, 1978), pp. 32-68; *Zen and the Birds of Appetite*, pp. 116 ff.

[21] Thomas Merton, *The Tears of the Blind Lions* (New York: New Directions, 1949), p. 21.

[22] Thomas Merton, *What Is Contemplation?* (Springfield, Ill.: Templegate Publishers, 1981), p. 32; *The Inner Experience*, unpublished, p. 63.

[23] Merton later adopted a suggestion from Jacques Maritain and referred to such persons as "masked contemplatives." (See *Inner Experience*, third draft, p. 63.)

[24] "The laity and the clergy who are absorbed in many active concerns are unable to give themselves to meditation and to a deeper study of divine and human things" (*Contemplation in a World of Action*, pp. 182-183).

[25] I use the word "monastic" rather than monks, so as to include women in contemplative orders as well as men.

[26] *Contemplation in a World of Action*, p. 186.

[27] I deliberately switch pronouns in referring to God, because I want to make clear than no one human image is in any way adequate to describe God. The image of human fatherhood is one we have long used to talk about God. But it is important to realize that it in no way expresses fully who God is. Scripture offers us a number of rich symbols to use in speaking about God: shepherd, savior, spouse, lover, etc. Among these symbols, that of mother is most

appropriate as a way of talking about God. If we restrict ourselves to only one image to describe God, we risk the danger of identifying the reality of God with that one image. To do so would be, in effect, to make that one image idolatrous.

[28] William H. Shannon, *Silence on Fire* (New York: Crossroad, 1991), p. 101.

[29] Norman P. Tanner, *Decrees of the Ecumenical Councils, Vol. 1* (Washington, D.C.: Georgetown University Press, 1990), p. 232.

[30] *Contemplation in a World of Action*, p. 185.

[31] *Contemplation in a World of Action*, p. 185.

[32] Thomas Merton, *The Mystic Life* (Chappaqua, N.Y.: Electronic Paperbacks, 1976), cassette no. 8.

PART ONE

Early Writings on Contemplation

1

What Is Contemplation?

There are thousands of Christians walking about the face of the earth bearing in their bodies the infinite God of Whom they know practically nothing. (17)

In her autobiography *My First Seventy Years*, Sister Madeleva tells of a student at St. Mary's College, Notre Dame, who became interested in the poetry of Thomas Merton and wrote to him asking for an explanation of contemplation. "His generous answer," Sister Madeleva recalls, "came in a manuscript entitled *What Is Contemplation?*, with permission to publish it at St. Mary's, if we wished." They indeed wished to publish it and did so on December 8, 1948. By the time they published it, its author was in process of rising to best-seller fame with *The Seven Storey Mountain*, which had been published three months earlier.

This small booklet, *What Is Contemplation?*,[1] represents Merton's first attempt to put into writing what he had read, studied and experienced about contemplation in his early years as a monk. It deals with traditional material on the contemplative life, hardly breaking new ground on the subject, as he draws his material from the Scriptures, the Fathers of the Church, Thomas Aquinas and writers on the mystical life like his Cistercian Father, Bernard of Clairvaux, and especially John of the Cross. Much of what he says would have been available in the writings of Reginald

Garrigou-Lagrange and Adolf Alfred Tanquerey that were standard reading in spiritual theology in seminaries and novitiates. The booklet does not bear the stamp of Merton's later literary *persona*. In fact, as you read this booklet, you cannot help but wonder what the young student thought of it. No doubt she was flattered that she should have received an entire manuscript in reply to her question. And when Merton became famous as the author of *The Seven Storey Mountain* a year later, she must have treasured this manuscript even more. But what did she think of its contents? Did it help her understand what contemplation was? Did it have any real meaning for her in her own life? Did it help her to move in the direction of contemplation? We cannot answer these questions for this anonymous student but we can perhaps put similar questions to ourselves as we look at the book's contents.

Although it is divided into nine sections, I propose to discuss this material in terms of three basic topics that I believe summarize the main content and thrust of the work: the call to contemplation, the kinds of contemplation and the three kinds of Christians. The discussion of these three topics will be followed by a brief reflection on the contribution this work makes toward clarifying Merton's understanding of contemplation in his early years in the monastery and also toward indicating directions in which his thought on contemplation might be expected to move.

The Call to Contemplation

Merton begins his booklet with a lament that so many Christians have practically no knowledge of God's immense love for them and the power of that love to make them happy. These people do not realize that the gift of contemplation, which is the deepest experience of God's love, is not "something essentially strange and esoteric reserved for a small class of almost unnatural beings and prohibited to everyone else" (7). They do not see that it is the work of the

Holy Spirit whose gifts are part of the normal equipment given to all Christians in Baptism—gifts that God gives presumably because he wishes them to be developed. "Therefore," Merton says, "If anyone should ask 'Who may desire this gift [of infused contemplation] and pray for it?' the answer is obvious: everybody" (11).

He finds justification for the claim that everyone is called to infused contemplation in the words of Jesus at the Last Supper, in which he promises union with God to the disciples and through them to us. Jesus said that he would send the Holy Spirit to us and that he and the Father would love us and come to abide with us. The abiding presence of God that Jesus promises is in a very true sense an experience of heavenly beatitude on earth. For the knowledge and love of God that comes from the abiding presence of the Trinity within us is "essentially the same beatitude as the blessed enjoy in heaven" (14).

Thus, Merton says, the seeds of perfect union with God—the seeds of contemplation[2] and sanctity—are planted in every Christian soul at Baptism. But it is a sad fact that in thousands of Christians these seeds lie dormant; they never grow. The reason is that so many Christians do not really desire to know God. They are content to remain "surface Christians" whose religious life is largely restricted to external practices. Because they lack any real desire to know God, he will never manifest the divine Self to them.

Merton quotes Thomas Aquinas on the absolute necessity of the desire to know God as a prerequisite for a true life of contemplation. In his commentary on the fourteenth chapter of John's Gospel, Aquinas says, "*Spiritualia non accipiuntur nisi desiderata*" ("Spiritual things are not received unless they are desired"). But he also adds, "*nec desiderata nisi aliqualiter cognita*" ("nor are they desired unless they are somehow known"). What he is saying is that there can be no desire for union with God, unless, in some measure at least, one has begun to experience such union. The paradox of the spiritual life is that we cannot know God unless we desire God, yet at the same time we cannot really desire God unless, to some degree at least, we have already come to know God. We cannot have an appetite for a particular food unless we have first tasted it; so we cannot have the desire for God unless we have first in some way tasted the joy of the divine presence. As Merton puts it: "The only way to find out anything about the joys of contemplation is *by experience*. We must taste and see that the Lord is sweet" (23).

> How do we acquire a taste for the things of the spirit? The only way is love. Jesus makes it clear that the interior life depends on love, when He says in the discourse at the Last Supper: If you love me...I will ask the Father and He will give you another paraclete.... He that loveth me shall be loved of my Father and I will love him and manifest myself to him" (John 14:15, 21). The love Jesus is talking about is not primarily feeling or sentiment; it is love at its deepest level, namely, loving obedience to His word. "If anyone loves me he will keep my word." Aquinas puts it clearly and simply: "It is obedience that makes a person fit to see God." (24)

Thus, desire based on some experience of love, love feeding desire and leading toward union, together with total uncompromising obedience to the will of Jesus—these are the dispositions needed in order to respond to the invitation, issued at Baptism, to achieve union with God in the experience of contemplation.

Kinds of Contemplation

Infused Contemplation

After discussing the call to contemplation (7-24), Merton devotes the rest of his booklet (25-79) to an explanation of what contemplation is. He makes it clear that there is only one kind of contemplation in its strict and correct sense: infused or pure or passive contemplation. This is a special gift of God that we simply cannot achieve by our own efforts;

it is a pure gift of God that involves a "direct and experimental"[3] contact with God as God is in the divine Self. It means emptying oneself of every created love to be filled with the love of God. It means going beyond all created images to receive the simple light of God's substantial presence.

Active Contemplation

There is a second type of prayer, analogous to infused contemplation, which Merton, following the tradition of Western mystical literature, calls active contemplation. Active contemplation, which is something that anyone can achieve by cooperating with God's ordinary grace, means a number of things to Merton. It is not restricted to a particular exercise or a single type of experience. It includes the use of reason, imagination and the affections of the will. It draws on the resources of theology, philosophy, art and music. It may involve vocal prayer, meditation or affective prayer. It introduces a person to the joys of the interior life, showing him how to seek God in the divine will and how to be attentive to God's presence. It builds in him the desire to please God rather than to enjoy the satisfactions of the world. It leads toward love and toward union with God in love.

Liturgy

The highest expression of active contemplation is the liturgy, which, with its rich fare of Scripture, theology, music, art and poetry, teaches one to be contemplative. Indeed, it may become the point of transition from active to passive contemplation. For, in the liturgy, Christ draws us to himself. But Christ is, quite literally, the "embodiment" of contemplation, since his humanity is perfectly united to the Godhead. Hence, by drawing us to himself, inevitably he draws us toward union with the Godhead and, therefore, toward infused contemplation. Hence Merton believed that liturgy may, not infrequently, be the occasion for moments of intuition akin to infused contemplation, especially when appropriate periods of silence are observed in the liturgy.

What makes active contemplation similar to infused contemplation is that the goal of both is union with God in love. What differentiates the two is that active contemplation is union with God in the liturgy of the Church or in the activities of one's life, whereas infused contemplation is union with God as God is in the divine Self. One way, perhaps, of expressing Merton's thought is to distinguish the immanence of God from his transcendence.[4] The immanence of God is the divine presence in all reality; the transcendence of God is the very Being of God. In infused contemplation, one experiences both; in active contemplation, one ordinarily experiences only the first.

Infused contemplation, therefore, because it involves experiencing God as she is in the divine Self, is contemplation in the strictest sense of the term, while active contemplation deserves the name of contemplation only by way of analogy. It must be pointed out, however, that the experience of the immanence of God in active contemplation can lead to a very deep love of God. Indeed, it could happen, in particular situations, that active contemplation could generate a deeper love of God than that achieved by some who may be pure contemplatives. "Such Christians as these," Merton says of those who live lives of active contemplation, "far from being excluded from perfection, may reach a higher degree of sanctity than others who have been apparently favored with a deeper interior life" (32-35). Infused contemplation, while it is the experience of God at a deeper level, does not necessarily mean a deeper love for God than that which can be achieved in active contemplation.

Three Types of Christians

It would seem correct to say that, in speaking of the interior life, Merton would distinguish three types of "practicing" Christians, namely: "surface Christians" (those who obey but do not really love God); "quasi-contemplatives" (those who love and are united with God in the activities of their lives); and pure contemplatives (those who love and experience God as God is in the divine Self).

"Surface Christians"

First of all, there are the "surface Christians," whose interior life, if indeed it may be called that at all, is "confined to a few routine exercises of piety and a few external acts of worship and service performed as a matter of duty" (12). Their predominant image of God is that of one who rewards and punishes. They seek not God but rewards. Their spiritual goal in life is to achieve heaven and to avoid hell. They respect God as a master; but their hearts belong not to God, but to their own ambitions, cares and comforts. They are not contemplative in any sense of the word; in no way do they taste the joys of union with God. They have no thought of seeking God's presence. They willfully remain at a distance from God. They live lives of divided allegiance, allowing God to maintain rights over the substance of their souls, but with their thoughts and desires turned not toward God but toward the world and external things. As far as experiencing God is concerned, they are in the same condition as men and women who refuse to acknowledge God at all.

"Quasi-contemplatives"[5]

Very different from "surface Christians" are those whom Merton describes as "quasi-contemplatives." These are Christians who truly love God and are united with God in the activities of their lives. They "serve God with great purity of soul and perfect self-sacrifice in the active life" (31). Their vocation to the active life does not allow them the solitude and silence required for a life of infused contemplation; nor do their temperaments suit them for such a life. They would probably be uncomfortable if they gave up all activity for a life of solitude.

This does not mean that they cannot live interior lives or that the only alternative for them is a life of "surface" Christianity. On the contrary, the promise of Christ that the three divine Persons will manifest themselves to all who love them is meant for them as well as for pure contemplatives. Though they may not be able to empty themselves of created things to lose themselves in God alone, as the pure contemplative tries to do, still they serve God with great purity of heart, expressed in fraternal charity, self-sacrifice and total abandonment to God's will in all that they do and suffer. They serve God in God's children on earth. They learn to find God in their activities, living and working in her company, remaining in the divine presence and tasting the deep peaceful joy of that presence (32).

Their prayer life may be very ordinary, not rising above the level of vocal and affective prayer. Yet, because they are conscious of God's presence, their humble prayer may result in a deep interior life that brings them to the threshold of contemplation. Hence, though they are living active lives in the world, they may be called "quasi-contemplatives."[6] They are not unfamiliar with graces akin to contemplation. Indeed, they may experience moments of true contemplation in their simple prayer life, in the liturgy, in the consciousness of God's presence in their lives as they go about fulfilling their daily responsibilities. They have fleeting moments, perhaps sometimes even prolonged periods of time, in which their intuition of oneness with God becomes a very vivid experience. Because of this union with God, immanent in their lives' activities, they may achieve a high degree of sanctity—perhaps even higher than some who have a genuine vocation to infused contemplation (32-35).

Pure Contemplatives

Besides the "surface Christians" and the "quasi-contemplatives," there is a third group of Christians who may be called pure contemplatives. These pure contemplatives who, Merton believes, will always be a small minority in the Christian community (30-31), are the people of the "desert," whose sole goal in life is to search for God and who find their sufficiency in God alone.[7] They live lives of solitude and silence in which they can empty themselves of all things outside of God, so that their emptiness can be filled with God's transcendent presence. They alone are contemplatives in the strict sense. Merton writes: "In the strict sense of the word, contemplation is a supernatural love and knowledge of God, simple and obscure, infused by him into the summit of the soul, giving it a direct and experimental[8] contact with Him" (36).

Following the tradition of the Fathers of the Church, Merton stresses the purity of love that is at the heart of true contemplation. It is pure in that it empties the soul of all affection for things that are not God. It is pure in that it desires no reward, not even the reward of contemplation. This is to say that the reward of pure love is not something outside of love itself; it is simply the ability to love. In the words of Bernard of Clairvaux: "*Amo quia amo, amo ut amem*" (I love simply because I love and I love in order to love).[9]

This disinterested love of God always brings peace and strength to the soul. Yet it would be a mistake to think "that infused contemplation is all sweetness and understanding and consolation and joy" (40). There are times when the peace it brings is almost buried under pain and darkness and aridity. There are times when the strength it gives seems to be shrouded in an extreme sense of helplessness and incapacity.

The reasons for this darkness and helplessness are to be found in the very nature of the contemplative experience. For contemplation is the light of God shining directly on the soul. But because the soul is weakened by original sin, the light of God affects the soul the way the light of the sun affects a diseased eye. It causes pain. The soul, diseased by its own selfishness, is shocked and repelled by the purity of God's light. The brightness of this light shatters the ideas of God that we have formed by our own reason. God, as God is in the divine Self, is not the God we imagined. It also shatters the ideas we have formed of ourselves. The flame of the divine light attacks our self-love and we no longer know who we are before God.

Thus, "infused contemplation, then, sooner or later brings with it a terrible interior revolution" (42). The God we thought we knew is taken away from us and our minds are no longer able to think of God. The joy of the divine presence is gone, because we no longer know the God who is present. The divine light has shattered all our ideas of God. We are not even sure that anyone is present at all. We who once loved God so ardently seem unable to love, because the object of love seems to have disappeared into impenetrable darkness. We no longer have anyone even to pray to; hence, "[g]one is the sweetness of prayer. Meditation becomes impossible, even hateful" (42). Liturgy turns into a boring exercise that appears to be without meaning. The ray of light becomes, for a time at least, "a ray of darkness" (45): It seems to remove everything we have known and loved, while leaving nothing in its place. One experiences the deep meaning of Saint John's words: "And the light shineth in darkness; and the darkness comprehended it not."[10]

This is a crucial point in the life of prayer. We want to depend on ourselves and make our own decisions, yet here we find ourselves called to wait for God to act. We want to know where we are going, yet here we find ourselves called to walk in emptiness with blind trust. We want to know at least that we are on the right path, yet here we find ourselves in a darkness that seems to deprive us of the certainty we once thought we had about God and about ourselves.

How can we know we are on the right path, especially when we see no path at all? How can we know whether this pain of separation from the God we once thought we knew is a real separation from God or the experience of a darkness wherein the true God is met more fully and deeply? How do we know whether what is happening to us is the beginning of infused contemplation or simply a growing distaste for the interior life that may signal an eventual return to a Christian life that is devoted largely to externals?

There are no easy answers to these questions; but the

surest test that infused contemplation is beginning to emerge from behind this cloud of darkness is "a powerful, mysterious and yet simple attraction which holds the soul prisoner in this darkness and obscurity" (51). Although we experience frustration, there is no desire to escape from the darkness and return to an easier stage of the spiritual life. At the same time, "there is a growing conviction that joy and peace and fulfillment are only to be found somewhere in this lonely night of aridity and faith" (52).

Then one day there is an illumination. The soul comes to realize that in this darkness it has truly found the living God. It is overwhelmed with the sense that God is present and that God's love surrounds the soul on all sides and absorbs it. The darkness does not cease to be darkness, but, by the strangest of all paradoxes, it has become brighter than the brightest day. Life is transformed and there is only one thought and one love: God alone. The soul has been awakened. It has entered on what writers on the mystical life have called the illuminative way. Truly awakened to the reality of God, it is being drawn toward union with God as God is in the divine Self.

How do we deal with this new experience, this awakening, this call to move from illumination to union with God? For help in answering this critical question, Merton turns to the writings of the great sixteenth-century Spanish mystic, Saint John of the Cross. Drawing on *The Dark Night*, *The Ascent of Mount Carmel* and *The Spiritual Canticle*, Merton offers several guidelines to help the awakened soul on the path toward contemplative union with God. These guidelines may be summarized as follows:

First of all, it is important that we know what God is doing in our souls and accept it. God's purpose is to bring us to "the threshold of an actual experimental[11] contact with the living God" (56).

John of the Cross says that in this dark night, "God secretly teaches the soul and instructs it in the perfection of love without its doing anything or understanding of what manner is this infused contemplation."[12]

If we realize what God is doing, we will not seek the very things God is trying to drive out of us; namely, the precise concepts we have had of God and the sweetness and consolation we have experienced in prayer. We must know when to leave meditation and affections behind. God wants to replace these created experiences with God's very presence: God wants to infuse into our souls God's light (to replace the concepts we had of God) and God's love (to replace the consolations and sweetness we had heretofore been experiencing in prayer). We must let God act! If we attempt by our own actions to increase the precision of our knowledge of God or to intensify our feelings of love, we will interfere with the work God is doing in us.

Second, we must find solitude as much as we can. We must live as much as possible in peace, quiet and retirement. We must do the tasks appointed to us as perfectly as we can with disinterested[13] love, wanting only to please God. We should not strive for spectacular "experiences," such as we read about in the lives of the great mystics.

> None of those graces (called *gratis datae*), ["gifts freely given" (by God)] can sanctify [us] nearly as well as this obscure and purifying light and love of God which is given to [us] to no other end than to make [us] perfect in His love (61).

Third, we must not be overanxious about our progress in prayer. "[We] have left the beaten track and are traveling by paths that cannot be charted and measured" (62). We must let God take care of our prayer and our progress in it.[14] We should seek only to purify our love of God more and more. We should seek only to abandon ourselves more and more perfectly to the divine will.

Fourth, we must accept the trials and crosses that God sends us, even though they baffle us. God is using them to form the divine image in us more and more perfectly.

Finally, and above all, we must realize that sanctity and pure contemplation are only to be found in the perfection of love.

The truly contemplative soul is not the one that has the most exalted visions of the divine essence but the one who is most closely united to God in the purity of love and allows itself to be absorbed and transformed into God by that love.

Let everything, pleasant or unpleasant, be a source and occasion of love. Merton quotes the celebrated passage from *The Spiritual Canticle* on the bee:

> Even as the bee extracts from all plants the honey that is in them and has no use for them for aught else save for that purpose, *even so the soul with great facility extracts the sweetness of love that is in all things that pass through it.* It loves God in each of them, whether pleasant or unpleasant.[15]

Such love leads to a holy indifference, the *apatheia* of which the Fathers of the Church speak, wherein the only thing that matters is to please the Beloved.

Merton concludes his "borrowings" from Saint John of the Cross with a quotation from *The Spiritual Canticle* on the value of contemplation:

> Let those that are great actives and think to girdle the world with their outward works take note that *they would bring far more profit to the Church and be far more pleasing to God if they spent even half this time in abiding with God in prayer....* Of a surety they would accomplish more with one piece of work than they now do with a thousand and that with far less labor.[16]

What Is Contemplation? leaves a number of questions unanswered, especially questions about the call to contemplation and the distinction between infused contemplation and active contemplation.

In the introduction Merton openly and with enthusiasm espouses the egalitarian view that all are called to contemplation. For all are given in Baptism the gifts of the Holy Spirit that are intended by God to produce as their fruit the life of contemplation. "Why," Merton asks, "do we think of the gift of contemplation, infused contemplation, mystical prayer, as something essentially strange and esoteric reserved for a small class of almost unnatural beings and prohibited to everyone else?" (7).

Yet, further on, he moves to an elitist view of contemplation, as he states quite clearly that few will achieve it. "The great majority of Christians," he says, "will never become pure contemplatives on earth" (30-31).[17]

He seems to resolve the discrepancy between these two perspectives initially in terms of the desire for contemplation. He writes: "God often measures His gifts by our desire to receive them" (8). This would seem to mean that the reason the majority of Christians never become pure contemplatives is that they lack the desire.

Yet later Merton appears to reduce the difference between pure contemplatives and "quasi-contemplatives," not to desire or its lack, but to a difference in life-style. Pure contemplatives have the silence and solitude necessary for the true contemplative experience; "quasi-contemplatives" do not. Merton admits that the latter, because of purity of heart, "maintained in them by obedience, fraternal charity, self-sacrifice and perfect abandonment to God's will...may reach a higher degree of sanctity than others who have been apparently favored with a deeper interior life" (32-35). This would certainly suggest that these "quasi-contemplatives" do indeed have a desire for union with God. It would appear, therefore, that life-style, rather than desire, is the practical determinant as to whether or not they can respond to the call to contemplation as a way of union with God.

If this is a correct reading of Merton's thought, it means that he is really saying that the call to infused contemplation, given theoretically to all, can in practice be responded to only in the monastic life or at most in a life-style that reproduces the solitude and silence that characterize the monastic life.

While this interpretation of Merton's thought severely limits the eligibility list for infused contemplatives, it does not mean that Merton saw the monastery as the only atmosphere conducive to sanctity. He certainly believed that sanctity is something that all men and women can achieve, whatever their state in life. For sanctity is primarily a matter of love.

Would Merton, perhaps, have been better advised to suggest that the call to sanctity, rather than the call to infused contemplation, is given to all, but that infused contemplation as a way to sanctity is restricted to the few? Would it have been enough for him to say that infused contemplation is a special and unique way to sanctity, but that there is also another way: the way of those he calls "quasi-contemplatives"?

Yet, answering these questions in the affirmative would still leave unanswered a whole other series of questions: Does union with God as God is in the divine Self (which is the goal of pure contemplation) produce of itself greater sanctity than union with God in the activities of one's life (which would ordinarily be the highest achievement possible to the "quasi-contemplative")? How does union with God in his transcendent Being differ from union with God in the activities of one's life? What does it mean to be united to God in the activities of one's life? Can a person be united with God in the activities of his life without, in some measure at least, being united with God as she is in the divine Self? Does the pure contemplative differ from the "quasi-contemplative," not in the sense that her union with God is different from that of the "quasi-contemplative," but simply in the sense that her experience of that union is different? If the seeds of contemplation are given to all in Baptism (and Merton states that they are), does this not mean that God wills those seeds to grow into contemplation? Yet if only the few actually achieve infused contemplation, does this mean that for the most part humans have managed to frustrate the plans God has for them? Is Merton's distinction between these two types of contemplatives based on a faulty dualism that separates God from God's creation? (This is a key question to keep in mind, as we continue discussing Merton's writing on contemplation.)

These questions, suggested but left unanswered by *What Is Contemplation?*, may well be kept in mind as we venture further into Merton's writings on the contemplative life.

One thing concerning *What Is Contemplation?* about

which there can be no question, is Merton's appropriation of the "apophatic way," the way of night and darkness, as his preferred approach to describing the contemplative experience. He speaks of "the curtain of darkness," "the cloud of obscurity," "the cloud of darkness," "the night of aridity and faith," "the night of faith," "the power of an obscure love," "the ray of darkness."

Yet it is important to realize that for Merton the darkness of the apophatic way must be understood dialectically.[18] It is one way of expressing the experience, but it never conveys the total experience. Thus it is darkness from our side (because the light of our concepts is put out), but not from God's side (for it is the very intensity of the divine light that causes the darkness). The darkness of the apophatic way is never complete and total darkness. That is why Merton speaks of the power of an obscure love. That is why he speaks of the ray of darkness, which is really a ray of light but so brilliant a light that it blinds us, as it leaves room for the activity of God. That is why the love that is obscure is yet a love that has power. That is why the "ray of darkness" is still a ray. "The darkness remains as dark as ever and yet, somehow, it seems to have become brighter than the brightest day" (53).

Merton's apophaticism will be developed in more detail in the discussion of his later works. This work sufficiently establishes him in the apophatic tradition.

Notes

[1] This booklet has been reprinted a number of times. Burns and Oates of London published it in 1950 with minor revisions. (The St. Mary's version concluded with prayer to the Virgin Mary; the Burns and Oates edition, being in their *Pater Noster* series, concluded with a prayer to the Father.) Templegate published the Burns and Oates edition in 1941 and again in 1960, in the United States. In 1981 Templegate did another reissue in a different format, with a series of Merton drawings, and with the text in 79 large-type pages.

[2] These words became the title of Merton's next book on the contemplative life, *Seeds of Contemplation*.

[3] At the time Merton was writing, the word "experimental" did not have the connection it has today with "experiment." Rather it was linked with "experience." Today we would use the word "experiential" in this context.

[4] See Thomas Merton, *The Silent Life* (New York: Farrar, Straus, Giroux, 1975).

[5] By "quasi-contemplatives" Merton seems to mean those whose interior lives involve active contemplation. Nowhere, however, does he speak of "active contemplatives." This may be because he considered such a term inappropriate and misleading, holding as he did that there is only one kind of contemplation in the strict sense of the term. In *The Inner Experience* Merton drops the term "quasi-contemplatives" and speaks of "hidden" or "masked" contemplatives. The latter term he got from Jacques Maritain, to whom on February 19, 1949, he writes: "Thank you for your kind remarks on *What Is Contemplation?*, and I especially like the term "masked contemplative," which expresses much better what I mean.

"As far as I know they are contemplatives, but they have no real way of knowing that they are, because their gifts of understanding and wisdom are not strong enough to enable them to recognize their experience for what it is. They know God by experience, but they can't interpret the experience. There must be very many like that even here and I think they sometimes get upset at the thought that they ought to be mystics and they are afraid that they are not" (*The Courage for Truth*, p. 24).

[6] In the 1981 revised edition, the term suggested by Maritain is incorporated into the text near the end of the section devoted to "quasi-contemplatives." It reads: "They enjoy a kind of masked contemplation" (*What Is Contemplation?*, p. 32).

[7] See *Silent Life*, pp. vii-xiv.

[8] Note again that "experimental" here means "experiential."

[9] Bernard of Clairvaux, Sermon 83 in Cantica, quoted in *What Is Contemplation?*, p. 40.

[10] John 1:5, King James Version.

[11] See note 8.

[12] John of the Cross, *The Dark Night of the Soul*, II, v. 1., trans. and ed., E. Allison Peers (New York: Image, 1990).

[13] "Disinterested" does not mean "lacking interest," but "free from self-interest and bias."

[14] See Romans 8:26, "Likewise the Spirit helps us in our weakness; for we do not know how to pray as we ought, but that very Spirit intercedes with sighs too deep for words."

[15] John of the Cross, *The Spiritual Canticle*, E. Allison Peers, trans. (London: Burns and Oates, 1978), chapter xxvii, quoted in *What Is Contemplation?*, pp. 65-66.

[16] *The Spiritual Canticle*, xxix, p. 3, quoted in *What Is Contemplation?*, p. 67.

[17] In *The Inner Experience* Merton will repeat this sentence or (perhaps better) will allow it to stand, since *The Inner Experience* is a revision of *What Is Contemplation?* See Chapter Four.

[18] *Dialectics* refers to a way of discussing facts or ideas that may appear contradictory with a view to some kind of resolution of the apparent contradictions.

2

Seeds of Contemplation

*God's love is like a river springing up in the depths of the
Divine Substance and flowing endlessly through His
creation, filling all things with life and goodness and
strength. (180)*

Seeds of Contemplation, Merton's first major publication[1] after
The Seven Storey Mountain, was published March 2, 1949. By
that time *The Seven Storey Mountain* had gone through several
hundred printings with sales in the hundred thousands. It is
not surprising, therefore, that *Seeds* received a good bit of
attention and achieved an almost instant popularity.

The book derives its title from a passage in Merton's
earlier work, *What Is Contemplation?*:

> The seeds of this perfect life (i.e., the life of contemplative
> union with God) are planted in every Christian soul at
> Baptism. But seeds must grow and develop before you reap
> the harvest. There are thousands of Christians walking
> about the face of the earth bearing in their bodies the
> infinite God of Whom they know practically nothing.... The
> seeds of contemplation and sanctity have been planted in
> those souls, but [in so many cases] they merely lie
> dormant.[2]

The first words of the introduction to *Seeds* describes the title
even more concretely:

> Every moment and every event of every man's life on earth

plants something in his soul. For just as the wind carries thousands of invisible and visible winged seeds, so the stream of time brings with it germs of spiritual vitality that come to rest imperceptibly in the minds and wills of men. Most of these unnumbered seeds perish and are lost, because men are not prepared to receive them: for such seeds as these cannot spring up anywhere except in the good soil of liberty and desire. (17)

Seeds of Contemplation is an invitation and a challenge to Merton's readers to bring these seeds to fruition and harvest in the good soil of liberty and desire. (Note the reference to *good soil*.) Perceptive readers will recognize that the seed-image in the title has its source in the New Testament. Each of the synoptic Gospels narrates the parable of the sower and the seed. In the parable the fruition of the seed depends on the kind of soil in which it is sown. It is only the *good soil* (not the soil that is a footpath or rocky or filled with thorns) that produces grain in due time. That this parable was very much on Merton's mind when he wrote this book is clear from the title he originally intended to give it: *The Soil and the Seeds of Contemplation*.[3] Since the gospel parables are not intended as stories that point a moral, but instead as challenges to the reader (often implicit in parables is the question: What about you?), it seems clear that Merton intended his book as a challenge to the reader. What kind of soil, he asks, will you choose to be for the seeds of contemplation that God has sown in you?

This introductory chapter moves into a lyric rhapsody about the tremendous harvest that would spring up if we looked for God in every moment and every event of our lives.

It is God's love that speaks to me in the birds and streams, but also behind the clamor of the city God speaks to me in His judgments, and all these things are seeds sent to me from His will.

If they would take root in my liberty, and if His will would grow from my freedom, I would become the love that He is, and my harvest would be His glory and my own

joy. And I would grow together with thousands and
thousands and millions of other freedoms into the gold of
one huge field praising God, loaded with increase, loaded
with corn. (18)

If it was his Abbot, Dom Frederic Dunne who directed[4]
Merton to write *The Seven Storey Mountain*, it was his
confessor, Dom Vital Klinski (a former abbot of Gethsemani),
who inspired the writing of *Seeds*. On December 29, 1946,
Merton recalls that he was told by Dom Vital "to teach
contemplation and especially to let people know, in what I
write, that the contemplative life is quite easy and accessible
and does not require extraordinary or strange efforts, just the
normal generosity required to strive for sanctity."[5]

Coming as it did in the wake of the highly popular *The
Seven Storey Mountain*, *Seeds* was fairly extensively reviewed.
The reviews were generally favorable, though in several cases
with reservations. Two reviewers (one in London, the other in
New York), while praising the book, point out its most
serious problem: the fact that, for the most part, it continues
the dualism which mars the text of *What Is Contemplation?*
The reviewer of *The [London] Times Literary Supplement* writes:
"There is so sharp a break and so deep a gulf between
'natural' and 'supernatural' that those who refuse the leap
must be pardoned."[6] In a similar critique Philip Burnham
says, in *The New York Times Book Review*: "At times a normally
reluctant reader may wonder if Thomas Merton...does not
view all natural joy and pleasure as too suspect; if he does
not separate nature and human nature from the
supernatural." The late Bede Griffiths, writing in *The
Downside Review*, notes the "ease and assurance" with which
the book is written and its fidelity to the great tradition of
Catholic mysticism. At the same time he expresses a certain
disquiet. "He still gives signs of the same superficial
mentality that marked *Elected Silence*. There is the same
childish contempt for the world and intolerance of anything
he cannot understand."[7] Pointing out Merton's unusual
insight into the mystical experience as oneness with God,
Griffiths suggests that Merton might be shocked to be told

45

that what he says about this oneness with God is "nearer the language of oriental mystics than of Catholic tradition." This remark of Bede Griffiths is noteworthy. For while Merton in one passage in *Seeds of Contemplation* speaks disparagingly of Eastern religions,[8] he will, in his final revision of this book (*New Seeds of Contemplation*),[9] take a friendlier and more appreciative approach.

Merton had his own problems with the book. He liked the book's cover (burlap—like that used on the walls of nightclubs, his publisher told him), but not its contents. "Every book I write is a mirror of my own character and conscience. I always open the final printed job with a faint hope of finding myself agreeable and I never do." He continues: "There is nothing to be proud of in this one either. It lacks warmth and human affection. I find in myself an underlying pride that I thought was all gone, but it is still there as bad as ever." He laments that a book club had taken it and called it a modern *Imitation of Christ*. "God forgive me," he wrote, "it is more like Swift than Thomas à Kempis.... The Passion of Christ," he grieved, "was too little in the book.... [It] is cold and cerebral."[10] (The reviewer from *The New York Times* had noted that "Merton does not dwell on the Gospel stories.")

On July 9, 1949, Merton expressed his misgivings about the book in a letter to Jacques Maritain: "I am revising the *Seeds of Contemplation* in which many statements are hasty and do not express my true meaning." He tells Maritain that the book is amazingly popular: forty thousand copies already in print. And with a secret (perhaps partly guilty) joy, he mentions that it has sold particularly well in Hollywood![11] A few days later he wrote, in the same vein, to Sister Therese Lentfoehr: "I am preparing a second edition of *Seeds* with a few emendations, hoping to tie up the loose ends and make things less likely to lead people astray."[12] The edition with these "few emendations" was published in December, 1949. A thorough rewrite would be published in 1962 as *New Seeds of Contemplation* (to be discussed in Chapter Six).

The book was a breath of fresh air. It was new and

different. It was not the kind of "religious" book people were accustomed to reading. What he writes about is not piety or devotion but spirituality. Piety and devotional literature tend to be about certain practices we should carry out in order to please God: saying prayers (like the rosary, novenas, the Stations of the Cross), going to Mass and confession, giving good example to others by our actions. Certainly these practices have their importance in the Christian life, for they are directed at improving our behavior. Spirituality, on the other hand, strives to deepen and transform our consciousness, to put us in touch with a world of reality below and above (indeed all around) our ordinary daily experience. We discover God, not as some remote, unreachable being, but as the very center of our being. With this discovery a new life dawns. We are liberated from selfishness. We come to discover our true selves that all the while have been hidden in God. We also find in God our inextricable link with our sisters and brothers of the human family. Compassion and unconditional love are born in our hearts.

Whereas devotional practices aim at a mediated relationship with God (mediated through the Church, through the sacraments), spirituality directs us toward an immediate experience of God, as God is in the divine Self. In 1949, hearing this kind of call was for many people something entirely new, perhaps even a bit scary; at the same time it was strangely attractive and appealing. Merton was telling them things about God and prayer that they had never read in their religion texts or catechisms or heard about in sermons. He was calling readers to penetrate the surface of words, to go beyond human formulations of the mystery of God in order to find God, "not in distinct and clear-cut definitions, but in the limpid obscurity of a single intuition that unites all dogmas in one simple Light, shining into the soul from God's eternity" (89). This is the experience of contemplation: something achieved without the mediation of words and symbols. It is what early Christian writers called "theology." Merton writes: "[T]heology does not truly begin to be theology until we have transcended the language and separate concepts of theologians" (90). He goes on, however, to add the *caveat* that when the contemplatives return from the depths of their experience of God and want to communicate what they have experienced to others (something they never can do fully, since words are never equal to the task), they must, nevertheless, strive for the kind of clarity of language which theologians have used to safeguard the tradition of faith. It is clear that Merton is speaking about the tradition of faith as preserved in the Catholic faith that he professed. Thus he expresses the earnest hope that the book "does not contain a line that is new to Catholic tradition or a single word that would perplex an orthodox theologian" (14). It seems clear, however, that people who did not share that Catholic tradition found the book nourishing for them also.

Different from *What Is Contemplation?*, *Seeds* is not a formal or systematic study of the contemplative experience. Merton describes it as "a collection of notes and personal reflections." It is a series of *pensées*, some developed to direct the reader's reflection, others given and then quickly dropped, leaving readers to their own reflections. It is a poetic reflection on contemplation, full of intuitions and insights. It is the work of a poet creating a book, as he is at the same time being created by God as a contemplative. "The poet," Merton writes, "enters into himself to create. The contemplative enters into God to be created" (71). Both these facets of Merton's personality—the poetic and the contemplative—are at work in this book. There is a freshness and creativity about it that produces moments of sheer poetry, like his description of the poverty and emptiness of contemplation, "We become like vessels empty of water that they may be filled with wine. We are like glass cleansed of dust and grime to receive the sun and vanish into its light" (178).

The book also suggests that Merton is writing about what he has come to know through experience. The words of the introduction have the ring of autobiography about them:

"[B]y receiving His will with joy and doing it with gladness I have His love in my heart, because my will is now the same as His love and I am on the way to becoming what He is, Who is Love" (19).

Interestingly, three reviewers suggest the autobiographical current in *Seeds*. Gerald G. Walsh of Fordham University writes: "In the present work the Trappist poet continues his autobiography." To him it represents Merton's arrival at the terrestrial paradise at the top of Purgatory: "It is a prose song full of the magic that makes the last seven cantos of Dante's *Purgatorio* so beautiful and bafflingly mysterious. Like Dante's Matelda, Thomas Merton is now laughing his way among the birds and brooks in the sweet Eden, which is a pledge of Eternal Peace."[13] In a similar vein, A. F. Wolfe writes that "Merton's devotional prism has caught reflections from Dante's Beatific Vision."[14] This theme—that contemplation is the return to the primeval garden of Eden—is one that is important to Merton and one that he will develop more explicitly in later works.

Emile Cailliet of Princeton University in his review picks up the autobiography motif, but in a different way. Describing *Seeds* as "an heroic book,"[15] he remarks that, while Merton hardly ever speaks of himself directly, whole sections of the book are autobiographical. He suggests a number of texts that surely have an autobiographical twist to them. Of whom but himself is he speaking, Cailliet asks, when he describes the man who planned to do spectacular things, who could not think of himself without a halo? "And when the events of his daily life keep reminding him of his own insignificance and mediocrity he is ashamed, and his pride refuses to swallow a truth at which no sane man should be surprised" (23). Cailliet cites other passages, for example, referring to a section where Merton describes solitude, at some length, he asks, "By what price those striking definitions of solitude?" (42). Or, my choice for a bit of autobiography in *Seeds*, who but himself is he describing when he writes: "As soon as God gets you in one monastery you want to be in another" (174). Vintage Merton!

I find Cailliet's suggestion—that we look for autobiography hidden in the text of *Seeds*—a happy insight and a most helpful way of reading this book. When Merton uses the word "you" in his text, he is often talking about himself, lamenting the undesirable things he sees in himself or reminding himself of goals he needs to work toward in his life. Approaching *Seeds* as hidden autobiography can help bring the text alive, serving as an antidote toward the attitude that might cross a reader's mind, namely, that the book is too abstract and impersonal. Cailliet's insight helps us to understand what Merton meant when he wrote: "Every book I write is a mirror of my own character and conscience."[16]

In writing about contemplation, Merton, here as elsewhere, struggles with the paradox of the gratuitousness of the contemplative experience and yet, at the same time, its naturalness. It "utterly transcends everything [we] are and can ever be." It raises us "above our natural capacity"; yet at the same time it is the very reason for our existence. In *What Is Contemplation?* Merton sees contemplation as the reason why we were baptized: It is the fruition of the gratuitous gifts of the Spirit offered to us in our Baptism. In *Seeds*, he wants to link contemplation with creation. Contemplation is the one thing for which we were all created. "Contemplation, by which we know and love God as He is in Himself, apprehending Him in a deep and vital experience which is beyond the reach of any natural understanding, is the reason for our creation by God" (144).

The ever-present paradox of contemplation that Merton consistently highlights is that, while it is above our nature, it is yet "the fulfillment of deep capacities in us." The life of heaven is a life of contemplation. "All those who reach the end for which they were created will therefore be contemplatives in heaven" (144). But we do not have to wait for heaven. The goal of contemplation can be achieved in this life—and not just by the few. "[M]any," Merton says, "are also destined to enter this supernatural element and breathe this new atmosphere while they are still on earth" (144). And it was to broadcast this message that Merton wrote his book.

As he says in the Author's Note at the beginning of the book: "[The book] has no other end or ideal in view than what should be the ordinary fulfillment of the Christian life of grace, and therefore everything that is said here can be applied to anyone, not only in the monastery, but also in the world" (15).

Notice how this seems to be a backing away from the more rigid position adopted in *What Is Contemplation?*, where he said: "The great majority of Christians will never become pure contemplatives on earth."[17] Here he is saying that many are destined to become contemplatives while still on earth. It may be that when he speaks of "many" being destined for contemplation, he has in mind what in the earlier book he called active contemplation, and not infused or pure contemplation. Yet this distinction, so carefully drawn in *What Is Contemplation?*, does not appear in *Seeds*.[18] What Merton seems to be talking about throughout *Seeds* is what he called, in the earlier book, infused or pure contemplation. It would seem fair, therefore, to say that in *Seeds* Merton seems to have modified his earlier position: Contemplation is not restricted to the few; many are destined to achieve its joys in this life.[19]

What is this experience of contemplation that is at once beyond our natural powers and yet also a fulfillment of deep capacities that God has put in us? As I indicated earlier, *Seeds* gives no systematic answer to this question. Contemplation is presented in a variety of ways: It is a precious multifaceted jewel which Merton turns so we can see different aspects of this rich and enriching experience. I propose in this chapter to discuss *Seeds* in terms of three unifying themes that seem to thread their way through the book: contemplation as discovery—of the true God, of the true self and of others; contemplation as an experience of freedom; and contemplation as an experience of darkness.

Contemplation as Discovery

Discovery of the True God

Contemplation is a discovery of our dependence on God and the implications of that dependence. "There exists," Merton says, "some point at which I can meet God in a real and experimental contact with His infinite actuality: and it is the point where my contingent being depends upon His Love" (31). The "point" Merton speaks of is a point of mysterious identity that is neither a created reality nor an uncreated reality but a "place" where both intersect. It is a point where, in a mystery beyond fathoming, we are one with God and we experience God.

The secret, of course, is that we must really meet God at this point. If we do not really meet God, this will mean that the God on whom we think we depend will be a fictitious god of our own making; and therefore a god we will never really meet, in fact cannot meet, for that god does not exist. It is nothing but an idol. But if we really meet God at this point of intersection of what is divine and what is human, the one we meet will be the true God as God is in the divine Self. For the God on whom we actually depend can only be the true God as that God truly is. Nothing less than the true God can be the one on whose love we depend for our very existence.

Our discovery of our dependence on God is in a way also God's "discovery" of our dependence on him. God "discovers" us as dependent on him the moment we begin to exist. God sees us in the divine Self and the divine Self in us. God "lives in [us], not only as [our] creator, but as [our] other and true self" (39). God discovers us in that pure contemplation that is the very reality of God. And we, being in God, swim in a sea of contemplation. As Merton puts it: "We become contemplatives when God discovers Himself in us." Since God's "discovery" of us coincides with our coming into being, it is true to say that we do not really *become* contemplatives. In a sense we already are contemplatives and always have been, because we exist in God who is pure contemplation. The problem is that we do not realize that we are contemplatives because we do not actualize our capacity. But the capacity is there, inherent in our dependence on God. For when we truly meet God at that point of dependence, it is a real and experiential contact with infinite divine actuality. We become at the center of our being the contemplatives we were always meant to be.

Because we are contemplatives in the very center of our being, the contemplative experience, when finally we reach it, is never a complete surprise to us. As Merton says: When we first taste the joys of contemplation,

> [I]t strikes us at once as utterly new and strangely familiar.... Although [we] had an entirely different notion of what it would be like, it turns out to be just what [we] seem to have known all along that it ought to be.... We enter a region which we had never even suspected, and yet it is this new world which seems familiar and obvious. (144-145)

In contemplation we return to a place where we have never been.

Discovery of the True Self

Contemplation is not only the discovery of the true God at our center; it is also the discovery at the same center of our true self.[20] For "the only way that I can be myself is to become identified with Him in Whom is hidden the reason and fulfillment of my existence" (29). God's love and mercy are the reason for our existence. His peace is the fulfillment of our existence. "[S]ince God alone possesses the secret of my identity, He alone can make me who I am or rather, He alone can make me who I will be when I at last fully begin to be" (29). For God bears in herself "the secret of who I am" (33). We find our true selves by finding her or, what amounts to the same thing. We "discover who [we are] and...possess [our] true identity by losing [ourselves] in Him" (46). "So it is with one who has vanished into God by pure contemplation. God alone is left. He is the only identity that acts there. He is the only one Who loves and knows and rejoices" (198).

Just as the God we discover at our center is not a false god, not an idol we have constructed by our imaginations, but the true God as God is in the divine Self, so the selves we discover in God cannot be the false selves we have constructed by our own desires and ambitions; they must be our true selves. We cannot live with an illusion of ourselves any more than we can live with an illusion of God.

That is why, before we can become who we are meant to be, we must recognize that we are "shadowed by an illusory person: a false self" (28). Our false selves exist, but at the level of illusion; they have no ultimate reality. They are the selves we imagine we are, not the selves that we are at our center. The great tragedy of human life is to go through it living as a self that we are not. This is what it means to experience the effects of original sin. Original sin, the effects of which survive Baptism, is a habitual state in which our acts tend to keep alive "the illusion that is opposed to God's reality living within me" (34). It is, therefore, the myth of original sin that begets the myth of the false self.

In fact, all sin, original or personal, starts from the assumption that our false selves are "the fundamental reality of life." We feed this illusion by self-seeking and self-aggrandizement. We construct the nothingness of the false self into what appears to be real. Our lives becomes an accumulation of accidents (in the Aristotelian sense) without substance.

> I am hollow, and my structure of pleasures and ambitions has no foundation. I am objectified in them. But they are destined by their very contingency to be destroyed. And when they are gone, there will be nothing left of me but my own nakedness and emptiness and hollowness, to tell me that I am a mistake. (29)

When Merton speaks of sin, he has in mind, not primarily a moral lapse whereby we choose what is in conflict with our better instincts, but an ontological lapse whereby we choose what is in conflict with our true being. It is not simply that we make mistakes. We *become* mistakes. For we become what we are not. But the mistake can be overcome, we can choose to drop the mask, the illusion, of our false selves and achieve our true identity in God. Indeed, from the moment we become capable of conscious acts of love, "our life becomes a series of choices between the fiction of our false-self, whom we feed with the illusions of passion and selfish appetite, and our true identity in the peace of God" (33-34).

Only God can teach us to make the right choices. He teaches us when we meet him at the center of our being; at the point of our dependence on him. That is why we must learn to "draw all the powers of the soul down into its deepest center to rest in silent expectancy for the coming of God, poised in tranquil and effortless concentration upon the point of [our] dependence on Him" (37). That is why the journey to our true identity is a journey along the way to contemplation. On that journey we learn to give up our false self, so that we can find our identity in God. And at the culmination of the journey God identifies "a created life with his own life, so that there is nothing left of any significance but God living in God."[21]

Discovery of Others

Contemplation is an experience in solitude, but it is not an experience in isolation. Contemplation leads us not only to God but also to other human persons. The point of dependence where we meet God is the same point at which we meet others, for they are no less dependent on God than we are. Meeting others, then, is an aspect of discovering our own identity, because we were never intended to exist separately. We must look for our identity not only in God but in other people. "The more I become identified with God [at my center], the more will I be identified with all the others who are identified with Him. His Love will live in all of us.... [W]e shall love one another and God with the same Love with which He loves us and Himself" (47).

While a contemplative must at some time go into the "desert," she must not go there to escape others, but in order to find them in God. It is dangerous to seek solitude merely because you want to be alone.

In his discourse at the Last Supper, Christ prayed that all might become one with the oneness he has with the Father in the Holy Spirit. When we achieve our true identity and become what God really intends us to be, we will discover that we love one another perfectly and that we all form the one mystical Person that is Christ living in us.

There is something incomplete about contemplation if it is not shared. That is why heaven, where the ultimate perfection of contemplation will be achieved, will not be a place of separate individuals, each with his own private vision of God; rather, it will be a sea of love flowing through the one Person of all the elect.

This sea of love in which we find our oneness with all is the life of the three Persons of God. In God there is no selfishness or isolation. "[T]he Three Selves of God are Three subsistent relations of selflessness, overflowing and superabounding in joy in the perfection of their Gift of their One Life to One another" (52).

This "circulation of love" in God "never finds a *self* that is capable of halting and absorbing it, but only another principle of communication and return" (52). This love of the three Persons is contemplation. Our joy and our destiny are to participate in this love, so that we can live entirely in and for God and one another.

Contemplation in this life is meant to reflect its heavenly counterpart. Even here on earth, "the more we are alone with God the more we are united with one another; and the silence of contemplation is deep and rich and endless society, not only with God but with men" (49).

And yet our efforts to achieve union with others in Christ is always a struggle. What is experienced with clarity in heaven is experienced only in obscurity in this life. For in heaven our thoughts of others can only draw us closer to God, whereas on earth, if we turn our thoughts directly to others in prayer, we may be distracted by their seeming separateness and so be withdrawn from union with God and likewise from union with them.

In heaven we meet others in the bright clarity of the purest contemplative vision; on earth we most often find them and God in a contemplation that is dark and obscure. But for the present it is in this darkness that we must try to find ourselves and others as we all truly are. The darkness becomes for us a sea of Love, if not Light, in which at last we become real and know that reality is to be found not in separateness but in union.

Contemplation as an Experience of Freedom

The seeds of contemplation that God plants in us can grow and develop only in the context of freedom. For they are seeds "planted in my liberty" (27). If we are to actualize our capacity for contemplation, then, we must become free persons. And Merton has much to say about what it means to be a free person.[22]

Perhaps the most important aspect of freedom, which in a sense encompasses its whole meaning, is the freedom to see things as they really are. This is the freedom that liberates me from anything that would tend "in one way or another to keep alive in me the illusion that is opposed to God's reality living within me" (34). This is the illusion of our false selves. As long as we perceive no greater subjective reality in us than our false selves, we have no freedom. We cannot seek God. We cannot become the contemplatives that we actually are. Our illusory selves may talk about contemplation, write about it, even try to become contemplative; but they can never succeed, for the subject of contemplation can only be a self that really exists. The shadow of the self cannot be contemplative any more than the shadow of a tree can produce fruit.

To have this freedom to see things as they are, we must also be free from selfishness, that is to say, from the desires and attachments that feed the false self. We must not use up our life accumulating pleasures and experiences and power and honors that clothe our false selves and attempt to construct their essential nothingness into something objectively real. We must escape "from the prison of our own self-hood" so as to "enter by love into union with the Life Who dwells and sings within the essence of every creature and in the core of our own souls" (22).

Until we have managed this escape, we will not be seeing things as they really are. Indeed, the very things that God has created to attract us to the divine self will keep us away from God. For we will linger on them, making them the objects of our self-seeking, instead of letting them lead us to God. It is only when we are delivered from self-seeking that we are free to seek God and nothing else. Freedom means, therefore, the complete destruction in us of all selfishness.

It is easier to speak about deliverance from selfishness than to achieve it. For selfishness is an elusive "reality" that at times we can identify only with great difficulty. For selfishness may be something of which we are conscious; but it may also mean something happening in us of which we are almost totally unaware. In other words, there may be obvious attachments in our lives that deter us from seeking God, and because they are obvious, we can readily recognize them and, it is to be hoped, deal with them. But there may also be attachments that are not so obvious: hidden and subtle attachments of which we are unaware and therefore not really able to deal with. For example, a contemplative may think that he is seeking God in his prayer when in reality he is seeking the consolations that God sometimes gives with prayer: recollection, interior peace and the sense of his presence. Clinging to these spiritual experiences can be, even if ever so unconsciously, an attachment to creatures that prevents us from truly seeking God and therefore blocks the way to true contemplation. "[R]ecollection is just as much a creature as an automobile. The sense of interior peace is no less created than a bottle of wine. The experimental awareness of the presence of God is just as truly a created thing as a glass of beer" (126).

Selfishness can hide itself under many guises. We need

the discernment to uncover its presence and its different forms. For until we are fully conscious that it is there, we can do nothing to free ourselves from it. What would it be like to be totally free? In a passage full of passion Merton offers a portrait of perfect freedom. His intent, we would hope, is not to discourage us, but to show how deep is the reality of freedom and how rare its perfect achievement.

> I wonder if there are twenty men alive in the world now who see things as they really are. That would mean that there were twenty men who were free, who were not dominated or even influenced by any attachment to any created thing or to their own selves or to any gift of God, even to the highest, the most supernaturally pure of His graces. I don't believe that there are twenty such men alive in the world. But there must be one or two. They are the ones who are holding everything together and keeping the universe from falling apart. (124)

The path to perfect freedom is a difficult one. For Merton it must always lead into the desert[23]; that is, into the place of silence and solitude. Only in solitude can we come to see things as they are. Only in solitude can we achieve that detachment that frees us to seek God in our lives. That is why Merton always saw the monastic setting as the ideal locus for contemplation. "[P]hysical solitude, exterior silence and real recollection are all morally necessary for anyone who wants to lead a contemplative life."[24]

Can one find sufficient solitude to become a contemplative in the urban setting in which most of us are destined to live out our lives? Merton would answer: Only with great, if not insurmountable, difficulty. In a celebrated passage, which impresses more by its earnestness than its practicability, Merton suggests how one may try to find solitude in the city.

> Do everything you can to avoid the amusements and the noise and the business of men. Keep as far away as you can from the places where they gather to cheat and insult one another, to exploit one another, to laugh at one another, or to mock one another with their false gestures of friendship.

Do not read their newspapers, if you can help it. Be glad if you can keep beyond the reach of their radios. Do not bother with their unearthly songs or their intolerable concerns for the way their bodies look and feel.

Do not smoke their cigarettes or drink the things they drink or share their preoccupation with different kinds of food. Do not complicate your life by looking at the pictures in their magazines.

Keep your eyes clean and your ears quiet and your mind serene. Breathe God's air. Work, if you can, under His sky.

But if you have to live in a city and work among machines and ride in the subways and eat in a place where the radio makes you deaf with spurious news and where the food destroys your life and the sentiments of those around you poison your heart with boredom, do not be upset, but accept it as the love of God and as a seed of solitude planted in your soul, and be glad of this suffering: for it will keep you alive to the next opportunity to escape from them and be alone in the healing silence of recollection and in the untroubled presence of God.[25]

Actualizing our capacity for contemplation requires an *existential freedom* that liberates us from the illusion of our false selves that would keep us living in a world of unreality. It calls, in addition, for a *moral freedom* that detaches us from the selfish desires, cares and ambitions—even spiritual ones—that interfere with our search for God.

There is yet another type of freedom needed for the contemplative experience, and that is what Merton calls *intellectual freedom*, or the freedom from concepts and images of created things. For the goal of contemplation is to meet at my center God as God is in the divine Self. And yet "we cannot know Him as He really is unless we pass beyond everything that can be imagined and enter into an obscurity without images and without the likeness of any created thing" (80).

To really meet God means that we have to pass beyond the kataphatic way that seeks to find God mirrored in the perfections of creatures. "No matter what perfection you predicate of Him, you have to add that He is not what we conceive by that term" (79). The apophatic way of meeting God in the darkness is the shorter and simpler way. For the living God is not a philosopher's abstraction. He "lies infinitely beyond the reach of anything our eyes can see or our minds can understand" (79). Neither is God the Being which the theologians speak of in the dogmas of faith. For the Truth of God as God is in the divine Self is apprehended:

> [N]ot in distinct and clear-cut definitions but in the limpid obscurity of a single intuition that unites all dogmas in one simple Light, shining into the soul directly from God's eternity, without the medium of created concept, without the intervention of symbols or of language or the likenesses of material things. (89)

The only one who can truly know God is God. If we are to truly know God, we must in some way be transformed into God. We must become somehow what she is. This is to say that the highest freedom possible to us is to know God as God is in the divine Self by loving identification with her in obscurity. The seeds "planted in [our] liberty" turn out to be not only the seeds of our identity, but the seeds of our identification with God.

Contemplation as an Experience of Darkness

Merton's obvious preference for the "shorter and simpler way" of apophaticism is evidenced by the more than fifty references to "darkness" (or equivalents such as "night," "cloud," or "obscurity") that appear in *Seeds of Contemplation*.

For Merton, all the exercises of the spiritual life (such as reading or meditation) are intended to lead us into the darkness. Thus, he says of meditation: If it "only produces images and ideas and affections that you can understand and feel and appreciate, it is not yet doing its full quota of work" (138).

Meditation achieves its purpose when it brings us to a point of bafflement and darkness, wherein we can no longer think of God or imagine God. Consequently, the only course left to us is to reach out to God by blind faith, and hope and love. When we reach this point, we must not be discouraged by the seeming futility of meditation; instead, we should relax "in a simple contemplative gaze that keeps [our] attention peacefully aware of Him hidden somewhere in this deep cloud" (139), into which we have entered.

Entering this cloud of darkness awakens our spirit to a new level of experience. This awakening is so unique an experience that by comparison the sharpest natural experience is like sleep. It is an awakening to the full possession of God, whom we yet possess in the darkness. For "our minds are most truly liberated from the weak created lights that are darkness in comparison to Him; it's then that we are filled with His infinite Light which is pure darkness to us" (89).

In the darkness the last vestiges of selfishness are taken away. "The deep and secret selfishness that is too close for us to identify is stripped away from our souls" (172) and in the darkness we are made free. The darkness becomes an atmosphere of breathless clarity in which we find peace, and the deep night becomes the brightness of the noonday sun, in which we find the One whom alone our heart desires. And we find ourselves on the threshold of a totally new experience, where we are no longer the subjects of an experience but are the experience itself. The duality between God and ourselves disappears. Merton attempts to clarify what this means: "What happens is that the separate entity that was you suddenly disappears and nothing is left but a pure freedom indistinguishable from infinite Freedom. Love identified with Love. Not two loves, one waiting for the other, striving for the other, seeking for the other, but Love Loving in Freedom."[26]

Contemplation finally becomes what it is really meant to be. "It is no longer something poured out of God into a created subject, so much as God living in God and identifying a created life with His own Life so that there is nothing left of any significance but God living in God" (196).

Notes

1 *What Is Contemplation?*, which had preceded it by some three months, was more a pamphlet than a full-length book.

2 *What Is Contemplation?*, p. 17.

3 On March 8, 1948, Merton wrote to Naomi Stone: "[James] Laughlin [of New Directions] is interested in another project that is underway, a book of more or less random thoughts about the contemplative life called: *The Soil and the Seeds of Contemplation*." *Witness to Freedom*, William H. Shannon, ed. (New York: Farrar, Straus, Giroux, 1994), p. 125.

4 There is some question whether writing *The Seven Storey Mountain* was Abbot Dunne's idea or Merton's. See William Shannon, *Silent Lamp: The Thomas Merton Story* (New York: Crossroad, 1992), pp. 131-133.

5 Thomas Merton, *Entering the Silence: Becoming a Monk and Writer: The Journals of Thomas Merton, Vol. 2* , Jonathan Montaldo, ed. (San Francisco: HarperSanFrancisco, 1996), p. 34. In *The Sign of Jonas* (New York: Harcourt Brace, 1953) the confessor is identified as Dom Gildas (p. 20).

6 *The [London] Times Literary Supplement*, December 23, 1949.

7 *The Downside Review*, 68 (1950), pp. 223-225.

8 See *Seeds*, p. 87, where Merton suggests that outside Christian faith there is no such thing as contemplation, "only the void of nirvana...or the sensual dreams of the Sufis." This statement was omitted in the revised edition of December 1949 and in *New Seeds*.

9 Thomas Merton, *New Seeds of Contemplation* (New York: New Directions, 1972).

10 *Sign of Jonas*, p. 165.

11 *Courage for Truth*, p. 25.

12 This sentence was omitted in the letters to Sister Therese in *Road to Joy*.

13 *Thought*, September, 1949.

14 *Saturday Review of Literature*, 32: 43 (April 16, 1949).

[15] *The Journal of Religion*, 29: July 1949.

[16] *Sign of Jonas*, p. 165.

[17] *What Is Contemplation?*, pp. 30-31.

[18] In *Seeds* Merton speaks about the activity of the contemplative, but not about active contemplation.

[19] It is my belief that Merton never completely resolved this ambiguity.

[20] This notion is developed in greater detail in *New Seeds*.

[21] See also *Seeds*, p. 198: "So it is with the one who has vanished into God by pure contemplation. God alone is left. He is the only identity that acts there. He is the only one Who knows and loves and rejoices."

[22] This notion is more fully developed in *New Seeds*.

[23] *Seeds*, pp. 57-58. See also p. 153: "The ordinary way to contemplation lies through a desert."

[24] See "Notes for a Philosophy of Solitude," in *Disputed Questions* (New York: Farrar, Straus, Giroux, 1960), pp. 177-207.

[25] *Seeds*, pp. 60-61. The exuberant *contemptus mundi* of this passage is toned down slightly in the December, 1949, revised edition of *Seeds*, extensively so in *New Seeds* (1962).

[26] *Seeds*, p. 195. Remember what I said in the Introduction about love as the bridge between the kataphatic way and the apophatic way.

3

The Ascent to Truth

*Far from teaching us to hate this world, John of the Cross is
telling us the way to love it and to understand it. (58)*

In the booklet *What Is Contemplation?*, Merton had made use
of the writings of Thomas Aquinas and John of the Cross to
explain what the gift of contemplation is and how to deal
with it when one receives it. This early work was too brief to
allow for any detailed understanding of the teachings of the
Angelic Doctor or of the saint of Carmel. Merton's obvious
interest in what these two saints had to say about
contemplation blossomed into a book that eventually came to
be called *The Ascent to Truth*. The book attempts to combine
the Scholasticism of Aquinas with the mystical doctrine of
John of the Cross.

Begun probably some time in December, 1948 (soon after
the publication of *What is Contemplation?*, but before the
publication of *Seeds*), this book was originally entitled *The
Cloud and the Fire*—a rather good title for a book on
contemplation, picking up as it does that wondrous sense of
God's presence with the people of Israel as they departed
from Egypt. Chapter 13 of Exodus describes that departure:
"The Lord went in front of them in a pillar of *cloud* by day, to
lead them along the way, and in a pillar of *fire* by night, to
give them light, so that they might travel by day and by
night."[1] In turn, Merton's manuscript came to be called *The*

School of the Spirit, and then *Ascent to Light*, finally yielding place to *The Ascent to Truth*.

This switching of titles suggests that Merton was encountering more than ordinary difficulty in writing this book.[2] He admits as much in *The Sign of Jonas* where he records on February 9, 1949:

> My work has been tied up in knots for two months—more. I have been trying to write *The Cloud and the Fire*, which is a book about contemplation and the theology of contemplation at that...I have a huge mass of half-digested notes, all mixed up, and I can't find my way around in them. My ideas are not fixed and clear....[3]

Six days later, on February 15, he writes:

> I had been thinking of tearing up *The Cloud and the Fire* for a long time. I haven't done that exactly, but I have simply stuffed it into an envelope, plans and all, and reconsidered what it was I was supposed to start.[4]

On February 20, 1949, he writes, in a more optimistic frame of mind: "With Our Lady's help the book, now changed and called *The School of the Spirit*, goes quite smoothly." This mood did not last for long. On April 29, he speaks once again of his frustration:

> I wonder how many plans I have made for this book, *The School of the Spirit*? Perhaps six—including the ones I made for it when it was called *The Cloud and the Fire*.[5] So I sit at the typewriter, with my fingers all wound up in a cat's cradle of strings, overwhelmed with the sense of my own stupidity and surrounded by not one but a multitude of literary dilemmas.... There exists an almost unlimited number of combinations in which you can arrange the statements you have jotted down so carefully on some eight hundred pages of various notebooks.[6]

It seems clear that Merton was having an attack of writer's block or, perhaps more simply, was writing in a genre in which he was uncomfortable. At any rate, sifting through some eight hundred pages of notes, he could not quite decide how to put them together. All he could say was: "All this undigested material is utterly terrifying, and fascinating at the same time." It is worth noting the verbs Merton uses: "terrifying" and "fascinating." These are verbs often used to describe the mystery of God, which was after all the ultimate subject of Merton's book.

The year passed and Merton failed to complete *The School of the Spirit*. On January 7, 1950, he wrote to Sister Therese Lentfoehr: "I do not mean to drop *The School of the Spirit* entirely. Only to take it up again from a more thorough Scriptural and Patristic viewpoint later on."[7] Another year passed. On January 8, 1951, he confided to Sister Therese that the book he had been writing "finally split into two that can be easier finished than one. This will content the publisher and save the author a few headaches."[8] The first part of the original book, which retained the title "*The School of the Spirit*,"[9] was never completed, at least not to Merton's satisfaction. The second part, which dealt with the doctrine of John of the Cross, became *The Ascent to Truth*.

The Ascent to Truth exhibits some of the battle scars Merton experienced in writing it. It would seem that he never quite got those "undigested notes" together.[10] The book does not read with the smoothness of *Seeds of Contemplation*; at times it is overly speculative and repetitious. There are lingering elements of the "Catholic" narrowness that becloud parts of *The Seven Storey Mountain*. Thus, in a chapter entitled "The Problem of Unbelief," he has words of scorn for people "who cannot believe in the revealed word of God," but "swallow everything they read in the newspapers" (30). Some fifteen years later he piped a very different tune in an essay he wrote for *Harper's* magazine which bore the title "Apologies to an Unbeliever." At the very beginning of that essay he tells the "unbeliever," "I recognize that I have been standing on your foot, and I am now at last getting off it, with these few mumbled sentences." But that was in 1966.

One wonders, too, whether Merton in his later years would have made the sweeping statement: "Theology is not made by mystics: mystics are formed by theology" (258). Certainly it is true that mysticism (at least Christian mysticism) cannot flourish in a theological vacuum, but does not the mystic have important data from his own experience to offer the theologian for his reflection? Did not Aquinas draw on the insights of mystics of the patristic age? Is it true to say that the mysticism of John of the Cross was formed by the theology of Aquinas, or would it be more correct to say that his mystical life was formed by God's grace and that the saint used the terminology of Aquinas to articulate his experience?

In a comparative graph he made in 1967 evaluating a number of his books, Merton described *The Ascent to Truth* as only "fair." It is difficult to fault his own evaluation.

To suggest shortcomings in the book is not to deny that it has value. His clarification of the ways of darkness and light in contemplation, the soundness of the ascetical discipline he presents, the way he clarifies the value and limitations of conceptual knowledge of God, his insistence on the crucial role played by our intelligence in the various stages that lead to contemplative union with God, his careful nuancing of the relationship between intelligence and love in the experience of God: All these elements of the book are of perennial concern to anyone interested in the contemplative vision of reality. There is much in this book that is worthwhile.

Yet the fact remains that this book has not had the appeal of his earlier work, *Seeds of Contemplation*; nor did it fare so well with the critics or the general public. The late Sister Therese Lentfoehr wrote a glowing review in *Renascence*.[11] Thus she says: "Among the important works of a significant author, frequently one book will stand out as in a special sense definitive and representative of that author's excellence. Of such caliber and status would seem to be Thomas Merton's *Ascent to Truth*."

Other reviewers were not so sanguine about the book. James A. Pike in his review in *The New York Times Book Review*[12] was put off by "the author's use of technical terms of scholastic philosophy—often without definition—side by side with breezy colloquialisms and homely illustrations." He wonders how a contemplative may know "that he is being now moved by a particular one of the seven gifts of the Holy Ghost and now by another...that his actions are 'active' or 'passive,' 'acquired' or 'infused'; that he is in one 'night' or another." The reviewer from *Blackfriars* found the first third of the book interesting and "very nearly a good book," but, from there on, except for some good passages here and there, "it falls to the ground."[13] The reviewer looked in vain for insights from early monasticism and from Merton's own Cistercian Order. This last criticism, it must be said, is a bit unfair, given that Merton's stated purpose was to show the link between the mysticism of John of the Cross and writings of Thomas Aquinas on human happiness.

One thing that emerges from the reviews and also from a careful reading of *Ascent* is that the limpid simplicity of *Seeds* is missing. Perhaps one explanation of the difference between these two works is the different perspective from which each was written. In all he wrote, Merton was very much of a traditionalist; that is to say, he always wrote with the utmost respect for the Christian tradition (and, in his later years, for other religious traditions). Sometimes he wrote out of the background of his own tradition, filtering that tradition through his own mind (as he did in *Seeds of Contemplation*); at other times he wrote about that tradition (which is what he does in *Ascent*). He was more successful in doing the first than the second. In writing about the tradition, he seems at times to get submerged in it and to become abstract and unduly speculative; in writing out of the background of the tradition, he is more truly himself, more concrete, more existential, more accessible. Despite his considerable background of learning, Merton is not at his best in writing scholarly works. Indeed, one of the problems of *Ascent* is that it is difficult to be sure what readers he had in mind. The book is hardly scholarly enough for the professional theologian and almost too scholarly, in some sections at least, for the general reader.

In *Ascent*, Merton sets for himself three main goals: (1) to define the nature of the contemplative experience; (2) to show the necessary ascetical discipline leading to that experience;

and (3) to give a brief sketch of mature contemplation. In working toward these goals, Merton draws on the principal writings of John of the Cross (*The Ascent of Mount Carmel, The Dark Night of the Soul, The Spiritual Canticle* and *The Living Flame*). He links the teaching of the Carmelite saint with the teachings of Thomas Aquinas, particularly with the five opening questions of the *"Prima Secundae"* of the *Summa Theologiae*, wherein Aquinas sketches his outline of the meaning of happiness and locates our last end in the highest contemplation of God. This Thomistic teaching, Merton says, "not only influenced Saint John of the Cross but actually provided him with the basic structure of his whole doctrine." He adds: "The mere fact that Saint John of the Cross was able to see the tremendous implications, for the contemplative life on earth, contained in a few simple, fundamental ideas of the Angelic Doctor about man's last end, is itself evidence of Saint John's theological genius" (132).

John's *ascetical* teaching—that complete detachment from creatures is necessary before one can arrive at union with God—builds on the doctrine of Aquinas that our last end cannot be found in anything created. His *mystical* teaching, that the goal of the spiritual quest consists (1) in contemplative union with God beyond concepts and images in the darkness of faith in this life, and (2) in the perfection of vision in the life to come, is but a reprise of Aquinas's theme that our happiness consists in nothing less than the vision of the very essence of God. His doctrine of detachment from creatures in order to achieve union with God are taken, sometimes word for word, from Aquinas's discussion of happiness.

The three goals Merton set for himself are not always developed in successive order, though they correspond roughly to the three divisions of the book: (1) "The Cloud and the Fire," (2) "Reason and Mysticism in Saint John of the Cross," and (3) "Doctrine and Experience." It can be said that these goals pervade his text and at times overlap one another. Nor is the link he attempts to forge between the theology of Aquinas and the mysticism of John of the Cross presented in any systematic way. He relates the one to the other as it suits the purpose of the particular chapter he is writing. Though there is a development in the book, a number of the chapters appear to be almost separate essays that could be read on their own.

This lack of any tidy developmental sequence in the book makes it difficult to try to summarize its contents in a few pages. In an attempt to bring a measure of unity into the discussion of a lengthy and somewhat complicated book, I have chosen to confine this summary to two topics which, to me, represent main thrusts in the book: (1) the *moral asceticism* of John of the Cross, by which I mean his teaching on the detachment that is so essential to the contemplative journey; and (2) his *intellectual asceticism*, by which I mean his insistence on the proper discipline of the intellect at the beginning of the journey toward God, during the course of that journey and even when its summit has been reached. This second topic is a special emphasis for Merton, because he was firmly convinced that "there is no such thing as a sanctity that is not intelligent" (325).

The moral asceticism of John of the Cross is an uncompromising call for complete detachment from creatures in order to arrive at union with God. It is an asceticism that is based on the teaching of Aquinas that our happiness cannot be found in creatures. In question two of the *"Prima Secundae"* (the First Part of the Second Part) of his *Summa Theologiae*, Aquinas parades before us one by one the created goods that one might look to for happiness—material possessions, honor, fame, power, bodily health, pleasure, the natural perfection of the soul—and one by one he eliminates them as candidates for the role of happiness in human life. No created good (which by its very nature lacks the fullness of goodness) can constitute human happiness. To be happy, we must be taken out of ourselves, not simply to a higher order of creation, but to the uncreated reality of God, to that Being who alone is the fullness of goodness.[14] God alone is our happiness.

But people can seek happiness in God only if they are not

seeking it in creatures, which means that they must be detached from creatures. In what does this detachment consist? Some might be tempted to say that it means total withdrawal from creatures insofar as this is possible. This is not the answer of John of the Cross. He is no Gnostic[15]: He denies neither the goodness of creatures nor the need to use them. He probes deeper to the very roots of the problem posed by creatures. *The problem is not in creatures but in ourselves.* It is not creatures but the *desire* for them that impedes our quest for God. John affirms without reservation "that the desire of creatures as ends in themselves cannot coexist with the desire of God as our true end" (57). The ascetical task is to rid ourselves, not of creatures, but of the desire to pursue them for their own sake apart from God. The words that follow are Saint John's call to detachment. They are lines which, Merton says, "have proved to be a terror and a scandal to many Christians" (52).

> In order to have pleasure in everything
> Desire to have pleasure in nothing.
> In order to arrive at possessing everything
> Desire to possess nothing.
> In order to arrive at being everything
> Desire to be nothing.
> In order to arrive at knowing everything
> Desire to know nothing.[16]

Merton's comments on these lines of John of the Cross are splendid:

> *Todo y Nada.* All and nothing. The two words contain the theology of Saint John of the Cross. Todo—all—is God, Who contains in Himself eminently the perfections of all things. For Him we are made. In Him we possess all things. But in order to possess Him Who is all, we must renounce the possession of anything that is less than God. But everything that can be seen, known, enjoyed, possessed in a finite manner, is less than God. Every desire for knowledge, possession, being that falls short of God must be blacked out. *Nada!* (53)

John is not wasting words, Merton warns us. We have to read him with close attention, as with merciless objectivity he identifies the enemy. It is not pleasure or possessions or knowledge. It is *desire*.[17] The secret of ascetical liberation is "the 'darkening' of all desire" (54). As Merton points out, John does not say: "In order to arrive at the knowledge of everything, know nothing," but "desire to know nothing." It is not pleasure, knowledge, possession or being as such that must be "darkened" and "mortified," but only the passion of desire for these things.

It is only by the "blacking out" of desire that we can begin to fulfill the greatest of the commandments: to love God with our whole heart, our whole soul and our whole strength. And for Saint John this commandment sums up the entire ascetical and mystical life.

Yet the passion of desire is strong and imperious in the human psyche. The ultimate perversion of that passion is reached when, instead of seeking creatures for the sake of creatures, people seek desire for the sake of desire. They may pursue created goods as goals that they hope will bring happiness. When one does not satisfy, they try another, and another. Finally, unable to locate happiness in anything they pursue, they may try to seek it in the very pursuit itself. Even when they see the futility of what they desire, they may continue to desire for the sake of desiring. The chase for pleasure then becomes the very pleasure that they seek. Desire for the sake of desire becomes a diversion,[18] whereby they fling themselves into exterior activities for their own sake—activities that benumb their spirits and distract them from the emptiness of their lives.

Desire—whether for a particular creature or desire turned back on itself—locks us in a prison of falsity and illusion from which we can be delivered only by discernment in the intellect and detachment in the will.

Discernment in the intellect and detachment in the will—both are necessary equipment for the ascetical journey. We cannot be freed from the desire for creatures until we know what creatures are and why it is futile to make them the object of desire. This is the task of discernment: It breaks through the web of illusion that desire spins around creatures, and reveals them in their true light. Discernment does not tell us that creatures are not good but only that they are not good enough to satisfy the longings of the human heart. Discernment gives eyes to detachment. Guided by the light of discernment, detachment frees us from all desires not centered on God. It delivers us from absorption in what is accidental and transitory. It refuses to let us be submerged by what is, ultimately, trivial and insignificant.

Discernment, by exposing creatures for what they are, and detachment, by disarming vain desires that would lead us astray, make us capable of a knowledge that is serene and a joy that is incorruptible. And we experience this serene knowledge and incorruptible joy not only in God but also in creatures. For once our knowledge and love find their fulfillment in God, we become free to find and enjoy in God the whole of God's creation.

Desiring to have pleasure in nothing, we have pleasure in everything. Desiring to possess nothing, we arrive at possessing everything. Desiring to know nothing, we arrive at knowing everything.

Far from teaching us to hate this world, John of the Cross tells us the way to love it and understand it. Paradoxically, we are able to be happy with creatures only when we no longer look to them as the source of our happiness.

The end of all ascetical discipline is freedom: the mind's freedom from illusion (achieved through discernment), and the will's freedom from desire (achieved through detachment). When we possess this freedom, we can know creatures and love them, without any fear that they will lead us away from God; for we have found them in God.

Contemplation is an experience of God that exceeds our natural capabilities. It is union with God beyond images and concepts, realized in this life in pure faith and in heaven in the beatific vision. Though this union with God—the highest possible experience of the divine reality—is beyond our natural powers, it is nonetheless true that the human intellect plays an important role—at the beginning and along the way—in our progressive ascent toward union with God. So does the human will. As I said above, one of Merton's principal concerns in *Ascent* is to clarify the role of intelligence in the contemplative journey and its relation to love.

The intellect has a role to play at the very beginning of the spiritual journey. Before we can go beyond images and concepts, we must have images and concepts to go beyond. By the natural power of human reason, we can arrive at a true, albeit limited, knowledge of God. We can know God in the concepts that come to us from created things, for all created things reflect the reality of God. They are footprints showing that God has passed by. The problem, of course, is that created things are but dim, imperfect, partial reflections. They tell us only that God has been there, not where God has gone. Concepts derived from created things are, therefore, never adequate to grasp the reality of God. They are limited; God's reality is unlimited.

Indeed, our concepts are limited even when we use them to signify created things. Concepts, though they give us an intellectual grasp of reality, are incapable of conveying the total concreteness of the reality they describe. Of necessity, they have limits and boundaries. If they did not have limits, we would not understand them. We define a tree differently from the way we define a horse. To define or conceptualize something is to place limits on it. The root of the English word *define* is the Latin word *finis*, which means "limit" or "limitation." To "de-fine"—that is, to place limits on something—is to say that it is this, not something else. What we cannot define (that is, put limits on) we cannot know. Thus, to take an example, we can know wisdom and justice insofar as they are different things. If we were to say that wisdom and justice are the same thing, one concept (or definition) would cancel out the other and neither would have meaning for us.

The limited character of all created concepts would seem to pose an insoluble problem when we try to rise from these concepts to a knowledge of God. The reality of God is one and undivided; it is unlimited. How can our diverse and limited concepts grasp in any way the undivided and unlimited reality of God?

Aquinas's way out of this dilemma is his teaching on the analogy of being—an approach to God that involves not only affirmation but also denial. Analogy means that the concepts we have of created things are verified in God, but always in a way different from the way they are true of creatures. As Merton writes:

> It is impossible for us to understand the notions of justice and mercy unless they are somehow divided from one another and opposed. In God, justice is mercy, mercy is justice, and both are wisdom and power and being, for all His attributes merge in one infinite Reality that elevates them beyond definition and comprehension. (92-93)

Every concept, therefore, that reason proposes to us about God tells us two things: (1) insofar as it is actually true of God, it tells us what God is: wise, just, merciful; (2) insofar as it is not true of God in any anthropomorphic or limited sense, it tells us what God is not. Thus, there are two ways of approaching God through concepts: the way of affirmation (the kataphatic way) and the way of denial (the apophatic way)[19]; and we need both. In Merton's words:

> We must affirm and deny at the same time. One cannot go without the other. If we go on affirming without denying, we end up by affirming that we have delimited the Being of God in our concepts. If we go on denying without affirming, we end up by denying that our concepts can tell the truth about Him in any way whatever. (94)

In a helpful image, Merton compares the ways of affirmation and denial to the takeoff and the flight of a plane. We make a statement about God: We affirm that He exists. This is the plane taking off. The plane rolls along the ground: We apply existence to God in the way it applies to us. But only for the moment. For, having affirmed, we now have to deny. The plane takes off into the air. It can do so only by "renouncing" its contact with the ground. So we cannot reach God in our concepts unless we renounce their limits and definitions. We take off from the "ground" of our affirmation and ascend into the "sky" of our denials. We know God—but imperfectly—in our affirmations. We know Him—but darkly—in our denials. Knowing God in our denials is to know Him by "unknowing" (94-98).

While reason through its affirmations and denials can speak to us of God as the divine reality is imaged in creatures, it cannot by itself make contact with God as God is in the divine Self. It can, however, tell us that such contact is possible. When it has made known all that creatures can say about God, and therefore can go no further by its own light, reason can tell that, over and above "the footprints He has left behind Him as He went on His way" (270-271), there is another light that can tell us where God has gone and where God is. This is the light of faith. Reason, admitting its own limitations, can yet show us that the only one who can tell us anything about God as God is in the divine Self is God. Reason can make known to us that God is able to communicate the divine Self to us so that what we cannot know about God by ourselves we can know through divine self-communication.

Faith is our response to this self-communication of God. It enables our intelligence "to make a firm and complete assent to divinely revealed truth, not on account of the clear intrinsic evidence of statements about God, but on the authority of God Himself revealing" (254). By faith we adhere to what we do not actually see; hence, the act of faith is not purely intellectual. It is elicited under the impulsion of the will. Because we believe what we do not see, faith is dark; because we believe under the impulsion of the will, faith is loving. That is why John of the Cross speaks of "this dark and loving knowledge, which is faith." [20]

The object of faith is not propositions about God, but God in the divine Self. "Faith terminates in God in the sense that every article of revealed truth ends in God or refers to God" (255). What faith attains to, therefore, is not just God revealed in the statements of faith, but God revealing, namely, God as God is in the divine Self.

Insofar as the object of faith is God revealed to us, faith is able to be expressed in propositions that tell us things about God that are beyond reason's light. Reason, while not able to arrive at these propositions by itself, can nevertheless reflect on them once they have been revealed. This it does in speculative theology and also, perhaps especially, in meditation. Moved by love, we become absorbed in new concepts about God that faith reveals. We thrill at a whole new level of understanding that opens up before us. New insights lead to new affective experiences of God and we go out to God in a deeper and more ardent love. Every new insight into God's reality becomes another reason for loving God.

Yet we cannot rest content simply with propositions about God. For faith attains not only to God revealed (in the propositions of faith) but to God revealing (that is, known in the divine Self, but in the darkness). Propositions, we must remember, are still concepts about God: They cannot reach God in the divine reality itself. They cannot unite us with God. Hence, while it is good to seek God in concepts, it is futile to expect that any conceptual knowledge, even that of faith, can lead us to union with God as God is.

That is why we have to know when the time has come to go beyond concepts into the dark but truer knowledge of God that lies beyond them. This is the moment when reason has to say "no" to reasoning. It is the moment when concepts have to become the diving board from which, at the divine bidding, we spring into the abyss of God. The call to contemplation is an invitation to turn our awareness of God from what is revealed about God to God who offers the revelation. This is the call to move from knowing God with clear concepts to knowing God in the darkness of "unknowing." We must allow the small matches which are our concepts ("intelligence," "love," "power") to be blown out by the tremendous reality of God bearing down upon us like a dark storm (106). We must plunge with abandon into the darkness of pure faith, where the soul knows God, "not because it beholds Him face to face, but because it is touched by Him in darkness" (256-257). "Faith takes man beyond the limits of his own finite intelligence. It is therefore "dark" to him, because he has no longer any faculty with which to see the infinite Truth of God" (152).

The way of pure faith is also the way of love. In the darkness in which we do not see God, we are united to God in the act of love. And this love of God in contemplative prayer makes a positive contribution to our knowledge of God. For "it gives the soul concrete possession of everything that is contained in the truths of faith." "Love gives us an experience, a taste of what we have not seen and are not yet able to see. Faith gives us full title to this treasure which is ours to possess in darkness. Love enters the darkness and lays hands upon what is our own!" (295).

In the darkness of pure faith, love gives us a positive experience of the transcendent quality of God's perfections which the propositions of faith can express only in a negative way. Thus, faith can tell us that God is good, but it must also add that God's goodness infinitely transcends all our ideas of goodness. Love can give us "a direct, positive experience of that abundant goodness which concepts could only declare to be beyond their knowledge." That is why love is able to "astound the intelligence with vivid reports of a transcendent Actuality which minds can only know, on earth, by a confession of ignorance. And so, when the mind admits that God is too great for our knowledge, Love replies: 'I know Him!'"[21]

These words of Merton are a beautiful and moving expression of love's experience plunged into the midnight of dark faith, but they are a poetic description and we must not overliteralize them. Though love's experience is real (it really touches God and is touched by God), strictly speaking, it is not knowledge. It is knowing by "unknowing." It is possession, but possession of what is not known. That is why it can never entirely satisfy the yearnings of the human soul. "[J]ust as conceptual knowledge creates anguish in the contemplative by reminding him how little he can know of God, so the possession of God by love, on earth, fills him with still greater agony because it tells him, even more clearly, that he can only rest in vision." (298)

Possessing God in the darkness by love is a far deeper experience than knowing God in the limited concepts of the intellect; yet possessing God in darkness only makes us yearn more fully to see God face to face. "Love does not heal our ignorance: mystical love is a sickness which vision alone can cure" (299). Even at the highest level of the mystical life, the experience of transforming union, "love cries out with a more and more ardent hunger and sweetly demands the satiation of perfect vision" (300).

This perfect vision which the soul, transformed in God, awaits at the threshold of heaven is "a clear intuition which in one glance takes in and, in a certain measure, comprehends everything that is obscurely revealed, in fragmentary fashion, by all the separate articles of faith, by all the truths revealed by God and even by those truths about God and His creation which reason can grasp" (303).

This is the summit of the mystical journey: It is seeing God, not through a glass darkly, but face to face, and knowing God as God knows the divine Self in its own reality.

As we saw earlier in *What is Contemplation?*, a point is reached in the contemplative ascent to God when the would-be contemplative realizes that she must abandon concepts of God in order to plunge into the darkness of pure faith. Two questions remain to be discussed: (1) What are the signs that identify that moment in the spiritual journey when one should stop seeking God by concepts?, and (2) Once we have entered into the contemplative experience in pure faith and love, does reason quietly remove itself from the scene, or does it still have its role to play?

John of the Cross suggests three signs which can help a person decide that she is ready to drop discursive meditation and all efforts to reach God by concepts. The first sign is the inability any longer to engage in fruitful meditation. Meditation which once brought joy to the soul becomes hard and wearisome. The second sign is a lack of interest in particular ways of representing God. Particular representations of God in the mind or the imagination, in a statue or a picture, no longer inspire devotion in the soul. This is a critical moment in a person's spiritual life. It means "the soul has come face to face with the distinction between God in Himself and God as He is contained in our concepts of Him" (232), and the first is immeasurably more attractive than the second. There is a growing distaste for representations of God "which are powerless to do justice to His infinite reality" (235). The third sign is a positive attraction for solitary contemplative prayer. In the words of Saint John: "The third and surest sign is that the soul takes pleasure in being alone, and waits with loving attentiveness upon God, without making any particular meditation, in inward peace and quietness and rest."[22]

What Saint John is describing is not a state of passivity. The soul is still engaged in an activity of the mind which is quite definite and precise; namely, attentiveness to God. "The difference," Merton suggests, "is not between activity and inactivity, but between two kinds of action—between reasoning and intuition. The soul gazes with the desire of love into the darkness where God is hidden and gradually loses sight of every other object" (233-234).

What is the role of reason when the soul crosses the divide between discursive meditation and the contemplative striving for God beyond concepts?[23] Its first task is to determine whether or not the moment has arrived to take this step. John of the Cross has laid down the guidelines; but guidelines must be applied. It is reason that makes the application. Reason gives the "go-ahead" to move to a higher level of the ascent to God.[24]

Reason must continue to operate in the night of faith. It must keep the contemplative traveling along the straight road of faith that leads to divine union. There is a type of mysticism that can lead people astray—a mysticism that thrives on unusual spiritual experiences: revelations or locutions or visions. John of the Cross does not deny that God can communicate with the soul of the mystic in these ways; but he does insist that such experiences should neither be sought after nor desired, since they cannot help us to know God in the divine Self. It is here that reason plays a decisive role. It must sift critically all spiritual experiences and reject those that fall outside the realms of pure faith. "Reason, acting in the service of faith, must question and evaluate and pass judgment on all our most intimate and spiritual aspirations.... The great paradox of Saint John of the Cross is that his asceticism of "night" cannot possibly be practiced without the light of reason. It is by the light of reason that we keep on traveling through the night of faith" (155).

Merton compares the soul's journey along the way of pure faith to the journey of a car along a dark road at night. The driver can keep to the road only by using his headlights. "The way of faith is necessarily obscure. We drive by night. Nevertheless our reason penetrates the darkness enough to show us a little of the road ahead. It is by the light of reason that we interpret the signposts and make out the landmarks along our way." (155)

Reason's task, therefore, in the ascent toward union with God, is to remove anything that would hinder the soul from receiving the inspiration of God. Saint Gregory Nazianzen calls the soul of the contemplative "an instrument played by the Holy Spirit" (181). From this instrument the Holy Spirit can bring forth harmonies and melodies we could never have dreamed of hearing. Reason's work is not to play the instrument but to tune the strings. "The Master Himself does not waste time tuning the instrument. He shows His servant, reason, how to do it and leaves him to do the work. If He then comes and finds the piano still out of tune, He does not bother to play anything on it" (182).

Reason must judge the right measure of self-denial that will keep the soul responsive to the "keys when they are struck by God" (182). By the active work of discrimination, which eliminates the movements of disordered passion and ill-regulated instincts, reason disposes the soul for passive union with God.

We have seen already how reason exercises its power of discrimination in the night of sense by enabling us to see what creatures are and what they are not. But its highest powers of discrimination are reserved for the night of the spirit, in which it helps us to discern what is and what is not of God. This is reason's highest function and its greatest glory.

Enough has been said to show the important place that John of the Cross assigns to reason in the life of contemplation. "Enter," he says, "into account with thy reason to do that which it counsels thee on the road to God, and it will be of greater worth to thee with respect to God than all the works thou doest without this counsel."[25] Reason serving under the standard of faith is an indispensable servant in our struggle for perfection. By reason alone, we can never hope to achieve union with God; but neither can we hope to achieve it without reason. To repeat Merton's words, quoted earlier: "There is no such thing as a sanctity that is not intelligent" (325).

Notes

[1] Exodus 13:21, emphasis added.

[2] On February 13, 1951, Merton's editor, Robert Giroux, suggested the title *The Ascent to Truth*. Merton wrote back wondering if "ascent" might be confused with "assent." He suggested *Ascent to Light*. As generally happens in such matters, the editor's suggestion prevailed.

[3] *Sign of Jonas*, p. 157.

[4] *Sign of Jonas*, pp. 160-161.

[5] "The Cloud and the Fire" is the title of the first of the three sections of *Ascent to Truth*.

[6] *Sign of Jonas*, p. 178.

[7] *Road to Joy*, p. 198.

[8] This quotation was unfortunately omitted from *Road to Joy*. It may

be found in an article by Sister Therese Lentfoehr, "The Spiritual Writer" in *Thomas Merton Monk*, Patrick Hart, ed. (New York: Sheed and Ward), 1974, p. 109.

[9] In the Trust agreement Merton states that *The School of the Spirit* (as well as *The Inner Experience*) was not to be published as a book. What actually remains of *The School of the Spirit* is something of a mystery. I have seen two typescripts of it. They are totally different from one another.

[10] His statement—about the unlimited number of combinations possible for the some eight hundred pages of notes he had—suggests that the final arrangement of the material may well have been somewhat arbitrary.

[11] *Renascence*, Vol. 4 (Spring 1952). I mean no disrespect to a lovely person, a fine poet and a dear friend when I say that it is difficult to think of the late Sister Therese Lentfoehr writing anything but a glowing review of a Merton book. As one who typed a number of his manuscripts, she was so deeply attached to him that she would have found it exceedingly difficult to say anything but the best about him.

[12] *The New York Times Book Review*, September 23, 1951.

[13] *Blackfriars*, 33: 144-46 (March 1952).

[14] "Now the object of the will is the universal good; just as the object of the intellect is the universal true. Hence it is evident that naught can lull the human will, save the universal good. This is to be found, not in any creature, but in God alone, because every creature is goodness by participation. Wherefore God alone can satisfy the human will, according to the words of Ps. CII, 5: 'Who satisfied your desire with good things.' Therefore God alone constitutes human happiness." *Summa Theologiae*, I, II, 2, 8.

[15] The Gnostics affirmed, among other things, the fundamental evil of created things.

[16] John of the Cross, *Ascent of Mount Carmel*, E. Allison Peers, ed. and trans. (Liguori, Mo.: Triumph, 1991), Vol. I, Bk. I, c. 13, n. 11, p. 62. Quoted in *Ascent to Truth*, pp. 52-53.

[17] In his later studies in Buddhism Merton would come to see that Buddhism also identifies desire (especially the desire to be a separate self) as the root of all human suffering.

[18] In "Notes for a Philosophy of Solitude" in *Disputed Questions*, Merton writes at some length about "diversion." He borrows the term from Blaise Pascal, who speaks of *divertissement* as inane activities which benumb our humanness. Merton sees it as a constant turning to superficial or meaningless actions to avoid facing the true realities of life. Just as "bread and circuses" served as the *divertissement* of ancient Rome, soap operas and situation comedies offer people in today's world something that may help them forget the banality and meaningless of much of life.

[19] See discussion of the kataphatic and apophatic ways in the Introduction.

[20] *Mount Carmel*, Bk. II, n. 24, p. 189. Quoted in *Ascent to Truth*, p. 255.

[21] *Ascent to Truth*, p. 296. Note once again how love is the bridge between the kataphatic tradition and the apophatic.

[22] *Mount Carmel*, Bk. II, c. 13, p. 116. Quoted in *Ascent to Truth*, p. 233.

[23] It should be clear that this "divide" is not crossed once and for all. There may be times when one who has tasted the joy of contemplation may experience the need for meditation.

[24] It should be clear that reason does not do this apart from or independently of the inspiration of God's grace.

[25] John of the Cross, *Maxims*, E. Allison Peers, ed. and trans. (Liguori, Mo.: Triumph, 1991), Vol. III, n. 41, p. 256. Quoted in *Ascent*, p. 179.

PART TWO

The Inner Landscape of Contemplation: Solitude

4

Thoughts in Solitude *and "Notes for a Philosophy of Solitude"*

Thoughts in Solitude

Let me seek, then, the gift of silence, and poverty, and
solitude, where everything I touch is turned into prayer:
where the sky is my prayer, the birds are my prayer, the wind
in the trees is my prayer, for God is all in all. (94)

One way of understanding the Merton story is to see it as his effort, not always successful, to turn loneliness into solitude. After his mother's death (when he was six years old), he was often alone and felt the pangs of loneliness. Yet there was something in him that was attracted to solitude. While at Oakham School he would regularly go off by himself to Brooke Hill, where he could be alone. He wrote of it in one of his novels: "I liked to be alone on top of it [Brooke Hill] and not have to talk to anyone...not have to listen to anyone else talk.... I just went up there to be there."[1] A rather insightful, even Zen-like, intuition for a lad of sixteen or seventeen. Noteworthy, too, is the fact that on the several trips he took to the continent while at Oakham, he always traveled alone. His two companions were the books he brought with him and the ever-present notebook for recording his reflections on what he experienced.

It should not be too surprising, then, that when Merton became a Catholic, his thoughts soon turned to the religious life and especially to a monastic order dedicated to solitude. Even after he had entered the Abbey of Gethsemani, he had periodic "attacks" of a yearning for more solitude than community life at Gethsemani afforded him. He openly admitted that Gethsemani was a second choice. He would have preferred to join a community of hermits, like the Carthusians, but that had been impossible in 1941 because at that time there were no Carthusians in America and war prevented him from joining them in Europe. During his early years in the monastery he was continually trying the patience of his abbot and confessor with his concern for greater solitude than Gethsemani could provide. Dom James Fox kept assuring him that he could have the solitude he needed at Gethsemani and wisely provided him with opportunities to be alone.

In January of 1953 he gave Merton permission to fix up an old abandoned tool shed in the woods behind the barns and use it as a kind of hermitage. He was allowed to spend several hours there each day. He named the "hermitage" St. Anne's. With the enthusiasm that came so readily to him when he had made a new discovery, he waxed with rapture about his "hermitage": "It seems to me that St. Anne's is what I have been waiting for and looking for all my life. Now for the first time, I am aware of what happens to a man who has really found his place in the scheme of things."[2] St. Anne's is the place where his own silence joins the silence of the world.

With his ever-present notebook with him at St. Anne's, it comes as no surprise that he would write a book about solitude. During the years 1953-1954, he wrote notes on spirituality that eventually became the book *Thoughts in Solitude*. It is important to note the preposition in the title. It is thoughts *in* solitude, not *on* solitude. One should not look here for a detailed study of the meaning of solitude (an approach to that would come a bit later in "Notes for a Philosophy of Solitude," which we will discuss in due time). It is a small book, undersized, with 124 pages and 37 chapters. (Its original title had been *Thirty-Seven Meditations*.) A kind of "scattering" of intuitions and reflections that came to him during his hours of silence at St. Anne's, its value lies not in a straight-line development of a theme, but rather in a dropping of ideas like fresh fruit from a tree. In his preface Merton suggests three topics that loosely connect the chapters with one another: (1) the meaning of solitude, (2) the human dialogue with God in silence, and (3) the interrelationship of our personal solitude with one another. Another way of trying to sum up the book is expressed in the prayer Merton addresses to God: "Let me seek, then, the gift of silence, and poverty, and solitude, where everything I touch is turned into prayer" (94).

Silence

The atmosphere of solitude is silence. We live in a world that seems to flee silence. It is an age of words. We are smothered by them, buried in them, bombarded by them on all sides. So much of our culture is media-driven. And the media are full of words. So often words make no deep impression upon us, because there are so many and because they arise not out of silence but out of busyness.

> If our life is poured out in useless words, we will never hear anything, will never become anything, and in the end, because we have said everything before we had anything to say we shall be left speechless.... (91)

These words of Merton remind me of the presidential debates between Gerald Ford and Jimmy Carter in 1976. In presidential debates, there is no real silence between words, because there is no real listening to the merits of what the other has said. During these debates in 1976, there was a power failure and the television sets in millions of homes suddenly became silent. The two candidates were left speechless. Their words trailed off into silence: not that fruitful silence that is the source of authentic words, but a barren silence that was only the cessation of language. Silence descended upon them and rendered them helpless. They did not know how to handle silence.

This mute picture of two powerful men reduced to silence by a failure of technology can be read as a parable of today's society. Our lives are so cluttered with words that we no longer know how to handle silence. Silence for all too many of us is simply a fruitless pause between words rather than a creative silence out of which deep and authentic words can emerge. Sated with words, we do not realize that we are starved for silence. Having lost the sense of our need for silence, we tend to fill the little silence we have with the noise of our radios and our televisions. Words and noises conspire to block silence out of our lives and, all too often, we are parties to the conspiracy.

During World War II, when our cities were blacked out at night, it was deemed advisable to move some of the children in New York City to the relative safety of the Catskill mountains. When they first arrived in the quiet stillness of the country, they were unable to sleep—it was too quiet! They were so accustomed to noise that the silence of the open country kept them awake. They could not relax with silence. Their predicament reflects our discomfort with silence. We don't seem able to relax with it either. When at a party there is a lull in the conversation, we reach desperately for more words to fill in the gap between words. Not knowing how to live with silence, we seem to resort to almost any device to avoid it.

Yet silence is the necessary ground for words that have something to say. Authentic silence is pregnant with words that will be born at the right time. But unless our words rise out of silence, they are apt to be curtains that cover reality rather than windows which reveal it. For only silence can reach that dimension of reality that is too deep for words. That is why when we speak out of silence, there is always silence left over. We cannot say all that we experience. We cannot put into words the totality of our silence. Words that come before silence rather than out of silence can come between us and God. "We put words between ourselves and things. Even God becomes another conceptual unreality in a no-man's land of language that no longer serves as a means of communion with reality" (85). We need the wordless contact with reality that comes only with silence. Silence is especially the "language" of the person who chooses to live a life of solitude. "The solitary life, being silent, clears away the smoke-screen of words that man has laid down between his mind and things. In solitude we remain face to face with the naked being of things.... When we have really met and known the world in silence, words do not separate us from the world nor from other men, nor from God, nor from ourselves because we no longer trust entirely in language to contain reality" (85-86).

I mentioned earlier that Merton's approach to the human person was as apophatic as his approach to God. Thus, it is, he would say, that I come to know myself only in silence, not by reflection on the self, but "by penetration to the mystery of my true self which is beyond words and concepts because it is utterly particular" (70). Vladimir Lossky captures well the particularity of the true self in his book *The Mystical Theology of the Eastern Church*: "When we wish to define, 'to characterize,' a person, we gather together individual characteristics, 'traits of character,' which are to be met with elsewhere in other individuals, and which because they belong to nature, are never absolutely 'personal.'" Finally, we admit that what is most dear to us in someone, what makes him himself, remains indefinable, for there is nothing in nature which properly pertains to the person, which is always unique and incomparable.[3] This is something, I believe, we all experience in dear friends. It is something that we experience when we come to know Thomas Merton. He was so clearly himself: a free spirit who escapes our efforts to describe or define him. This unique particularity is also true of ourselves. Our self-knowledge never fully grasps who we are. It never fully describes us. There is always "more of us" left over. For this self-knowledge "opens out into the silence and the 'subjectivity' of God's own self" (70). We "see" God with the eyes of our inner self which is not separate from

God. We hear God with the ears of our "heart" which are attuned to the silence of God (see 51, 13).

In the depths of silence which is beyond words, we encounter God whom no eye can see and whom we can never name, yet in whom "we live and move and have our being."[4] In silence's depths, beyond words, there is no separation between "I" and "Not I." For God is all in all.

All this means that we must come to see that there is much more to life than the fleeting fragments of it that we catch in our words. Life is not an uninterrupted flow of words which is finally silenced only by death. Rather life, if it is true and authentic, develops in silence, comes to the surface in authentic words and returns to a deeper silence; and at the end of life we speak our final word—our Amen to life—which ushers us into the silence of God.[5]

Poverty

Closely linked with silence, the language of the solitary, is poverty, which is the solitary's way of dealing with reality, especially his own reality. Poverty may be thought of as a freedom from possessions that includes the freedom from the desire to possess things. This is generally what we have in mind when we speak of poverty: having nothing. But at a deeper level there is an ontological poverty which means *being* nothing. The poverty that seeks to be free of any attachment to possessions, material or spiritual, is essential to the true solitary. But the deeper kind of poverty—the poverty that names our nothingness—is not something one works to achieve. It is already there from the moment we exist. Part of the package of being a creature, ontological poverty is the most fundamental reality of our being, whether we understand it or not. As the Zen saying puts it: "If you understand, things are just as they are; if you do not understand, things are just as they are." We are totally dependent on God, whether we understand or not. But what a difference it makes when we do understand!

This ontological poverty calls us to the habitual

realization that God is everything and that, apart from God, we are nothing. It brings us an intuition of our contingency: our total dependence on God. In life and in death we belong entirely to God. What folly it is then to live our lives as if God were not involved. "The more we are content with our own poverty the closer we are to God for then we accept our poverty in peace, expecting nothing from ourselves and everything from God" (53).

It is only in the realization of our helplessness, our total dependence on God, that we can experience the deep need we have for the mercy of God. When we see helplessness in others, we are moved to pity and compassion. Graphic pictures of emaciated children dying from starvation tug at our hearts and we untie our purse strings to offer our help. In ontological poverty, we stand before God poor and helpless. But "when we understand the true nature of His love for us, we will prefer to come to Him poor and helpless. We will never be ashamed of our distress. Distress is our advantage when we have nothing to seek but mercy" (36). The surest sign that we appreciate God's love for us is "the appreciation of our own poverty in the light of His infinite mercy" (37). For, paradoxically, it is our poverty that stakes our claim on God's mercy.

Mercy is a term that looms large in Merton's vocabulary. That wonderful voice of God that concludes the pages of volume two of the Merton journals is a triumphant divine cry of mercy:

> What was cruel has become merciful. What is now merciful was never cruel. I have always overshadowed Jonas with my mercy, and cruelty I know not at all. Have you had sight of me, Jonas, my child? Mercy within mercy within mercy.... I loved what was most frail. I looked upon what was nothing. I touched what was without substance, and within what is not, I am.[6]

Poverty, because it sees reality as it is and therefore as nothing apart from God, protects us from illusions. It is so easy for us to live with our illusions. It is illusion to make possessions the goal of our lives. It is illusion to be puffed up with the sense of our own importance. It is illusion to be attached to a false self that exists only in our imagination. The meaning of the false self is something to which Merton will attach great importance in his writing on contemplation. His thoughts are especially spelled out in *The Inner Experience* and in *New Seeds of Contemplation*. I will save further reflection on this important aspect of his anthropology till later.

Solitude

Solitude may be interior or exterior. It may be a matter of the heart or a matter of place or it may be both. To strive for an inner spirit of solitude (which means to find quiet and silent time in our lives) is a necessary goal for anyone who wants to grow spiritually. Some are called to an exterior solitude: to trust themselves completely "to the silence of a wide landscape of woods and hills, or sea, or desert; to sit still while the sun comes up over that land.... To pray and work in the morning and to labor and rest in the afternoon, and to sit still again in meditation in the evening when night falls upon the land and when silence fills itself with darkness and with stars" (101). This is surely a special vocation—to belong so completely to silence, to let it soak into one's bones and be the very substance of one's life.

It is also a risky vocation. It makes sense only as a gift of oneself to God, never as a way of getting something. We must beware of the person who seeks solitude to achieve something else, even if that something else is contemplation. A person does not become a solitary in order to have a "spiritual life." "Do you suppose," Merton writes, "I have a spiritual life? I have none. I am silence, I am poverty, I am solitude, for I have renounced spirituality to find God."[7]

It was his longing for exterior solitude that Merton struggled with in his earliest days in the monastery and periodically at various periods in his life. Even when he was allowed to live as a hermit on the grounds of Gethsemani in August of 1965, he was never quite content that he had achieved the solitude to which he was being called. Probably his clearest and most mature articulation of what solitude meant to him is to be found in an essay published in 1960 in *Disputed Questions*. Though the book was published in 1960, the various drafts of this essay were begun much earlier. It is to this essay that I now wish to turn.

"Notes for a Philosophy of Solitude" in *Disputed Questions*

There have always been, and always will be, persons who are alone in the midst of society without realizing why (195).

Merton considered "Notes for a Philosophy of Solitude" (DQ, 177-207) one of his most important pieces of writing. In his journal, under the date of December 4, 1965 he quotes from Rainer Maria Rilke: "A work of art is good only if it has sprung from necessity" and muses on a few of his own writings that came from a kind of necessity. He lists only a few, among them "Philosophy of Solitude."[8] On December 20, 1962, he writes to John Wu, Sr.: "I am glad you like 'Philosophy of Solitude.' It is one of the things I have most wanted to say, perhaps the only thing I have said that *needed* to be said."[9] To June Yungblut, who was preparing to do some post-doctoral work on his writings, he says in a letter of March 6, 1968: "The 'Notes on the Philosophy of Solitude' in *Disputed Questions* is very central."[10]

The censors of the Cistercian Order did not view this article in quite the same way. They saw it as an overzealous defense of the solitary life (that is, the hermit life) and a subtle criticism of the cenobitic life (life in community).[11] They were especially critical of what they saw as "a direct attack on Superiors, Confessors or Directors of souls." Moreover, they thought it showed too much trust in the individual's discernment of the will of God and, in consequence, a "lack of trust and respect for the Authority established by God."[12]

Merton voiced his frustrations with the censorship in a letter of May 30, 1960 to Sister Therese Lentfoehr:

> I wrote an article on solitude, and any one would think that it was an obscene novel, the way they landed on it. There is in the Order a kind of terror of any mention of the solitary life, no doubt because the tradition in this regard is unpalatable among us: we have decided that the cenobitic life is the ne plus ultra, and we have to struggle by main force to keep ourselves convinced of this. Such absurdities arise from the arbitrary fantasies of institutional thought, thinking for the outfit rather than in accordance with truth and the full tradition of the Church. But I really got in trouble.[13]

After this general statement of difficulties with the censors and his perception of the reasons for them, he goes on in this letter to describe them more concretely:

> I rewrote the thing three times and these rewritings were further developments of an original version written in 1955 or earlier and published only in French and Italian.[14] I never could get that one past the American censors (the others did not give it a second thought!). Finally when I thought I had the whole thing simon pure, the censor declared that I was making "a direct attack on Superiors and the authority of the Church." This was for a sentence that ran somewhat like: "Those who say interior solitude is sufficient do not realize what they are saying." This was taken to mean superiors, as if no one else would ever think of saying such a thing.
>
> In another sentence, where [sic] I said that the principal anguish of the solitary life was that the hermit did not have anyone to guide him and the will of God pressed upon him with immediacy or something like that. Overlooking the fact that I said this was a source of anguish, they picked that up and said I was preaching against authority and spiritual direction and saying that everyone should seek to be directly guided by the Holy Ghost. You never saw such a stupid mess. The Abbot General [Gabriel Sortais][15] picked

this up and flew into one of his rages, which can be very stormy and I was all but consigned to the nether regions as a contumacious heretic.[16]

While the censors were debating the fate of his article, Merton proceeded to have it published, uncensored, by his friend Victor Hammer, in a small edition of one hundred fifty copies. To complicate matters still further, he titled this edition *The Solitary Life.*[17]

The struggle with the censors proved to be not all bad. As Merton undertook to change his text to suit the censors, new ideas entered the text and eventually enriched the essay that finally appeared in *Disputed Questions*. The original article, which appeared only in French and Italian, was very clearly a defense of the hermit life. In a footnote at the beginning of the *Disputed Questions* essay Merton tells us that he had extended the article's horizons and that it now applied to solitaries who had no necessary connection with the monastic life. It was to be an explanation of the solitary life, not a defense of hermits. "The 'solitary' of these pages," he writes, "is never necessarily a 'monk' (juridically) at all. He may well be a layman, and of the sort most remote from cloistered life, like Thoreau or Emily Dickinson" (DQ, 177). That may well have been his intent, but, as one reads this essay, it is difficult to avoid the impression that, consciously or not, Merton is talking about his own struggle to achieve at Gethsemani a greater degree of solitude and the frustrations he experienced in that struggle.

If the censors for the Order experienced a certain frustration about this essay, I must admit that I did also—though for reasons quite different from theirs. I was puzzled and upset, because the essay seemed to defy my efforts to summarize it. Here was a bit of Merton writing which I had long admired; yet when I tried to trace the development of its thought, I could not find the key to that development. Finally, I was moved to look more closely at the title of the book and its physical structure. The table of contents lists the title as "Philosophy of Solitude," but the essay itself bears the title: "Notes for a Philosophy of Solitude." The picture became clearer. I had been misled by the abbreviated title in the table of contents. Merton's actual title suggests that he was not writing a philosophy of solitude, but some notes out of which such a philosophy might be developed. A glance at the structure of the essay was also revealing. There are three parts to the essay and within each part paragraphs or groups of paragraphs are numbered: nine such numbered sets of paragraphs in Part One; twenty-two in Part Two and twelve in Part Three. I recognized this as a technique Merton had employed elsewhere. In *No Man Is an Island*, he uses numbered paragraphs and describes the book as "musings" about questions that were important to him. "They do not take in a broad view of all that matters. They are simply observations of a few things that seem to me to matter."[18]

The light at last dawned for me. I was looking for a full-blown philosophy of solitude; he was simply giving "notes" one might use to construct such a philosophy. I had been looking for a structure in which one idea would consecutively build on another to develop an intended theme. What was actually presented to me was one idea suggesting another and, whenever it suited the author, an idea returned to again. There was not so much a progression of thoughts leading to a specific conclusion, but more often a laying of one thought alongside another without any pretense at completeness.

Settling in my own mind the methodology I believed Merton was following proved a freeing experience. My task, as I see it, is to point out some of the richness the article holds for me, inviting readers to share what I have mined in this "field of gold," but also encouraging them to look for the riches they can discover there. Or, to change the metaphor, the richness of this article is not that of a finely cut diamond, but the richness of a diamond in the rough.

PART ONE: THE TYRANNY OF DIVERSION

In Part One I note four topics that seem important to me:

Solitariness and Society

All human beings are solitary. Most people, though, are averse to being alone or feeling alone (the latter is possible even in the society of others). Solitariness is something we cannot escape even if we want to: It is built into the human condition. No matter how gregarious our lives may be, there will always be those times—and they are by no means few—when we will be alone. Perhaps it happens at night, when we cannot sleep. Even if someone is sleeping next to us, we are still alone. Questions flood our minds: some petty and inconsequential, others profound and inexplicable. We have to face them—alone. Even in a crowd we can experience solitariness, when, for instance, we have no bonding with anyone who is there. And if solitariness stalks us all through life, it makes its final appearance at life's end. No matter how surrounded by loved ones we may be, each of us dies her or his death. We all die alone.

The solitariness of our lives is complemented by that other element that is part of human life: We live in the midst of people. We belong to society. If our society becomes community, it can give meaning to our solitariness by turning it into true solitude, where we experience the unitive relationships we have with our sisters and brothers in that community. On the other hand, society can degenerate into a mere collectivity that cannot know solitude and uses every effort possible to avoid the solitariness that life inevitably imposes upon us.

Diversion

Society, seen as collectivity, while it cannot give us a way of escaping our solitariness entirely, does everything it can to help us forget it. This it does by enticing us to live fictitious lives, lives in which we are out of touch with reality and

101

become victims of diversion. This notion of diversion Merton borrowed from Blaise Pascal. Pascal writes about *divertissement*, by which he means systematic and planned distraction, which makes it possible, as Merton puts it, for a person "to avoid his own company for twenty-four hours a day" (DQ, 178). Diversion means engagement in inane activities that benumb our humanness. It is the constant turning to superficial or meaningless actions as a way to avoid facing the realities of daily human life. Merton calls diversion a tyranny, because it controls our lives and deprives us of the freedom to be our real selves.

The words Merton uses to describe what diversion leads to or what it springs from are illuminating: "illusion," "fiction," "stupor," "apathy." They evoke a vision of someone who is in a daydream, out of touch, in a daze. Such persons may function well on the surface, but they never reach the deeper realities of life, since these are precisely what diversion enables them to avoid. "[T]he function of diversion is simply to anesthetize the individual as individual and to plunge him into the warm apathetic stupor of a collectivity which, like himself, wishes to remain amused" (DQ, 178). Today's soap operas and situation comedies take the place of the "bread and circuses" that served as *divertissement* in ancient Rome. There was plenty wrong with Roman society and the Roman emperors offered the diversion of food and entertainment to make people forget the banality and meaninglessness of their lives. Our society does much the same and has ever so much more in the way of sophisticated technological tools to accomplish it.

The Solitary's Rejection of Diversion

The solitary is the one who renounces the call to live by diversion. She refuses to walk away from reality. Rather the solitary is determined to seek the truly real and live with it, whatever the cost. She must face straight on the anguish of realizing that "underneath the apparently logical pattern of a more or less 'well-organized' and rational life, there lies an abyss of irrationality, confusion, pointlessness and indeed of apparent chaos" (DQ, 179). The solitary person pricks the bubble of the tight self-contained illusion that the devotees of diversion build about themselves and their little world. The solitary is prepared to live with life's incomprehensibility rather than ignore it or pretend it isn't there.

Faith: True and False

One of the essentials of interior solitude, Merton writes, is that "it is the actualization of a faith in which a man takes responsibility for his own inner life" (DQ, 180). Faith is a plunge into the mystery of life. When it seeks to avoid that mystery by having recourse to conventional formulas, without ever probing their meaning, faith itself can become a form of diversion. A faith of pre-packaged, unthought-out answers to all the important issues of life is a diversionary faith. Persons of true faith travel, not without difficulty, toward the heart of mystery. Such a person discovers that "his mystery and the mystery of God merge into one reality, which is the only reality" (DQ, 180). This reality is that God lives in us and we in God. Our heart beats in the heart of God.

Summing up this first part of the essay, I would suggest that Merton is telling us that there are three levels at which we can live. First, there is the phenomenal level, where harmony seems to exist or, if it doesn't, we are able to divert ourselves from the disharmony and live insulated as far as possible from the disturbing, the troublesome and the burdensome. This is the level of diversion, where people live with a good deal of fiction in their lives.

There is a second level of human existence, which might be called the existential level. This is the level, where below the surface realities of life, we are in direct contact with life's complexities, incongruities, contradictions and absurdities. This is the level which the solitary chooses to explore and from which he refuses to be diverted.

The third is the contemplative level. The solitary realizes

his potential as a contemplative and breaks through the level of seeming meaninglessness and enters into the mystery of the true self and, in doing so, enters at the same time into the mystery of God. It is at this level that life's contradictions and absurdities are resolved. This is what Merton is talking about when he refers, in *Conjectures of a Guilty Bystander*, to Julian of Norwich and her "eschatological secret," namely, her conviction that "all will be well. All manner of things will be well." The Lord comes to us with the final answer to the world's anguish. The "Last Day" will bring not destruction and revenge, but mercy and life. "All partial expectations will be exploded and everything will be made right."[19]

PART TWO: IN THE SEA OF PERILS

Moving from this ideal presentation of the solitary life, Merton goes on to discuss the perils the solitary has to face and the qualities needed to face them.

False Solitude

One of the pitfalls solitaries have to face is the danger of separating themselves from society in order to affirm their individuality. False solitaries want at all costs to be noticed by society, through admiration and approval or even, if need be, through opposition. In either case they are getting what they desire: attention. There may be a bit of autobiography in Merton's description of the false solitary. In July, 1956, at a conference at St. John's University, Collegeville, Minnesota, Dr. Gregory Zilboorg, a psychiatrist and well-known convert to Catholicism, taunted Merton (I can't think of a milder term that would do justice to the situation) that Merton's desire to be a hermit was pathological. What he really wanted, Zilboorg said, was a hermitage in Times Square with a large sign over it saying: "HERMIT."[20] Merton was aware— perhaps more aware than Zilboorg—of the danger of a false solitude that leads to separation and is simply another form of diversion. The true solitary, Merton knew, does not renounce people or anything that is basic and human about relationship with people.

Responsibility for One's Own Inner Life

Taking responsibility for their own inner lives, persons of solitude refuse to live by the social images that their society sees as beneficial and praiseworthy in its members. They are not willing to substitute society's words, slogans and concepts for genuine experiences of their own. They are called to exercise a prophetic role. They despise the criminal arrogance of their own nation as well as that of the "enemy." They despise the hidden aggressions in themselves as much as the self-seeking aggressiveness of politicians. They reject the fictitious symbols that often substitute for genuine social unity, but they are one with everyone in the peril and anguish of a common humanity. They share with everyone a common essential human solitude—a solitude that was assumed by Christ and which, in Christ, becomes mysteriously identified with the solitude of God (see DQ, 187-188).

The Social Witness of Solitude

Solitaries have a definite function in society. Though outwardly separated from other people, they witness to the primacy of the spiritual and to the mystical character of the Church. "...[A] Christian hermit can, by being alone, paradoxically live even closer to the heart of the Church than one who is in the midst of her apostolic activities" (DQ, 192).

In the version submitted to the censors, Merton followed the above statement by saying: "The life and unity of the Church are, and must be, visible. But that does not mean that they are exclusively or even primarily visible." This statement was pounced on by one of the censors, who saw in it the danger of stressing the invisible aspect of the Church at the expense of the visible. It might lead to such wrong ideas as "no need to belong to a visible Church" or "immediate personal illumination by the Holy Spirit." Merton dropped the controversial sentence, but did insist that the solitary, by listening to the Holy Spirit and to his conscience, is able to offer a different perspective on society: a perspective that values not productivity and usefulness, but love, compassion and concern for all of God's people. The solitary is not, as so many people seem to think, simply a dynamo of prayer who substitutes for those who haven't the time to pray. He is first and foremost a witness for everyone to a singleness of purpose that exposes for what they really are the fictions that diversion throws in our eyes in its efforts to blind us to reality.

PART THREE: SPIRITUAL POVERTY

The Poverty of the Solitary

Being a solitary does not mean that one will be free from distraction (and be a great contemplative) and from worries and concern (and thus able to live a life without care). Quite the contrary, the solitary's prayer may be poorer than that of the monk[21] who lives in community. Solitaries may have ulcers like the rest of humanity. They may have to face doubts, not just about abstract truths, but doubts that question the very roots of their own existence and that undermine the reason for the life they are striving to live. "It is this doubt which reduces him finally to silence, and in the silence which ceases to ask questions, he receives the only certitude he knows: The presence of God in the midst of uncertainty and nothingness.... He knows where he is going, but he is not 'sure of his way,' he just knows by going there. He does not see the way beforehand, and when he arrives, he arrives. His arrivals are usually departures from anything that resembles a 'way.' That is his way. But he cannot understand it. Neither can we" (DQ, 202-203).

The Immediacy of the Will of God

Reflecting on the place of the will of God in the solitary, Merton wrote: "The terror of the lonely life is the immediacy with which the will of God presses upon our[22] soul. It is much easier, and gentler, and more secure to have the will of God filtered to us quietly through society: through decrees of men, through the orders of others." As you can readily suspect, Merton once again runs afoul of the censors. To satisfy them, he changed the "immediacy" of God's will to "the mystery and uncertainty with which the will of God presses upon our soul" (DQ, 204). He added also that to deal with this uncertainty, one needs the guidance of "directors and superiors." It was a capitulation that almost completely altered what he intended to say, but he had no other choice.

Exterior Solitude

Merton's final brush with the censors came in his defense of exterior solitude against those who would deny it as a necessity or at least as a significant value. "It is often said," he tells us, "that exterior solitude is not only dangerous, but totally unnecessary. Unnecessary because all that really matters is interior solitude. And this can be obtained without physical isolation" (DQ, 205). Merton's comment, cited by the censor, reads: "There is in this statement a truth more terrible than can be imagined by those who so glibly make it, as a justification for their own lives crowded with diversion." One wonders: Was Merton being reckless or naïve? As you may easily expect he was forced once again to change a sentence: this one seen by the censor as "a direct attack on Superiors, Confessors or Directors of souls."[23] Merton's accommodation to the censor read: "There is in this statement a truth more terrible than can be imagined by those who make it, so readily and with little awareness of the irony implicit in their words" (DQ, 205). He explains the irony. One who is called to solitude, but is required to live in community, finds that the trivial bonds that bind him or her to community break one by one and are replaced by a deeper bond: a wordless communion of love. The solitary in his very solitude loves those in community, in fact loves them perhaps for the first time. I doubt that this change pleased the censor. Still, it was allowed to pass. Merton had a way of wearing down the opposition of censors!

This essay comes to a stunning conclusion in which Merton uses a theme he had developed the year before in his unpublished book, *The Inner Experience* and which he will explore even more fully in the year to come in *New Seeds of Contemplation*: the theme of the gradual disappearance of an ephemeral self and the emergence of a self that endures. This true self is not something possessed or acquired. It is not an object at all, it is not a thing. It is not the shallow "I" of the individual, but the deep "I" of the spirit. As Merton puts it: "[I]n this inmost 'I' my solitude meets the solitude of every other man and the solitude of God" (DQ, 207). The inmost "I" is beyond separateness, limitation, and selfish affirmation. "It is only this inmost and solitary 'I' that truly loves with the love and the spirit of Christ. This 'I' is Christ Himself living in us: and we, in Him, living in the Father" (DQ, 207).

Notes

[1] "The Straits of Dover" (unpublished journal in Merton archives of St. Bonaventure University library).

[2] Thomas Merton, *A Search for Solitude: Pursuing the Monk's True Life: The Journals of Thomas Merton, Vol. 3,*f Lawrence S. Cunningham, ed. (New York: HarperSanFrancisco, 1996), p. 32.

[3] Vladimir Lossky, *The Mystical Theology of the Eastern Church* (Cambridge: James Clark and Co., 1957 [original French ed., 1944]), p. 121.

[4] Acts 17:28.

[5] See Thomas Merton, *No Man Is an Island* (New York: Harcourt Brace, 1955), p. 261.

[6] *Search for Solitude*, p. 488.

[7] *Entering the Silence*, p. 463.

[8] There are only a few others that he includes. *Thoughts in Solitude* is one of them. The others are *Chuang Tzu, Guilty Bystander,* some of the poems in *Emblems, Sign of Jonas, Seven Storey Mountain, Thirty Poems.* "The rest," he says, "is trash...I would say the writing on Zen was 'necessary' too. And some of *Behavior of Titans.*" Thomas Merton, *Dancing in the Water of Life,* Robert E. Daggy, ed. (*The Journals of Thomas Merton, Vol. 5*) (New York: Harper Collins, 1997), p. 349.

[9] *Hidden Ground of Love*, p. 624, emphasis added.

[10] *Hidden Ground of Love*, p. 642.

[11] The hermit is a monk who lives alone. The cenobitic life is the life of monks in community.

[12] Censor's "Reflections on the Ms. 'Notes for a Philosophy of Solitude'" in the archives of the Merton Center at Bellarmine College, Louisville, Kentucky.

[13] *Road to Joy*, pp. 235-236.

[14] The French version, *Dans le desert de Dieu*, was published in Temoignages, Paris, March, 1955. My translation appears in the Spring 1991 issue of the *Merton Seasonal*.

[15] Merton is hardly fair to the Abbot General who wrote him a firm but conciliatory letter, urging him to think more seriously about his filial relationship to the Church but at the same time expressing his fondness for Merton.

[16] *Road to Joy*, pp. 235-236.

[17] In 1977, when the censors seemed to be out of the picture, "The Solitary Life" was published in a book called *The Monastic Journey*, edited by Brother Patrick Hart and published by Sheed, Ward and McMeel.

[18] Thomas Merton, *No Man Is an Island*, p. xiv.

[19] Thomas Merton, *Conjectures of a Guilty Bystander*, p. 212.

[20] See *Silent Lamp*, p. 172.

[21] Note how in the latter part of his essay Merton seems to slip into a monastic terminology, speaking of "monks" and "hermits." This

reflects that this essay is a rewrite of an earlier French article that was intended as a defense of the hermit life. His attempt to widen the horizons of the essay was not completely successful.

[22] Is Merton suggesting here that he is telling his own story?

[23] Censor's report, unpublished, archives of the Thomas Merton Center, Louisville, Kentucky.

PART THREE

Later Writings on Contemplation

5

The Inner Experience

The first thing that you have to do, before you even start thinking about such a thing as contemplation, is to try to recover your basic natural unity, to reintegrate your compartmentalized being into a coordinated and simple whole, and learn to live as a unified human person (3).

During the summer of 1959, Merton produced a full-length book devoted to the topic of contemplation. It was intended as a rewrite and update of *What Is Contemplation?* It turned out to be an almost entirely new work. The title he initially gave to this book was *The Dark Path*; the title he finally decided upon was *The Inner Experience*. On July 4, 1959, Merton wrote to Sister Therese Lentfoehr: "At the moment, guess what, I am rewriting *What Is Contemplation?* It will be a patchy job. But I have been wanting to do it. I may revise other early material too."[1] Merton confided to Sister Therese his reason for wanting to revise some of his earlier writing:

> It is all very unsatisfactory to me. In fact a lot of it disgusts me. I was much too superficial and too cerebral at the time. I seem to have ignored the wholeness and integrity of life, and concentrated on a kind of angelism in contemplation. That was when I was a rip-roaring Trappist, I guess. Now that I am a little less perfect I seem to have a saner perspective. And that too seems to be not according to the manuals, doesn't it?[2]

Merton apparently spent a great deal of time during the summer of 1959 working on this revision of *What Is Contemplation?* On September 9, 1959, his journal entry suggests that he had done "some rewriting on *Inner Experience* which is now I think a respectable book."[3] On September 29, 1959, he was able to report to Sister Therese: "I finished a book this summer called *The Inner Experience*, which started out to be a simple revision of *What Is Contemplation?*, but turned into something new, and just about full-length." Although he stated that he had finished the book, he was apparently not satisfied with it. For he goes on to say: "It has to be revised and has been sitting here on the desk waiting for revision for some time, but I refuse to work around the house as they are blasting around on all sides with jackhammers and other machines and it is impossible to think. The novices have been making a good share of this noise, trying to put a couple of new showers in our crowded cellar."[4] Presumably the new showers were installed and the jackhammers and machines eventually stopped their blasting, but Merton never got around to revising the manuscript of *The Inner Experience*. In his journal, under the date of September 29, 1959, the very day he had written to Sister Therese, he again expresses a desire to revise it: "My last ms. ("The Inner Experience") lies on the desk untouched. I want to revise it. I want to clean up that room. And get rid of a lot of things and clear the deck for action."[5] There is no indication that the revision occurred. In volume five of the journals under the date of August 23, 1963, he is still talking about revising it, but again there is no proof that he did so at the time.

Four Drafts of the Manuscript

The manuscript that Merton wrote survives in four typescripts that are housed at the Thomas Merton Studies Center at Bellarmine College in Louisville, Kentucky. The first draft is made up almost entirely of new material into which Merton apparently intended to insert the contents of *What Is Contemplation?* The second draft contains some material from that earlier work. Draft three has in it about ninety percent of the text of *What Is Contemplation?* plus much additional material. It is this additional material that is of particular interest, since it was written eleven years later. Draft four is practically identical with the third draft, though pages 77 and 78 are numbered in the fourth draft as pages 77a and 77b. This means that the pagination of draft four from this point is one page off from the pagination of draft three. Thus, draft three runs to 151 pages; draft four, only to 150. Draft four also differs from the third draft in that it has a number of handwritten notations added to the text.[6] These notations are relatively few and do not in any sense constitute a major revision of *The Inner Experience*. Thus, for all practical purposes, it can be said that the latest draft of this typescript which we possess dates from September, 1959. There is no indication that Merton made any of the changes he kept intending to make until the summer of 1968.

Minor Revision in 1968

When in August of 1968 he was preparing to leave Gethsemani for his journey to Asia, he did a bit of "cleaning up" at the hermitage, as he had been told that others would be using it during his absence. One day, as he was in the midst of this cleaning up, he went to Louisville, where he paid a visit to his longtime friend and former teacher, Daniel Walsh. Walsh was in his office at Bellarmine College, but was on the point of leaving to give a lecture to the Carmelite nuns in the monastery across the street from the college. "I won't detain you," Merton said, "I just dropped in to give you a gift on the anniversary of your ordination to the priesthood." He handed Walsh a large manila envelope and said: "It is something I wrote a long time ago, but wondered what the response would be if it were published. I had previously decided against it. But recently I reread it and made some corrections and additions [7] which you will note. Give it to the Carmelites to read and one day tell me what they think."[8] He also suggested that Walsh might show it to his Bellarmine students and get their reactions. The large manila envelope contained the manuscript of *The Inner Experience*. The changes (which he had made after rereading the manuscript recently) were minor: a word, phrase or sentence here or there plus one paragraph of about 125 words.[9] Merton was clearly asking Walsh's advice as to whether or not it was publishable. Four years after Merton's death, Walsh wrote to Father Flavian, the abbot of Gethsemani, to tell him of his conversation with Merton.[10] He expressed the strong conviction that *The Inner Experience* should be published. Father Flavian agreed with him, as he very much admired the manuscript. Unfortunately, when the Merton Legacy Trust was set up in 1967, Merton had included a stipulation that *The Inner Experience* and also *The School of the Spirit* were not to be published as books.[11] Father Flavian, after consulting John Ford, the lawyer for the Trust, decided not to involve the monastery in the legal proceedings that would be required to "break" this provision of the Trust Agreement.[12]

In the appendix at the end of this book there are three diagrams. The first (A) indicates the relationship of the four drafts to one another in terms of their content. The second diagram (B) shows the common material between *The Inner Experience* (draft four) and *What Is Contemplation?*

The text I shall be quoting from is the most complete text—what I have called "draft four." As Diagram A in the appendix indicates, there is some confusion about the division of *The Inner Experience* into chapters. He was not exaggerating when he told Sister Therese that it would be "a patchy job." There are two Chapters IV. He then skips to Chapter VII. Following Chapter VII are two unnumbered chapters which one would expect to be Chapters VIII and IX, yet they are followed by a chapter numbered IX. Finally Chapters X to XV follow in order. How does one approach this "patchy job"? With some difficulty. The book is probably proof that Merton's pen (typewriter) almost always lagged behind the thoughts that seemed so readily to "invade" his inquiring mind. He is certainly open to the charge of writing too much and refining his writing too little. Michael Casey has put well the excitement of reading this work and the confusion it often seems to engender. "It is like stepping into a rehearsal, a workshop, or a busy kitchen."[13] But it's as if that rehearsal or workshop or busy kitchen was frozen in time without its full product ever emerging. It's like being stopped at the top of a roller coaster: the ride is enjoyable but never quite makes it to a satisfactory landing.

One thing can be said with certainty: *The Inner Experience* fits well with our discussion of what Merton had to say about contemplation. In 1959, Merton once again makes clear how important contemplation is to the Christian life. He makes it the central focus of the text of *The Inner Experience*. Thus on September 12, 1959, he wrote to Czeslaw Milosz: "I have just been finishing another book, *The Inner Experience*, a wider view of the same thing, contemplation, with more references to Oriental ideas. There is to me nothing but this that counts, but everything can enter into it."[14]

This text from the letter to Milosz sums up some of the main points Merton will take up in various parts of *The Inner Experience*. Merton makes clear in this letter that (1) *The Inner Experience* is about contemplation; (2) it will offer a more complete statement about contemplation ("a wider view") than his previous writings; (3) links will be established with Eastern religious thought; (4) contemplation is connected with, and unifies, the totality of human life ("nothing counts more" than contemplation; "everything can enter into it"). I invite the reader to keep these four points in mind as we journey through the pages of this unfinished manuscript. Especially important in this letter is the link Merton forges with Eastern religious thought. This marks the first appearance of a new element in his writings, namely, a turning to the East, to the experience of contemplation outside the Christian faith, as a way of enriching his understanding of Christian contemplation. In *Seeds of Contemplation* he had spoken disparagingly about Oriental mystics.[15] Still in the grips of a dualism that would differentiate the natural and the supernatural, he had at that time seen the Oriental experience as purely natural: They did not therefore reach the transcendent reality. That was ten years earlier. Now in 1959 he is much more open to a positive approach to Oriental writings.

I propose to discuss *The Inner Experience* in three parts. In the first part (pages 1-54) Merton discusses the question: Who is it that contemplates? In Part Two (pages 55-103) the topic is kinds of contemplation. Part Three (pages 104-150) deals with issues related to contemplation.

The Identity of the One Who Contemplates

The Inner Experience begins with a preliminary warning against living divided lives. One of the struggles we all face is the danger of letting our lives be divided into compartments, each having its separate place in our lives, none of them connected with the others. It's as if we become a number of different persons. If one could take a photo of our lives, they would look a bit like many modern offices in which each person, working in the same huge space, has her own cubicle, marked off and physically separate from all the others. We already have too many compartments in our lives. Do not, Merton cautions us, set up another compartment, label it "contemplation," and proclaim that it is the only one that really matters.

The worst thing that can happen to a person who is already divided into a dozen different compartments is to seal off yet another compartment and tell her that this one is more important than all the others and that one must henceforth exercise a special care in keeping it separate from them (3).

In the first of what will be quite a few references to Eastern religion and culture, Merton suggests that this kind of division within us, this "being distracted" (literally "being pulled apart") is more likely to be a problem for people in the

West than in the East: "The Eastern traditions have the advantage of disposing people more naturally for contemplation."[16] Merton goes on to say:

The first thing that you have to do, before you can even start thinking about such a thing as contemplation, is to try to recover your basic natural unity, to reintegrate your compartmentalized being into a coordinated and simple whole, and to learn to live as a unified human person (3).

Clearly, then, when Merton writes about "contemplation," it is not just one of a number of elements in our lives that he considered important. It is the one element that can bring unity into our often scattered lives. It is what really matters; there is nothing that counts more. As he puts it in his letter to Milosz: "Everything can enter into it." It "decompartmentalizes" our lives and brings unity to the persons we are. Once we have reintegrated our being and coordinated our lives into a simple whole, then we can have some confidence that when we say "I" that there "is really someone present to support the pronoun [we] have uttered" (3).

Much of what Merton wrote about contemplation in his earlier works tended to be derivative: his own "take" on what can be found in Scripture and recognized Christian writers from the past, e.g., Thomas Aquinas and John of the Cross. *The Inner Experience* offers much more of his own original thinking about contemplation. Much of that thinking is an attempt to discuss the question: Who is the subject of the contemplative experience? Suppose I want to make contemplation a reality in my life, what must I do? First of all, I have to get in touch with my own identity. I have to answer the question: "Who is the 'I' who wants to be a contemplative?"

The False Self

Don't jump too quickly to a response, Merton cautions us. The answer is not as easily arrived at as one might at first think. He is raising a problem he had hinted at ten years earlier in *Seeds of Contemplation*, when he wrote: "Everyone of us is shadowed by an illusory person: a false self."[17] Now the false self takes up a good bit of our time and energy, yet, except in a very superficial sense, the false self does not exist. If it does not exist, it clearly cannot be the subject of a contemplative experience. It is crucial, therefore that we know what Merton means by the false self if we are to understand his answer to the question: Who is it that contemplates? He uses a variety of synonyms for this "false self." In *The Inner Experience* he prefers to use the term "exterior self." This self, by whatever term one uses to designate it, has, he tells us, no substantive reality. It is a self of changing emotions: now up, now down. It is a self that has no voice of its own: It speaks the voice of the anonymous collectivity. In our day the media are often the source from which this self derives its opinions and judgments. It is a self that has objectified itself (that is made itself into an object that can be talked about and described). It has therefore lost any awareness of its own subjectivity. It quite literally does not know itself. It exists, not at any deep level of reality, but only in our egocentric desires: the desire to possess, to manipulate, to achieve, to be praised, to be recognized, to be fulfilled. If its environment happens to be religious and it hears about contemplation, it will probably want to be a contemplative. He will even, Merton says, make contemplative faces at himself like a child in front of a mirror.

> He will cultivate the contemplative look that seems appropriate to him and that he likes to see in himself. And the fact that his busy narcissism is turned within and feeds upon itself in stillness and secret love, will make him believe that his experience of himself is an experience of God. (5)

In this way the external or false self fabricates a contemplative identity, delights in it, without realizing that there is nobody there. The false self simply does not exist.

The Hidden, Interior, True Self

The first step toward true contemplation, then, is to renounce this illusory self and to learn that there is another self in us (the only one that really exists): the spiritual self which alone can be contemplative. This true self [18] does not seek fulfillment. It is content to be and in its being it finds fulfillment, because its being is rooted in God.

This true self in a person is his or her own subjectivity. It is the interior "I," that has no projects. It seeks to accomplish nothing, not even contemplation. It is in touch with its own being, aware that its being is one with God. Therefore in what it does, it is led not by any egotistical desires (because it has none), but by the promptings of God's own Spirit. It is this inner self, present in all of us but lying dormant in most of us, that must be awakened if we are to experience the life of contemplation. This awakening is not so much something that we acquire and therefore "have," but something that we are. This is to say that we do not really become contemplatives. We always are contemplatives in the depths of our being. But we have to become aware of what we are. We have to become who we are.

What can we know about our inner self? Not very much actually in the form of conceptual knowledge. For the inner self is not something that we can define and then deduce its characteristics from the definition. Why? Because it is not an object or a thing. It is "not a part of our being, like a motor in a car. It is our entire substantial being itself on its highest, most personal, most existential level. It is like life and it is life; it is our spiritual life when it is most alive" (6). What this means is that the inner self can only be known as God is known: that is, apophatically. For it is as secret as God himself and evades every concept by which we try to seize hold of it. It is satisfied to be. It just is.

In an interesting and suggestive metaphor, Merton compares the inner self to a "shy animal" that emerges only in an atmosphere of peace, silence and detachment. There is nothing we can do to coax it to manifest itself. "All we can do with any spiritual discipline is produce within ourselves something of the silence, the humility, the detachment, the purity of heart and the indifference which are required if the inner self is to make some shy, unpredictable manifestation of his presence" (6).

It is the inner self that gives depth and reality to every truly spiritual experience. Indeed, every in-depth experience, whether religious or moral or artistic, is to some extent an experience of the inner self. A sense of peace when you have been reconciled to someone from whom you have been estranged, the joy in listening to a Mozart or Beethoven symphony, the pleasure enjoyed through gazing upon a Rublev icon or a Van Gogh painting—depth experiences of this sort do indeed bring us glimpses of the inner self. Yet, as is always true of the inner self, such experiences are difficult to articulate. There is a certain incommunicability about them. No matter what you say or how clever you may be at saying it, there is always so much more of the experience left over, unable to be put into words.

It must be remarked that such experiences that lead us into the realms of the inner self are harder to come by in our busy, competitive, overactive society. In the longest addition he made to *The Inner Experience* in 1968, Merton wrote: that "a certain cultural and spiritual atmosphere favors the secret and spontaneous development of the inner self." He continues:

> The ancient cultural traditions both of the East and of the West, having a religious and sapiential nature, favored the interior life and indeed transmitted certain materials, in the form of archetypal symbols, liturgical rites, art, poetry, philosophy and myth which nourished the inner self from childhood to maturity. In such a cultural setting, no one needs to be self-conscious about his interior life, and subjectivity does not run the risk of being diverted into morbidity and excess. Unfortunately such a cultural setting no longer exists in the west or is no longer common property. It is something that has to be laboriously recovered by an educated and enlightened minority.[19]

A Zen Experience

Merton sees in the Zen experience of satori (enlightenment) an example, on the natural level, of a spiritual awakening that reveals the inner self. For satori is a revolutionary spiritual experience in which, after a long period of purification, there is a kind of inner explosion that blasts the false exterior self to pieces and leaves a person with nothing but her inner self, or, as the Buddhists would say, with nothing but the original face with which she was born. The result is a definitive realization of the nothingness of the exterior self and in consequence the liberation of the real self, the inner "I." Merton is careful to point out, however, that to describe the experience in these words is to use Western terms. "The real self in Zen language is beyond the division between self and non-self."[20]

The Zen example Merton uses is the experience of Chao-pien, a Zen disciple and a Chinese official who sits quietly in his office with his mind at rest (we might see this as simple quiet prayer). But Chao-pien had reached a point of inner maturity, where, as Merton puts it, "the secret pressure of the inner self was ready to break unexpectedly forth and revolutionize his whole being in Satori." A sudden clap of thunder and the "doors" of the inner consciousness fly open and reveal his "original face." The exterior self is not only revealed in its nothingness, but it is seen never to have existed in the first place. Here is Chao-pien's story in a simple four-line poem:

> Devoid of thought, I sat quietly by the desk in my official room
> With my fountain-mind undisturbed, as serene as water;
> A sudden crash of thunder, the mind-doors burst open
> And lo, there sits the old man in all his homeliness. (10)

Perhaps at first reflection, the reader of this poem may be disappointed. Why isn't this sudden breakthrough of consciousness an exciting, even terrifying experience? What does satori effect if it simply leaves an old man sitting in his room "in all his homeliness"? The answer is that, contrary to what we might expect, our inner self is "utterly simple, humble, poor and unassuming" (10).

The inner self is not an ideal self, especially not an imaginary, perfect creature fabricated to measure up to our compulsive need for greatness, heroism and infallibility. On the contrary, the real "I" is just simply ourselves and nothing more. Nothing more, nothing less. Our self as we are in the eyes of God, to use Christian terms. Our self in all our uniqueness, dignity, littleness and ineffable greatness: the greatness we have received from God our Father and that we share with him because he is our Father and "in him we live and move and have our being."[21]

The discovery of the inner self, which the Buddhist experiences in satori, is also the experience of Christian mystics; but with this difference: Zen seems to make no effort to go beyond the inner self, whereas Christian mysticism sees the discovery of the inner self as a stepping-stone to an awareness of God. The Christian mystic passes beyond the inner "I" and "sails into an immense darkness" in which he confronts "the 'I AM' of the Almighty" (11). God reveals the divine Self interiorly as dwelling in the inmost self.

Merton draws a distinction between the Zen writers whose interest seems to be exclusively in what is actually given in the experience and mystics in the Christian, Jewish and Islamic traditions. For the latter there is an infinite metaphysical gulf between our being and God's, between our own inner "I" and the "I" of God. There is therefore, Merton insists, a distinction between the experience of our inner self and our awareness that God reveals the divine Self to us through our inner self. Yet Merton does not seem to be entirely consistent. A few pages later, drawing on the Christian tradition (specifically Augustine, Tauler and John of the Cross) he seems to blur this distinction. He writes:

> Since our inmost 'I' is the perfect image of God, then when that 'I' awakens, he finds within himself the Presence of Him Whose image he is. And, by a paradox beyond all human expression, God and the soul seem to have but one single 'I.' They are (by divine grace) as though one single

person. They breathe and live and act as one. Neither of the 'two' is seen as object. (16)

There is pure subjectivity beyond all duality.

The awakening of the inner self and the awareness of God that it involves demand a strict spiritual discipline in the life of the would-be contemplative. It is not possible to find one's inmost center and know God there, as long as we are preoccupied with the desires of the outward, false self. In Merton's words:

> Freedom to enter the inner sanctuary of our being is denied to those who are held back by dependence on self-gratification and sense satisfaction, whether it be a matter of pleasure-seeking, love of comfort, or proneness to anger, self-assertion, pride, vanity, greed, and all the rest. (14)

There is a price to be paid if one wants to be a contemplative. The cost is demanding, yet at the same time freeing.

What frees us is faith: not just as an assent to revealed truths, but as a personal and direct acceptance of God in the divine Self. Faith means a turning to God and a turning away from creatures. It is a blacking out of the visible in order to see the invisible. Yet this needs to be properly understood. It is not a purely negative experience. Quite the contrary. Faith is a light so bright that it dazzles the mind and darkens all vision of other realities. Its brilliance appears at first to blind us, but only for the moment. For, as we gradually accustom ourselves to the light, we see all of reality transfigured by faith and filled with the light of God. We see the same external objects as we did before, but we view them in a different way. They no longer lead us or trap us. They are no longer objects of desire or fear. We see them as God's gifts to us. They are important to us at their own level of reality, but they can never claim ultimacy in our lives.

The Inner Self and Objects in the World

The inner self, therefore, does stand in a definite relationship to the world of objects, but it has a view of the world radically different from that of the exterior self. Whereas the latter tends to look at things from an economic or technical or hedonistic viewpoint, the interior self sees the world, not in bewildering complexity, but in unity. Objects in the external world are not things to be manipulated for pleasure or profit; rather, they are seen with an "immediacy" of vision that does not allow them to become objects of desire or greed or fear. To use a Zen expression, the inner self sees objects "without affirmation or denial." It simply sees what it sees. It sees only what is there. "It does not take refuge behind a screen of conceptual prejudices and verbalistic extortions" (17).

Merton contrasts a child's vision of a tree with a lumberman's vision. The child sees the tree in a way that is utterly simple and uncolored by ulterior motives. The lumberman, when he sees a tree, may be aware of its beauty but his vision is conditioned by motives of profit and considerations of business. He cannot just "see" the tree.

The Inner Self and Subjects in the World

The inner self is not only related to objects in the world; it also stands in a definite relationship to other subjects, to persons. It sees others not as limitations of itself, but as its complement, its other self. Indeed, no one can arrive at a true awareness of his own inner reality, unless he has first become aware of himself as a member of a group; that is, "as an 'I' confronted with a 'thou' that completes and fulfills his own being" (19). The Christian is not merely "alone with the Alone"; he is one with all his brothers and sisters in Christ. His union with them is a unity of love that transcends affirmation or denial. Since the spirit of Christ dwells in us all, we become, in the mysterious phrase of Saint Augustine, "one Christ loving Himself."

This is not to deny that the inner self is the sanctuary of our most personal and individual solitude; it is to say that, "what is most personal and solitary in us is what is united with the 'Thou' that confronts us" (20). Without question, a certain withdrawal is necessary in our lives for the perspective that solitude alone can give.[22] But it must be a withdrawal not for the purpose of separation but in the interest of a higher unity. Mere withdrawal without a return to freedom in action can only lead to "a static, death-like inertia of spirit" (22) in which there is no awakening at all.

The Inner Self and the Worshiping Community

Real contact with the world of things and with the societal community of men and women is essential for the awakening of the inner self. Equally important is contact with the worshiping community. For all authentic forms of social worship attempt in some manner to provide a religious experience in which the members of the religious group can transcend their individual selves and the group to find themselves and the group at a higher level. This means that all truly serious and spiritual forms of worship aspire at least implicitly to lead their participants to a contemplative awakening of the individual and the community.

But when forms of religious and liturgical worship lose their initial impulse of fervor they tend to become noisy and superactive and in the process easily forget the contemplative element so essential to authentic worship. This was one of the problems we had to deal with as the Second Vatican Council called us to more active participation in the liturgy. It was all too easy to forget that contemplative silence can be a way of participating in worship and must be an element in any true form of worship. In some contexts liturgy became a marathon of activity that left a community spiritually (and physically) breathless. Nor was sufficient care always taken to relate liturgy to daily life. Even after Vatican II it was possible to let liturgy be a wonderful celebration of community without any real connection with the daily living of the members of the worshiping community.

When the contemplative dimension of worship is lost,

one of two things happens. Either the participants concentrate on rites and forms for their own sake or for the sake of placating the deity they worship; or they tend to seek an artificial kind of togetherness at a superficial level that does not allow them to transcend themselves or the group. Liturgy becomes at best a celebration of human community at a purely horizontal level, with no transcendent reference. In either case the liturgical forms fail in their purpose: Instead of enabling the believer to penetrate to his inmost being, they serve only to stir up the unconscious emotions of the exterior self. It was against this type of liturgy—worship that had lost its impulse toward interiority and no longer had any relationship with the daily lives of people—that the Old Testament prophets inveighed. It was this kind of ritual that activates the lips but not the heart that Jesus rebuked in the Pharisees.

Contemplative Unity and the Genesis Myth of the Fall

Why is it that contemplation seems so difficult for us, when it appears to be the one way for us to live authentically? Why is it that our lives seem to be in the command of a false self that in reality does not even exist? Why is it that we are so out of touch with what is most real in us? The Christian response to these questions is the myth of the fall described in the third chapter of Genesis. God's original blessing to humanity was the gift of self-awareness, which is simply to say that humans were created as contemplatives. God's original blessing was the gift of the true self. The myth of the "fall" suggests the puzzling, unexplainable, yet undeniable, fact that we are alienated from that true self. This alienation we call original sin.[23] The fall was a fall from the unity of the contemplative vision into a condition of multiplicity, distraction and exteriority. Alienated from their inmost spiritual selves, humans looked outward, not inward. As a result, they were enslaved by an inexorable concern for the exterior, the passing, the illusory, the trivial. No longer able to recognize their own identity in God, they found themselves utterly exiled not only from God but also from their own true selves. The human temptation in this state was for a person "to seek God and happiness outside himself" (34). Thus, his search for God became in fact a flight from God and from his inmost self—a flight that inevitably took him further and further from reality. This state or estrangement in realms of unreality is what is meant by original sin.[24]

Our task after the fall is to return to paradise, to recover our lost identity. We have to return to God, that is to say, to "that infinite abyss of pure reality" (35) in which alone our own reality is grounded. This return is made possible by the death and Resurrection of Jesus Christ, in which we are invited to participate. Our participation consists in a spiritual death in which our exterior self is destroyed and by a spiritual resurrection in which our inner self rises from the "dead" by faith and we begin to live again in Christ. It is as if original sin means that we have forgotten who we are and by our participation in Christ's Resurrection we "remember" our true selves. We become aware of who we are.

Merton sees in the precision of the Nicaean and Chalcedon formulation of the mystery of the Incarnation, not simply a theological nicety, but a necessary expression of the central truth of all history.[25] For it is only in recognizing Christ as the God-man that we can hope once again to achieve our lost union with God. God had to be revealed as human so that all might become one with the risen Jesus and in him recover the original blessing of our oneness with God.

Because Christ assumed a human nature which is in every respect literally and perfectly human and because that human nature belongs to the Person of the Word of God, everything human in Christ is at the same time divine. The thoughts and actions of Christ are the works of a divine Person. His very existence is the existence of a divine Person. In him we see a human being who is in every respect identical with ourselves as far as his human nature is concerned, yet who at the same time lives on a completely transcendent divine level of consciousness and being.

By becoming human, Christ makes it possible for us to be divinized. As Athanasius, the great exponent of orthodox Christology, declared, in a formula borrowed from Saint Irenaeus: "God became human in order that humans might become divine." Christ did not merely reestablish for us a favorable juridical relation with God; he elevated, changed, and transformed us into God. Our radical divinization takes place in Baptism; but the divine life remains hidden and dormant within us until it is more fully developed by a life of asceticism and charity and, on a higher level, contemplation. In referring to our divinization, Merton is bringing up a doctrine very dear to the Greek Fathers. Christian tradition through the centuries has seen two reasons for the Incarnation: (1) to free us from original sin, and (2) to actualize in us the capacity for divinity that is in us from the moment of our existence. Western Christianity has tended to emphasize the first and to stress the overcoming of a sinful state in humans; Eastern Christianity is more comfortable with the second approach to understanding why God became human in Jesus.

The Christian is called by the Gospel to renew in her life the self-emptying and self-transformation by which God became human. "Just as the Word emptied Himself of His divine and transcendent nobility in order to 'descend' to the human level, so we must empty ourselves of what is human in the ignoble sense of the word, which really means what is less than human," in order that we may be raised to the level of God. This does not mean the destruction of anything that belongs to human nature as it was assumed by Christ. It does mean "a radical cutting off of what was not assumed by Him because it was not capable of being divinized" (40).

This "radical cutting off" must apply to everything that focuses on and perpetuates our exterior and illusory self to the detriment of our interior and true self. The inner self is renewed in Christ and becomes the "new man" of whom Saint Paul speaks. This "new man" is the contemplative, who through participation in the Christ-life is assimilated to the hypostatic union,[26] the union of the divine and human in Christ. In Christ we become God's sons and daughters. As Paul says to the Romans: "[I]t is that very Spirit bearing witness with our spirit that we are children of God."[27] This testimony of the Spirit to our inmost self (i.e., our spirit) is what Merton means by Christian contemplation.

Kinds of Contemplation

Following the topic of the identity of the one who contemplates, Merton discusses a variety of material that may best be classified under the general title of "Kinds of Contemplation," with particular emphasis on "infused" contemplation. While it contains some excellent insights on the contemplative life, this section is the least coordinated part of the book. It exhibits the "patchwork" characteristic that he spoke of in his letter to Sister Therese. Sections of *What Is Contemplation?*, some of them quite lengthy, are inserted into the text at various points, and not always harmoniously. Several ways of handling the subject of contemplation are discussed in the text, but Merton never relates them to one another. He speaks of the distinction he had made in *What Is Contemplation?* between infused (or passive) contemplation and active contemplation.

Passive and Active Contemplation

Passive contemplation is the passive intuition of our inmost self and of God. It is an understanding of contemplation that is primarily theological; for it is not empirically verifiable, since it is being known to us only as a truth that comes to us from God's revelation. Christ's words in John's Gospel that he will "manifest Himself" to those who love him suggests a divine activity which the one who contemplates is unable to bring about by his own efforts (hence Merton's use of the word "passive"). In classical mystical terminology, such a grace is effected "in us and without us" (*in nobis et sine nobis*).

Active contemplation, on the other hand, is effected in us, but with our cooperation (*in nobis et non sine nobis*). Passive contemplation involves no conceptual mediation: It is without concepts and images. It is essentially apophatic. Active contemplation uses concepts and judgments and acts of faith. It may be a springboard for moments of genuine contemplative intuition.

Active contemplation is the deliberate and sustained effort to discover the will of God in the events of life and to lead one's life in harmony with the divine will. This involves three things: (1) It means being alive to the signs of the times—being in tune with what is most genuine in the movements of the day. (2) It means confronting reality with a sense of awe. (It is this sense of awe and reverence that distinguishes active contemplation from a kind of aesthetic contemplation that rests in the beauty of abstract truth.) This sense of awe moves us to reverence people simply for the wonder of who they are as places of God's presence. Indeed we see all of creation as sacred and as God's gift to us that we must not abuse or exploit. (3) It means being in touch with our own inner life, directing that life according to our inner truth and striving for unity in that life nourished by meditation, reading and participating in the liturgical life of the Church.

I find the distinction Merton makes between discursive reading and contemplative reading particularly helpful. In discursive reading we pass from one thought to another, as we follow the author's development of his ideas. And if our reading is attentive we may be drawn to expressing some thoughts of our own.

> "Reading becomes contemplative when, instead of reasoning, we abandon the sequence of the author's thoughts in order not only to follow our own thoughts (meditation), but simply *to rise above thought and penetrate into the mystery of truth which is experienced intuitively as present and actual.* We meditate with our mind, which is 'part of' our being. But we contemplate with our whole being and not just with one of its parts." (57)

In a culture that prides itself on speed in everything, including reading, we need to learn how to slow down at times and read in a contemplative way.

In active contemplation one is also nourished by the liturgy of the Church. In fact, Merton believes, liturgy is "the ordinary focus of active contemplation" (59). For, in the liturgy, one enters into the Church's contemplation of the great mysteries of faith. Liturgies of the Word, announcing the Gospel (the kerygma), put us in touch with the mystery of salvation. As we hear the Word of salvation, it enters the depths of our being and awakens anew in us our divine life as sons and daughters of God. Eucharistic liturgies unite the Christian sacramentally with the risen Lord; for they symbolize and effect the mystical union of the believer with Christ in love. In active participation in the liturgy we thus join with the whole Church in contemplating the mysteries of faith.

Active contemplation also means union with God in the activities of one's life. This is the normal way to contemplation for the great majority of Christians. They are "hidden contemplatives" or, in the term he borrowed from Jacques Maritain, "masked contemplatives." They abandon themselves to the will of God and keep in touch with the realities of the present moment; that is to say, the inner and spiritual realities, not the surface emotions and excitements which in reality are nothing but illusion. They swim with the living stream of life, remaining in contact with God in the hiddenness and ordinariness of the present moment and the tasks it brings. In this way, ordinary activities—such as walking down a street, sweeping a floor, taking a stroll in the woods—can be enriched with a contemplative sense of the presence of God. Being in touch with God in this way is "one of the simplest and most secure ways of living a life of prayer, and one of the safest" (64). Those who follow this way may achieve a high degree of sanctity—even greater perhaps than that of those who are "juridically" called to live lives of contemplation.

Natural Contemplation and Mystical Theology

As another way of approaching the kinds of contemplation, Merton turns to the Greek Fathers and elaborates on the distinction they drew between natural contemplation (*theoria physike*) and mystical theology (*theologia*).[28] Natural contemplation is "the intuition of divine things in and through the reflections of God in nature and in the symbols of revelation" (66). Such contemplation presupposes a long ascetic preparation that delivers one from attachment to exterior things and produces a purity of heart and a singleness of view that enables one to see straight into the nature of things as they are. "Natural" contemplation is natural, not in its origin, but in its object: It is "the contemplation of the divine in nature, not contemplation of the divine by our natural powers" (66-67). Such contemplation, while it implies ascetic preparation on the part of the contemplative, is mystical in that it is God's gift of enlightenment, enabling us really to see the created world as it is and to see the symbols of God's presence with which it is filled.

Theologia, or pure contemplation (what Merton had earlier called infused contemplation), is "the direct quasi-experimental [i.e., experiential] contact with God beyond all thought, that is, without the medium of concepts" (67). Since it brooks no medium between God and our inmost spirit, it is in this sense direct contact with God. Such direct contact with God is not a matter of spiritual effort or intellectual learning. It is an identification with God by love, for it is love that constitutes in us the likeness of God. At the same time, it is a meeting with God in the darkness of unknowing. This embrace in darkness is absolutely essential to pure contemplation, because, with the elimination of concepts and images, all natural lights are put out. One knows God through one's "own divinized subjectivity." Saint Gregory of Nyssa aptly compares the mystic to Moses ascending Mount Sinai and entering into the dark cloud where he is face to face with God. The inmost self ascends into the darkness with no concepts at all. Then he can touch, or rather be touched by, God. In the cloud of unknowing, "the gap between our spirit as subject and God as object is finally closed and in the embrace of mystical love we know that we and He are one" (69).

But the cloud into which we enter has not only a light shining in the darkness; it has also a fire that wages a relentless attack against the last vestiges of self-love that remain in us. There are times when this fire strips us of all the consolations we once enjoyed in prayer, and we are left in a state of terrible inward anguish in which we seem no longer able to pray or to love. This anguish may at times be accentuated when conflicts arise between the inward light of God, however dimly perceived, and the outward claims made on our obedience by the community in which we live. Such conflicts are not unlikely, since the call into the darkness is a call to leave familiar and conventional patterns of thought and action.

In the midst of this anguish and these conflicts, we must come to realize that God is drawing us to a deeper emptying of all that is incompatible with his love. We become indifferent to ourselves and even to our spiritual ambitions. Knowing that we are one with God in love, we gradually cease to worry about ourselves and about useless questions. We learn to leave "all decisions to God in the wordlessness of a present that knows no explanations, no projects and no plans" (73). As Eckhart says: Mystical love of God is a "love that asks no questions" (73).

The Movement From an Exterior Life to an Interior One

The discovery of God in the inmost depths of our being, Merton says, marks a "shift from the exterior life to an interior life in the strict sense of the word" (85). For, while the term "interior life" can be a valid description of a life that strives for prayer and self-discipline, the interior life properly so called actually comes alive only when "this inner and spiritual consciousness has been awakened" (85). Until we make this shift to an interior life, our spirituality will remain largely a matter of external practices.

The paradox of the contemplative way, therefore, always involves a darkening and blinding of the exterior self and an awakening and enlightening of the inner self. The time comes when it is necessary to darken and put to sleep the discursive and rational lights that one was familiar with in meditation. This is no easy task and can be done only with the help of God's grace. For one tends to feel guilty about relaxing and resting in the darkness; and there is a strong inclination to climb back into the safety and security of the boat of habit and convention.

In a striking analogy Merton compares this critical point in the life of a contemplative to the battle of Jacob with the angel.[29] "It is the battle of our own strength, lodged in the exterior self, with the strength of God, which is the life and actuality of our inner self" (88). It is a battle that takes place in the darkness. The angel, our inner self, wounds a nerve in our thigh, so that ever afterwards we limp; that is to say, our natural powers are crippled. Though we do not overcome our antagonist, yet we do not let him go till he blesses us. And when we are blessed, we receive a new name, Israel, which means "He who sees God." And this new name makes us contemplatives. But when we ask the name of our antagonist, no answer is given us, for our inmost self is unknown, just as God himself is unknown.

John of the Cross defines this battle in terms of a twofold purification. First there is the dark night of the senses, which is a purification of the exterior and interior senses that brings one to the threshold of contemplation. Second, there is the dark night of the spirit, in which even the interior self is purified. "In the first night the exterior man 'dies' to rise and become the inner man; in the second night the interior man dies and rises so completely united to God that the two are one" (89). It is "as if the soul itself were God and God were the soul." In the words of John of the Cross, the soul is completely lost in God, "as a drop of water in a flagon of pure wine."

Issues Related to Contemplation

The Desire for Contemplation

If we desire to be contemplatives, how do we know what it actually is that we desire? There is no easy answer to this question. Contemplation is knowing God as unknown and by unknowing, "an apophatic grasp of Him Who is" (109). As such it cannot be satisfactorily explained to one who has not had the experience; at the same time, one who has had it can recognize it in others. This is because contemplation is a common religious phenomenon that is not limited to any age or place or society. Whether it is thought of as natural or supernatural, it is an experience that is possible for anyone who sincerely seeks the truth and responds to God's grace. That is why anyone can desire it.

Yet those who would desire it must renounce all preconceived notions about what it is and open themselves to a completely new experience. Moreover, they must put aside all ambition to achieve it. One can only desire it by "not desiring" it. Anyone who thinks of contemplation as something lofty and spectacular that he seeks to accomplish cannot receive the intuition of that reality that is at once transcendent and at the same time immanent in his ordinary self.

Those who know that they do not know and who open themselves to the truth without pride in their own capacities and without personal ambition may indeed experience the desire for contemplative freedom arising in themselves unobserved. Then they are on the road to contemplation, because, paradoxically, they didn't even know there was such a road.

Sin and Guilt

To take the first step toward contemplative freedom one needs not so much an awareness of what lies at the end of the road—the experience of God—as a clear view of the obstacle that blocks the road at the very beginning: the obstacle of sin. This is especially necessary today. For we live in an age that has lost the sense of sin and replaced it with a sense of guilt. A sense of sin can be a productive experience, leading to conversion of spirit. A sense of guilt, on the other hand, can actually deaden our realization of the meaning of sin in our lives.

Guilt is a kind of prurient feeling of naughtiness for having violated the taboos of one's religion. It is a sense of oppression from the outside: an experience of anxiety in which one feels that he is going to be called to account for a misdeed. I experience guilt when I think that someone else believes me to be in the wrong.

Guilt can be dealt with in two ways: (1) by gestures of piety that symbolize good intentions and therefore assuage conscience and obscure the sense of sin; or (2) by transferring guilt to the group and thereby escaping personal responsibility. This tendency to make sin a collective responsibility rather than a personal one is very strong in our day. The more collective responsibility becomes, the more nebulous it is. Then the most terrible crimes can be accepted without a tremor, because the guilt is "theirs," not "mine." Witness, Merton suggests, the willingness of the majority of "believers" to accept nuclear war with all its implications, and with scarcely a murmur of protest.

Sin is something much deeper and more existential than guilt. It is a sense of inner falsity: not just the realization that I have done wrong, but that in some real sense I *am* wrong.

It is a sense of evil in myself, not because I have violated a law outside myself, but because I have violated the inmost laws of my own being which are, at the same time, the laws of God who dwells in me. The sense of sin is the sense of being deeply and deliberately false to my inmost being and therefore to my likeness to God (112).

Merton sees as part of the mission of the contemplative "to keep alive in the world the sense of sin," and to nurture, at least in himself, a sense of personal responsibility before God as well as a personal independence from collective irresponsibility. In fulfilling this mission, the contemplative is the descendant of the Old Testament prophets, who were called to confront the people of Israel with the reality of sin and make them see the difference between sin and legal guilt. Legal guilt could be set right by rituals, but sin cut them off from God. The prophets did not preach an abstract morality: They called people to accept the concrete will of God.

The contemplative, like the prophet, is aware not only of his own sins but of the sins of the world, which he takes upon himself, because he cannot dissociate himself from the world in which he lives or from the deeds of other people. In an age that has known Auschwitz and Dachau, our contemplation "is something darker and more fearsome than the contemplation of the Church Fathers" (115). For it must embody a deep sorrow and a healing sense of repentance in the face of the mystery of evil that stands as a wall between us and God. Contemplation that would shrink from the burden of our days and refuse to share the misery of others would only be an escape into unreality and spiritual illusion.

Our age, perhaps more than any other, has experienced the absence of God. Indeed, in some circles it has been proclaimed that God is dead. In such an age, God must often seem to be "absent" from our contemplation. The truth is that never more than today God makes the divine presence felt by "being absent." Our contemplation, therefore, need not be a vain struggle to try to make God present, but rather an acceptance of apparent emptiness and absence, while we realize, if only dimly, that in the nothingness that seems to engulf us God is more surely present.

Contemplation and Technology

In discussing the practical problems that deter efforts to live a contemplative life in today's world, Merton develops a theme that is familiar to those who have read his books of social criticism: that the technological society we live in and the television culture it has engendered have all but destroyed our natural disposition to contemplation. In pre-industrial ages—and in some primitive societies today—people were formed by their tradition and culture. Even if they could not read or write, they possessed a fund of important and vital knowledge as an integral part of their lives. A wholesome simplicity and a healthy self-confidence prepared them for and disposed them toward the contemplative experience. The technological orientation of contemporary society, with its tendency to manipulate persons and cast them into a single mold, beclouds the natural and spontaneous signs of spirituality. Imagination, originality and freshness of response to reality that tended to characterize pre-industrial societies have been replaced, in our technological world, by fears and anxieties and the compulsion to conform that assail contemporary men and women from all sides. The result is that the disposition to contemplation that was once natural to the human person has to be recovered and learned.

The Monastic Life

Where can a person find the proper setting where in silence and detachment he can learn the ways of the interior life? The most obvious answer is a monastic or contemplative community. The monastery provides a way of life that is supposed to be oriented toward contemplation. It is a place where you find yourself living among contemplatives and where spiritual direction is readily available. Indeed, the community life of the monastery is a kind of "sacrament" of the presence of God. This at least is the ideal expressed in the Rule of Saint Benedict—a Rule which through the centuries has proven itself adaptable to new situations and which offers a wholesome combination of liturgy, labor, study and contemplation.

In practice, however, there is often a gap between the ideal and the real situation that exists. A monastery is a community of "juridical" contemplatives—that is, a community of men or women whose very way of life involves a commitment to contemplation—but, there are, Merton believed, all too many monasteries that "contain few or no real contemplatives" (118). The rigidly institutional character of monastic life today can inhibit contemplative development. The factory-like atmosphere of very large monasteries requires so many jobs to be done that the things that are most necessary tend to be forgotten. Though the monastic life is based, in theory, on a medieval pattern, the tempo is often that of a modern place of business, with none of the seemingly aimless leisure and thoughtlessness of time that the contemplative spirit requires. The monastery has not remained immune from the influences of technology.

Merton speaks of the large influx of vocations to the monastic life and the emergence of new types of monasteries occurring in his time. He was writing forty years ago. The vocation picture is quite different at the beginning of a new century. Nonetheless he warns that disappointment awaits anyone who might expect contemporary monks to carry the torch of culture through a new dark age, as monks of medieval times had preserved human culture in the dark ages of the past.[30] From his own experience as master of novices, Merton came to realize that the influx in large numbers of hopeful candidates seeking to enter upon the monastic life created a unique set of problems. There is nothing in the monastic rule, Merton points out, to prepare the monastery for the arrival of the television addict. It can no longer be taken for granted that young postulants who seek admission to the monastery really know their own minds or have their lives together. Most often they are immature and lack the background of a true liberal education. They may have gone through a process of education, but much of it had little to do with real life. It may have taught them ways to control things and to manipulate persons, but not how to be free from external compulsions and how to open themselves to their own inner truth. They are formless bundles of unrelated factual knowledge that is largely superficial and not integrated into their lives. They do not really "know" what they know, for what they have "learned" has not been personally appropriated by them. Their lives are often a pitiful mixture of pseudo-sophistication and utter vacuity.

Moreover, the television culture, in which they have been indoctrinated, encourages passivity and receptivity, but unfortunately of the wrong kind. Certainly, the passivity and receptivity that are the fruits of an active and relentless struggle against all that captivates and enslaves the senses, the emotions and the will are qualities essential to contemplation. But such qualities are not conducive to contemplation if they are the result of the inertia and uncritical absorption of material and temporal "values" poured out of a television set. Young candidates who are formed (or deformed) by such a culture are not simply unprepared for the contemplative life; they are unprepared for any kind of human life.

If monasteries are going to accept such undeveloped candidates, before they enter the novitiate they need to be in separate communities of postulants. Merton is talking about an environment in which they can be given not only an elementary religious formation but also the opportunities for normal human experience, in which they will be able to find a certain amount of depth in their lives and come to appreciate the value of silence and of being alone with themselves.

Such things, Merton believes, cannot be done in a novitiate. You cannot teach asceticism to someone who has not had, in any depth, truly human experiences. You cannot speak of "mortification" of the senses to someone who has never had the pleasure of using his senses normally and innocently in the enjoyment of the good things of nature. Only one who has learned to see with his own eyes and taste with his own tongue and experience reality with his whole being can ever begin to understand the meaning of ascetic discipline.

Saint Teresa of Avila, in Chapter VI of the *Book of Foundations*, counsels those who have been led into exaggerations and delusions in their prayer life to distract themselves deliberately from what they think to be spiritual, in order "to keep in touch with ordinary human realities of life" (129). A person has to be attuned to what is truly human before she can be ascetical—or contemplative.

Contemplative Life in the World

The cloistered monk in his contemplative quest has the support of an institutional structure geared to contemplation. He has also an atmosphere of solitude that protects him in part at least from the pressures and distractions of secular life. The layperson intent on an interior life has neither the structure nor the atmosphere conducive to the spiritual quest. If he wishes to enjoy even an elementary life of prayer, he must be willing to face the ceaseless struggle to keep free from the collective pressures that subject him to the spirit of the world and deaden his sensitivity to the spirit of God. This struggle involves two things. First, it means reducing the conflicts in his life by cutting down contacts with the world and subjection to secular concerns. This requires reducing the need for pleasure, comfort, prestige and success and embracing a life of relative poverty and detachment. Second, it means putting up with the conflicts that remain: the noise, the agitation, the lack of time, the constant contact with a secular mentality which seems to engulf us on all sides and from which we can never be wholly delivered.

Lay people should seek some kind of structure, however informal, that will join them with others of similar intent, perhaps with the help of a priest who is truly interested in contemplation, and possibly in contact with a contemplative community. Merton envisions the possibility of a contemplative Third Order attached to a Cistercian or Carthusian monastery. Such a group of lay people could provide its members with books, conferences, spiritual direction, perhaps even a quiet spot in the country to go to for brief periods of prayer and solitude.

Structure is not enough; there is also the need of creating the atmosphere of quiet and solitude so essential to spiritual growth. Merton offers three suggestions toward this goal. I leave the readers to reflect on whether or not his suggestions make practical sense in their lives.

First, lay people interested in the interior life should seek a place to live and an occupation to engage in that will offer them opportunities for solitude. Even though it might entail some economic sacrifice, they might move to the country or to a small town, where they would have more opportunity to think and to get their lives together. The relative poverty that such a move might involve would liberate them from the pitiless struggle to keep their standards of life at the level of the rest of society. As regards occupation, probably not everyone is ready to embrace the life of a forest ranger or a lighthouse keeper or a night watchman, but, Merton asks, what is wrong with farming? One has to ask if Merton is becoming more naïve and unreal as he becomes more concrete. Clearly the basic principles he enunciates make sense. His examples hardly seem very practical or even possible for the vast majority of people. Perhaps readers might want, at this point, to reflect on what places and occupations, open to them, are most conducive to a contemplative way of life.

Second, they might rearrange the schedule of their daily activities so as to enjoy those parts of the day which are quiet because the world does not value them. The early hours of the morning, when most people are asleep, offer you the opportunity of having the whole world to yourself so that you can taste the peace of solitude. Dawn is a peaceful, mysterious contemplative time of the day—a time that speaks of new life and new beginnings. It is well suited to symbolize the continual interior spiritual renewal that must characterize our life in Christ.

Third, they should make special efforts to keep Sunday as a day of contemplation. Sunday is sacred to the mystery of the Resurrection. It is a time to contemplate all that God has done for us, and especially what he has done in Christ. It is not, therefore, just a pause in the week, but "a burst of light out of a sacred eternity" (133) entering into the otherwise ceaseless round of secular time.

We should stop working and rushing around on Sunday,

not just to rest so that we can start over again on Monday, but to collect our wits and to realize the relative meaninglessness of the secular business that fills the other six days of the week.

On Sunday we can taste the satisfaction of the peace that only Christ can give—a peace which, if we orient our work toward it, can filter through the rest of the week. "Sunday reminds us of the peace that should filter through the whole week when our work is properly oriented" (134).

Fourth, a layperson intent on living an interior life must not attempt to be a monk in the world. His prayer life cannot be pure contemplation; he must be content to be what Merton calls a "masked contemplative." For active virtue and good works must necessarily play a large part in his "contemplative" life. He must be faithful to the duties of his state in life, whether as head of a family, member of a profession or citizen of his country. Married Christians must see their contemplation linked closely with their married life. Indeed, their expression of married love is a symbol of the human desire for God and for oneness with him. The Greek Fathers believed that, before the fall, Adam and Eve were literally one flesh, one single being. The fall divided them into two, and ever after, sexual love has been an effort to recover that lost unity. Yet perfect unity cannot be realized by man and woman. It can be realized only in Christ who has married human nature and united it to God in his own Person. Sexual union is a symbol, however frail and incomplete, of that perfect union of humanity with God effected in the Incarnation. Since the love of married Christians mirrors, though dimly and incompletely, the perfection of Christian love, their contemplative spirituality must be rooted and centered in the mystery of Christian marriage.

The Future of the Contemplative Life

In the final pages of *The Inner Experience*, Merton discusses the future of the contemplative life in the contemporary world. Contemplation today, he insists, cannot consist merely in withdrawal into a subjective peace that evades responsibility for the world, of which the contemplative, like everyone else, is after all a part. The contemplative must learn in his withdrawal the unique contribution he can make to that world.

A contemplative is not just a person who separates herself from others and goes off to meditate while they struggle to make a living. Contemplatives cannot forget the world and its struggles in order to sit absorbed in prayer, "while bombers swarm in the air" (143) above them. The contemplative is one who lives a life that tends toward unity. True, contemplatives must begin by separating themselves from the ordinary activities of other people so that in recollection and solitude they can find the inner center of their lives, which remains inaccessible as long as they are immersed in an exterior life.

But contemplation is not intended to be a life of permanent withdrawal. The contemplative is not one who is less interested than others in what is going on in the world; if anything, contemplatives should be more interested— precisely because they are contemplatives. Indeed, they should not only be more interested in what happens, they should be more perceptive of the real issues at stake. For if they have achieved true purity of heart, they are less likely to be involved in the surface confusion that most people take for reality. They will have a more spiritual grasp of what is "real" and "actual," a deeper appreciation of values that are permanent, human and truly spiritual.

The contemplative's contribution to the world will not be that of the specialist, skilled in political science or economics or any other particular discipline, but that of the person who is whole and unified in his own being and who seeks to communicate an intuition of wholeness and unity to others. Because he is in touch with what is most deeply real, he is attuned to the Logos of his own time, with a compassion for people's deepest sufferings and a sensitivity to their most viable hopes. He has an understanding of history: a contemplative view of a humanity moving toward that final unity of all things at the Parousia of the Lord, a unity which he must not simply anticipate passively but must help to bring about actively by his own creative freedom. He is humble enough not to engage in a Promethean struggle to divinize himself by his own techniques and powers, wise enough to realize that "the free cooperation of his creative love with the love of God will lead him to fulfill his own true call to divinity as a son of God" (145).

Above all else, the contemplative can offer an insight into human freedom to her contemporaries who seek emancipation and liberty but whose tragedy is that they seek it in the wrong way and by means that lead only to deeper enslavement. The contemplative can teach the world that freedom is rooted, not in us, but in God. We can be free only when we participate in the freedom of God. To be free is to renounce the struggle to dominate others and the slavery of being dominated by our own desires. Freedom means liberation from our false, manipulative self in order to discover our true and free self in God. Then, like Adam and Eve in paradise before the fall, we can walk as free persons with our God in the cool of the evening breeze.

Appendix to Chapter Five

In 1961, two years after he had finished *The Inner Experience*, Merton was working on his large-scale revision of *Seeds of Contemplation*. Sometime during Lent of that year he put together a selection of prayers for the use of the novices and students of the Abbey of Gethsemani. The prayers were drawn from a variety of Christian sources—from the Gospels, the Desert Elders, writers from the sixth century, the Cistercian fathers of the twelfth century, fourteenth-century mystics, sixteenth-century Carmelites, twentieth-century writers. In all there are 53 pages of selected prayers.

What I am interested in here is not the text of the prayers. While the selection certainly represents a rich gathering of prayers, many of them are in older translations—the only ones existing in 1961. Since then many of the works he quotes have been issued in more modern translations. Also the works of many of the writers whom he quotes are much more easily available than they were in 1961. There is little need, therefore, to reproduce these prayers.

My interest lies in the preface he wrote to this prayer collection. It is only one page, of about 370 words, but it is packed with meaning about the life of prayer. In a sentence that sums up a whole theology of prayer, he writes: Prayer is not only the "lifting up of the mind and heart to God," but it is also the response to God within us, the discovery of God within us; it leads ultimately to the discovery and fulfillment of our own true being in God. Prayer, in other words, is not just something that we do; it is a perspective-giving element that directs our whole life. Prayer involves "mutuality." It is not just that we seek God. God seeks us, indeed more than we seek God. Prayer means entering into "mystery." This means that, when we do not enter into mystery, we do not pray. Prayer is a discovery of our own creaturehood, our own dependence on God. Recognizing our dependence becomes a recognition of the God on whom we depend. Recognizing our sinfulness is recognizing the mercy this God extends to us. Prayer is taking joy in our poverty and God's mercy.

Here is the text of Merton's Preface:

---■---

Prayer is not only the "lifting up of the mind and heart to God," but it is also the response to God within us; it leads ultimately to the discovery and fulfillment of our own true self in God.

We should not, therefore, regard prayer simply as a cry from our own heart seeking an answer from God: for if we are moved to prayer by divine grace, then our prayer is also our response to God seeking the love of our own hearts. Let us recognize, then, that our supernatural desires are a response to His infinitely mysterious desires.

*He seeks us more than we seek Him. If we love Him, He
has first loved us. But let us recognize, too, that we do not
know ourselves and we know Him still less. We do not
understand our own needs and desires: how can we clearly
understand His desires in our regard? Prayer then is
always shrouded in mystery. To pray is to enter into
mystery, and when we do not enter into the unknown, we
do not pray. If we want everything in our prayer-life to be
abundantly clear at all times, we will by that very fact
defeat our prayer-life.*

*Prayer is an expression of our complete dependence on a
hidden and mysterious God. It is therefore nourished by
humility, by a sense of indigence, and by compunction. We
should never seek to reach some supposed "summit of
prayer" out of spiritual ambition. For this would be a sure
way to frustrate our own intentions. We should seek to
enter deep into the life of prayer not in order that we may
glory in it as in an "achievement," however spiritual, but
because in this way we can come close to the Lord Who
seeks to do us good, Who seeks to give us His mercy, and to
surround us with His love. To love prayer is, then, to love
our own poverty and His mercy.*

Notes

[1] This would suggest that *The Inner Experience*, besides including the
booklet *What is Contemplation?*, contains other materials written
before 1959. I believe that some such earlier material has been
incorporated into *Inner Experience*, but I have not been able to
identify it or its source.

[2] *Road to Joy*, p. 233.

[3] *Search for Solitude*, p. 327.

[4] *Road to Joy*, pp. 233-234.

[5] *Road to Joy*, p. 332.

[6] It seems odd that draft three has corrected the pagination of draft
four! The only drafts that are so designated by Merton are draft

two and draft three. What I have called "draft four" was so designated by me, not by Merton. It may have been typed before three (or about the same time), but it is on what I have called "draft four" that Merton made corrections that are not found in draft three. Hence in terms of Merton's later modifications "draft four" seems clearly to be the final draft.

[7] I am convinced that these were the only changes Merton made in his manuscript. Raymond Bailey in his book *Thomas Merton on Mysticism* (New York: Doubleday, 1975), p. 230, cites Brother Patrick Hart as saying that the first draft of *The Inner Experience* was written in 1961. Brother Patrick has told me that this was incorrect. Anne E. Carr in her fine work, *A Search for Wisdom and Spirit: Thomas Merton's Theology of the Self* (Notre Dame, Ind.: University of Notre Dame Press, 1988), states on page 153 that "Merton finished the fourth draft shortly before he left for Asia in 1968." It would be more correct to say that he made minor corrections and brief additions in 1968.

[8] Daniel Walsh to Father Flavian, May 6, 1972. Archives, Abbey of Gethsemani.

[9] In the fourth draft, there are approximately 450 words changed or added. Of those words, 125 are an insert that comes early in the manuscript. A manuscript page is approximately 430 words. This means that, all together, the additions amount to a little over a page of manuscript—hardly a large addition to a manuscript of 150 pages. The additions are mostly for clarification; they add little to the work that is new.

[10] Daniel Walsh to Father Flavian, May 6, 1972. Archives, Abbey of Gethsemani.

[11] *Road to Joy*, p. 301.

[12] Conversation with Brother Patrick Hart.

[13] Michael Casey, "Notes on Thomas Merton's 'Inner Experience'" *Tjurunga* 44 (1993), pp. 30-55.

[14] *Courage for Truth*, 63.

[15] *Seeds*, pp. 31-32.

[16] *Inner Experience*, p. 3. It is worth noting that this sentence is one of those additions Merton made in 1968.

[17] *Seeds*, p. 28.

[18] Merton uses various synonyms for this "spiritual" self, such as "true" self, "inner" self, "interior" self.

[19] *Inner Experience,* insert, p. 7. This insert, because it was long, was written on the back of the previous page in Merton's own hand.

[20] *Inner Experience,* insert, p. 8. Merton inserted this sentence directly into the text in his own handwriting. This and the previous insert are examples of the minor changes he made in the manuscript before handing it over to Daniel Walsh in 1968.

[21] Acts 7:28. See also *Inner Experience,* p. 10.

[22] See the earlier discussion of *Thoughts in Solitude* and "Notes for a Philosophy of Solitude" in Chapter Four.

[23] When we speak of the fall as original sin, we are using the term "sin" analogically. It expresses the existential reality of our alienation from God and creation, though with no attempt to assign to anyone in particular the responsibility for this alienation.

[24] Merton points to the deep symbolic meaning the Greek Fathers found in the Genesis story of the fall. The forbidden tree in the garden is the tree of self which we are not supposed to see or notice. When we take notice of it, we are divided within ourselves and alienated from external reality. (See *Inner Experience,* p. 34.)

[25] Merton's writings seem to show no acquaintance with contemporary Christological thought.

[26] The uniting of the divine and human nature of Jesus Christ in one person. The Greek word for "person" is *hypostasis.*

[27] Romans 8:16.

[28] Merton chooses to ignore the controversy about the differences between "infused" and "acquired" contemplation—a controversy of the 1920's and 1930's discussed by such theologians as Garrigou-Lagrange.

[29] See Genesis, 33:24-29.

[30] This represents a drastic departure from the enthusiastic apologia for the monastic life that is found in the pages of *The Seven Storey Mountain.* Because of the renewal of monastic life that began in the 1960's under the influence of the Second Vatican Council—a

renewal in which his own writings played a significant role— Merton's later writings present a somewhat more hopeful and optimistic picture of the monastic life for the contemporary world. It is true to say, though, that in his later journals, for example, he continues to ask questions about the meaning and viability of the monastic life in the world of his day.

6

New Seeds of
Contemplation

*The only true joy on earth is to escape from the prison of our
own false self, and enter by love into union with the Life Who
dwells and sings within the essence of every creature and in
the core of our own souls. (25)*

Seeds of Contemplation, published in 1949, sold forty thousand
copies in its first four months. It was reprinted at least ten
times. One can legitimately wonder if it would have achieved
such amazing success had it not followed the exceedingly
popular best-seller, *The Seven Storey Mountain*. Despite its
popularity, Merton was not happy with it; and beginning
with the seventh printing, published December 19, 1949, the
book was issued in a revised edition. This revision, though
not substantive with regard to content,[1] is different in outlook
from the original edition. In 1962 a second revision was
published which not only picked up and amplified the new
outlook evident in the first revision but was sufficiently
altered and enlarged in content to justify Merton's statement
in the preface that "it is in many ways a completely new
book," and to warrant the use of the adjective "New" in the
title of this final revision.[2] *Seeds of Contemplation* proved to be
a very popular book, as the number of printings testify; nor
was its popularity confined to English-speaking readers: it
has been translated into thirteen languages.[3] *New Seeds of*

Contemplation, which is the only edition remaining in print, has continued to be a favorite among longtime Merton readers, as also among those who have just recently "discovered" Merton. *New Seeds* has had five foreign-language translations.

The purpose of this chapter is to explore the new insights into the contemplative experience that a reading of *New Seeds* will offer to one who has already read *Seeds of Contemplation* (though I should point out that it is not necessary to have read *Seeds* before reading *New Seeds*). What is the difference in outlook and in content that one finds in the third edition of this "spiritual classic"? One way of answering this question is to consider what Merton himself has to say about the three different editions. Each of the three versions has an Author's Note. In addition, each of the two later versions has a preface in which Merton introduces the new version to his readers.

The Author's Note is identical in the first and second editions. There is, however, an interesting addition and an equally interesting omission in the Author's Note of *New Seeds*. The addition is a footnote appended to his statement in *Seeds*: "These are the kinds of thoughts that might have occurred to any Cistercian monk." In the footnote Merton writes, not without a touch of humor, that not all his confreres saw his work as representative of authentic Cistercian tradition: "In the twelve years since this was written and published, not a few Cistercians have vehemently denied that these thoughts were either characteristic or worthy of a normal Cistercian, which is perhaps quite true" (xiv).

The omission in the Author's Note of *New Seeds* is even more significant. In the two earlier versions, Merton had expressed the hope that his book did not "contain a line that is new to Catholic tradition or a single word that would perplex an orthodox theologian." In *New Seeds* the text is revised to read simply: "We sincerely hope that it does not contain a line that is new to Christian tradition." The substitution of the word "Christian" for "Catholic" indicates that Merton had a wider readership in mind for *New Seeds*.

The fact that he is no longer worried that his writing might "perplex an orthodox theologian" suggests a broadening of his theological perspective. He is moving toward a theology that will be less rigid and more pluralistic than the theological framework in which he had felt obliged to write during his earlier days in the monastery. Merton is serving notice that a new type of writing could be expected from him in the future: something simpler, less abstract and more existential. David had become uncomfortable in Saul's armor!

The movement away from a strict dogmatic framework had already been foreshadowed in the preface to the 1949 revised edition, which, as I mentioned above, is different in outlook from the unrevised edition. The new outlook is a change in methodology. Merton warns his readers not to search his book for precise theological statements. "The author is *talking about spiritual things from the point of view of experience* rather than in the concise terms of dogmatic theology" (xii, emphasis added).

This is not only a warning but a promise: a promise of the experiential direction that Merton's writings will take in the future. It must be said that his next work on the spiritual life, *The Ascent to Truth*, did not fulfill this promise for it is cast largely in a dogmatic framework. (But, as I pointed out earlier, Merton was less than satisfied with this book.) The promise does find fulfillment in *The Inner Experience*, which, except for the older material incorporated into it, has a perspective that is definitely experiential and existential. Indeed, *The Inner Experience* may be seen as a kind of watershed between the theological ratiocinations of *What Is Contemplation?* and *The Ascent to Truth* and the obvious emphasis on experience that characterizes *New Seeds, Contemplative Prayer (The Climate of Monastic Prayer), Zen and the Birds of Appetite*, sections of *Conjectures of a Guilty Bystander*, and essays in *Contemplation in a World of Action*, as well as other works not so immediately related to the topic of contemplation. Merton remained true to the promise he had made in the preface to the revised edition of *Seeds*.

The preface of *New Seeds*, written twelve years later,

reaffirms Merton's commitment to write about spiritual things in the light of experience. But between the writing of these two prefaces an important change had taken place in Merton's understanding of "experience." By 1962, "experience" had taken on a broader and deeper meaning for him. The "experience" of which he spoke in the preface to the revised edition of *Seeds* was the limited experience of a young monk who just eight years earlier had fled the world and exchanged its gregariousness for the isolation of a Trappist monastery and who, moreover, reveled in that isolation, dreaming of an even deeper withdrawal from the world as he wrestled with the "temptation" of becoming a Carthusian. There is a touch of truth in the caricature Merton would later draw of himself as "the man who spurned New York, spat on Chicago and tromped on Louisville, heading for the woods with Thoreau in one pocket, John of the Cross in another and holding the Bible open at the Apocalypse."[4]

The twelve years following the publication of *Seeds* were important years of growth for Merton. His flight from the world came to be tempered by a compassion for people and a growing sense that if his contemplation was to be authentic, he must learn to share the joys and sorrows of others, their thoughts, their needs, their aspirations. In *Seeds* Merton speaks of unity with others, but it is a unity read about in books or discovered in prayer, rather than a grasp of solidarity with other people that is brought to prayer, so that unity can be experienced at a deeper level. In *New Seeds* the intuition of unity is more concrete and existential. In the first two versions of *Seeds* the locus of contemplation is "a citadel"[5]; in *New Seeds*, it is "a wide impregnable country" (228). As Donald Grayston has pointed out: "Both [terms] are images of security in the life of the spirit; but the first suggests enclosure, the second openness and freedom. In the citadel dwells one inhabitant; in the wide country there is room for an infinite number."[6]

During the twelve years that preceded the writing of *New Seeds*, Merton's contacts with others within the monastery broadened as he was given the responsibility of directing the scholastics and, later, the novices.[7] His contacts with people outside the monastery grew also, as his correspondence (largely generated by his writings) expanded and as increasing numbers of people arrived at the monastery gate to seek his counsel and to share their experiences with him. He became better informed on events and movements going on in the world, as friends (like Wilbur H. Ferry and James Laughlin) sent him clippings, articles and books, and as various groups (e.g., the Catholic Peace Movement) solicited his involvement and the power of his pen to shed the light of Christian truth on the social issues of the day. *New Seeds* was written by a Merton whose outlook was significantly different from what you find in *The Seven Storey Mountain* or in *The Sign of Jonas*. The change had been progressive and had begun long before 1961 (when he was revising *Seeds*). In my biography of Merton, *The Silent Lamp*, I suggested 1958 as the year the change became especially evident. It is interesting— even a bit amusing—to compare in the three editions of *Seeds* the changing "counsel" he gives his readers about the reading of newspapers:

> *First edition*: "Do not read their newspapers, if you can help it."[8]

> *Second edition*: "Do not read their newspapers, unless you are really obliged to keep track of what is going on."[9]

> *Third edition*: (*New Seeds*) "Do not read their advertisements." (84)

As he moved from the "citadel" to the "wide impregnable country," new realms of experience opened up for him that he could carry back with him to his solitude—a solitude in which he could probe not only the depths of his own heart but, increasingly, the deepest realities of the heart of the world. He never lost his conviction that contemplation demands solitude—a proper withdrawal from the world— and he was always (well, almost always) faithful to that demand. But solitude does not mean isolation from concern for people. Indeed, such concern is the very condition for fruitful contemplation. "[C]ontemplation is out of the question for anyone who does not try to cultivate compassion for other men" (77). But the solitude in which *New Seeds* was written was a solitude that had been enriched by contact with the solitude and loneliness of many other people. Merton expressed it well in the preface to *New Seeds*:

> More than twelve years has passed between the first and second redactions of this text. When the book was first written, the author had no experience in confronting the needs and problems of other men. The book was written in a kind of isolation, in which the author was alone with his own experience of the contemplative life.... The second writing has been no less solitary than the first: but the author's solitude has been modified by contact with other solitudes; with the loneliness, the simplicity, the perplexity of novices and scholastics of his monastic community; with the loneliness of people outside any monastery; with the loneliness of people outside the Church. (ix-x)

In all three versions of *Seeds*, Merton is writing about what he had experienced; but by the time he came to write *New Seeds*, "experience" had taken on new and richer meanings. Its horizons had been vastly broadened. That is why *New Seeds*, rather than either of its predecessors, is appropriately described as the "spiritual classic."

Anyone who attempts to articulate the contemplative experience must choose some kind of conceptual context— some systematic way of using words—in which to place what he has to say about that experience. Only then can he hope to make his experience in some way intelligible to others. In his early writings on contemplation, notably in *The Ascent to Truth*, Merton chose as his context the traditional Western approach to mystical writing represented, at its best, by Thomas Aquinas and John of the Cross. This approach stresses the activities of the various faculties of the soul— memory, imagination, intellect and will—involved in the activity of prayer. It sharply distinguishes the supernatural activities of these faculties (i.e., what happens when they are elevated by the infused virtues and the gifts of the Holy Spirit) from their natural mode of operation. Such an approach assumes the body/soul dichotomy and speaks of prayer as the activity of the soul rather than the person. It is an approach that tends to be abstract, highly analytical, often unduly complex and quite definitely dualistic. Abounding in precise definitions, subtle distinctions and minute explanations, it is inclined to be overly cerebral and, in the hands of writers less gifted than Thomas Aquinas and John of the Cross, to take the life and exhilaration out of the description of prayer. Prayer becomes complex and contemplation difficult to achieve except by an elite few.

I have pointed out that Merton had served notice in the December, 1949, Preface that he was abandoning this approach in writing about contemplation. What he did not mention in that Preface was that, at the very time he said this, he was already one year into the final writing of a book in this Scholastic tradition.[10] Whatever is to be thought about Merton's inconsistency in saying in December, 1949, that he would no longer write about spiritual things "in the concise terms of dogmatic theology," when he was in the midst of writing a book that did just that, it is quite clear that in 1962, when he came to publish *New Seeds*, Merton had without doubt gotten the Scholastic approach out of his system.

The conceptual context of *New Seeds* is worlds apart from the Scholastic setting out of which *The Ascent to Truth* emerged. It is a context that cannot be clearly identified. It is, I venture to say, a mixed bag, including elements of existentialism,[11] Christian personalism[12] and Zen.[13] There are existential insights. Thus, for example, he writes: "For the contemplative there is no *cogito* ('I think') and no *ergo* ('therefore'), but only SUM, I am."[14] This represents an obvious moving out of the Cartesian thought-pattern that has dominated Western thought since the seventeenth century. In Descartes's philosophy we can only conceive of another (even God) as an object that we look at subjectively (9). Merton speaks also of "the tragic anguish of doubt mercilessly examining the spurious 'faith' of everyday life" (12)—surely an existentialist theme.

There are also insights of Christian personalism. Here

Merton is clearly borrowing from the Neo-Thomism of the early twentieth century, represented at its best by Daniel Walsh (his longtime friend and teacher), Etienne Gilson (whose book *The Spirit of Medieval Philosophy*[15] had made a deep impression on him while he was still a student at Columbia) and Jacques Maritain (with whom he carried on a long and fruitful correspondence). The note of personalism is introduced early in the text. Thus, Merton writes: "We must remember that this superficial 'I' is not our real self. It is our 'individuality' and our 'empirical self,' but it is not truly the hidden and mysterious person in whom we subsist before the eyes of God" (7). Christian contemplation, he writes, is "supremely personalistic" (153). Note how he identifies the person with "our real self" and individual with the "empirical self." More and more, as we have already seen in *The Inner Experience*, his writing on contemplation will be dominated by the contrast between the real self and the empirical self.

There is also, one is tempted to say especially, in the context of *New Seeds* the influence and flavor of Zen. From the very beginning, the book abounds in expressions, intuitions, insights, and nuances that suggest Merton's appropriation of the language of Zen. Contemplation, like Zen, cannot be taught. "It is impossible for one man to teach another 'how to become a contemplative.' One might as well write a book: 'how to be an angel'" (x). Moreover, contemplation, again like Zen, "cannot be clearly explained" (6). It cannot be captured in definitions or distinctions. "It can only be hinted at, suggested, pointed to [a typical Zen term], symbolized." The more one tries to analyze it, "the more he empties it of its real content, for it is beyond the reach of verbalization and rationalization" (6). It is, moreover, beyond the duality of knowing or unknowing. There is no adequate psychology of contemplation, for contemplation is not to be found in the superficial consciousness which can be reached by reflection. This reflection and this consciousness are precisely part of that empirical self which "dies" and is cast aside like a soiled garment in the genuine awakening of the contemplative. For contemplation is nothing less than "life itself, fully awake, fully alive, fully aware that it is alive" (1).

To describe an experience as "genuine awakening," as "life itself," as "full awareness," as something that can only be "pointed to," as something beyond dualities and beyond the reach of verbalization, is to use a language that would be recognized as Zen even by the most casual student of this Japanese approach to reality. Aldhelm Cameron-Brown has written of *New Seeds*: "...A suspicion which has been growing throughout the book is verified at the end, when Basho's frog plops onto the last page and we realize that Thomas Merton has come under the influence of Zen."[16] Indeed he has and it is more than a suspicion. When, in 1965, Merton wrote the preface to the Japanese edition of *Seeds of Contemplation*, he highlights his affinity with the monks of Zen: "The author of this book can say that he feels closer to the Zen monks of ancient Japan than to the busy impatient men of the West."[17]

New Thoughts on Contemplation[18]

Merton begins *New Seeds* with an entirely new chapter, entitled "What Is Contemplation?" The title strikes a familiar note: It recalls Merton's earliest writing on the subject of contemplation—the brief work he had produced in response to a theology student's request for an answer to the question that became the title of that earlier work and has now become the title of the initial chapter of *New Seeds*. Merton, it is fair to say, was less confident in 1962 that he could give an adequate answer to this question than he had been in 1948 when he sent to St. Mary's School of Theology, with permission to publish, the booklet *What Is Contemplation?* The deeper his experience of contemplation, the more reluctant he became to articulate the meaning of an experience for which there can be no explanations. To jump for a moment to a later period of Merton's life, I want to mention a letter he wrote in 1967 to students at Smith College. These students had spent an evening reading and discussing his works. Some of them wrote to him about the experience. In reply, he told them that he believed that they had come to see a reality most precious—and most available too, yet at the same time incomprehensible. It is "the Reality that is present to us and in us." However we name that reality, the simple fact is that "by being attentive, by learning to listen (or recovering the natural capacity to listen which cannot be learned any more than breathing) we can find ourselves engulfed in such happiness that it cannot be explained: the happiness of being one with everything in that hidden ground of love for which there can be no explanations.[19]

The attentiveness of which Merton speaks (and awareness and awakedness are synonyms he often uses) is not so much something we do, but something we are. Attentiveness is not the same thing as thinking. Thinking tends to divide: It implies a subject thinking and an object that is thought about. Attentiveness or awareness, on the other hand, is a very different experience: It reduces the distance between us and what we are aware of. A deep sense of attentive awareness closes the gap between us and what we are aware of. It brings together and unites. In fact in a deep experience of attentive awareness, the subject/object dichotomy disappears. We are not aware of something. We are simply aware. This attentive awareness is what Merton means by contemplation.

He is making clear that we are not subjects who discover God as an object. It is rather that our subjectivity becomes one with the subjectivity of God. In that oneness we find ourselves "at one with everything." In Chapter Two of *New Seeds* he writes: "Contemplation is the experiential grasp of reality as subjective, not so much 'mine' (which would signify 'belonging to an external self') but myself in existential mystery. Contemplation does not arrive at reality after a process of deduction, but by an intuitive wakening in which our free and personal reality becomes fully alive in its existential depths, which open out into the mystery of God" (8-9).

Awareness of God, then, is not awareness of an object. It

is pure awareness, simple attentiveness. In Merton's words:

> There is 'no such thing' as God because God is neither a
> 'what' nor a "thing' but a pure 'Who.' He is the 'Thou'
> before whom our inmost 'I' springs into awareness [*and
> love. He is the living God, Yahweh, I AM, who calls us into being
> out of nothingness, so that we stand before Him made in His
> image and reflecting His infinite being in our littleness and
> reply: 'I am,' and so with Saint Paul we awaken to the paradox
> that beyond our natural being we have a higher being 'in Christ'
> which makes us as if we were not and as if he alone were in us.*]

This significant statement that I have put in italics is an
addition which Merton made to the French edition.[20]

This kind of writing is significantly different writing from
the booklet of 1948. It is writing that is new and fresh and
exciting. It was not the "stuff" on the topic of contemplation
one might find in the standard manuals of spiritual and
mystical theology (manuals Merton had studied in his
preparation for the priesthood). True, in *New Seeds*, Merton is
still writing out of the background of a Christian tradition,
but describing contemplation in such a way that much of
what he says could be understood and accepted by people
belonging to other religious traditions. This does not mean
that he abandoned the Western Christian tradition on the
contemplative experience. (Many of the descriptive
statements in Chapter One are distinctly Christian. Moreover,
there is a large section of new material in Chapter Twenty-
One on the importance of the humanity of Christ to the
Christian contemplative.) But he considerably expands the
perimeters of that experience. He had come to realize that
contemplation, far from being a Catholic monopoly, is an
experience that is shared by many religious traditions.
Indeed, he was, more and more, prepared to say that other
religious traditions—e.g., the Christian East and some of the
religions of Asia—may well have been more faithful to the
contemplative dimension of life than the Christian West, with
its accent on action and material progress. His widening
contact with the religions of Asia, notably Buddhism, gave
him not only a deep respect for the mystical elements of these

religions, it also gave him a new vocabulary to describe the experience of contemplation. *New Seeds* is an effort to harmonize the vocabulary of Western mystical literature, and some of its more modern expressions, with the vocabulary of other religious traditions; and the harmony appears convincing.

The first chapter of *New Seeds*, though relatively brief, abounds in statements descriptive of the contemplative experience, any one of which the unwary reader might be tempted to take as a definition of contemplation. But in spite of what Grayston calls "his inveterate tendency in this direction," Merton does not intend these statements as definitions. They are different ways of attempting to express what in reality, as I have suggested so many times already, is undefinable.

He begins by describing contemplation as a state of heightened consciousness—an insight that would be congenial to most any contemplative tradition. "Contemplation," he writes, "is the highest expression of man's intellectual and spiritual life. It is that life itself, fully awake, fully active, fully aware that it is alive" (1). One is reminded of Evelyn Underhill's statement: "Only the mystic can be called a whole man, since in others half the powers of the self always sleep."[21]

This heightened consciousness does not mean being conscious of a particular object of perception; rather, it is pure consciousness, which Merton describes in a variety of ways: "spontaneous awe at the sacredness of life, of being"; "gratitude for life, for awareness and for being"; a "breakthrough...to a new level of reality"; "vivid awareness" of "the reality" of "the Source of life and being"; "an awakening to the Real within all that is real" (1, 3).

The language of Zen and Christian mysticism vie with one another as Merton continues to pile description upon description. Contemplation is "the experience of the transcendent and inexpressible God" (2). It is being "[t]ouched by Him Who has no hands" (3); yet the "touch" is real, for it is "felt" at the very roots of our limited being. It is being "called by Him who has no voice" (3), yet whose word is heard in the depths of our heart. For we are words who respond to God or, rather, who echo the word God speaks in us. And as an echo is not really distinct from the word whose resonance it is, so contemplation is a deep resonance in the inmost center of our spirit in which our very life "loses its separate voice" (3) and resounds the word God speaks in us. "Contemplation is the awareness and realization, even in some sense experience, of what each Christian obscurely believes: 'It is now no longer I that live, but Christ lives in me.' It is awakening, enlightenment, the amazing intuitive grasp by which love gains certitude of God's creative and dynamic intervention in our daily life." It is being "carried away by Him into His own realm, His own mystery and His own freedom" (5).

Yet when all the descriptions have been made and all the analogies drawn, one must say: but nothing of all this can tell you what contemplation truly is. For contemplation is an experience that is rich in meaning but "poor in concepts and poorer still in reasoning" (5). No description or analogy can begin to convey the reality of the experience, for it is "too deep to be grasped in images, in words or even in clear concepts. It can be suggested by words, by symbols, but in the very moment of trying to indicate what it knows the contemplative mind takes back what it has said, and denies what it has affirmed. For in contemplation we know by 'unknowing.' Or better, we know beyond all knowing and 'unknowing'" (1-2).

Here it is important to remember what was said in the Introduction about the difference between the kataphatic and apophatic way of speaking about God. The contemplative experience of God cannot be expressed in kataphatic terms alone. In the very act of saying that it is "this," one must, with equal emphasis, assert that it is "not this." Indeed, it is beyond "this" and "not this." For this reason, therefore, Chapter One, "What Is Contemplation?" necessarily spills over into Chapter Two, "What Contemplation Is Not." For "[c]ontemplation is always beyond our own knowledge, beyond our own light, beyond systems, beyond explanations, beyond discourse, beyond dialogue, beyond our own self" (2).

The message of Merton's affirmations and negations is clear. He is not saying: If you do "this" and "this," you will probably become a contemplative. Rather, he is saying: If you are a contemplative or at least open to the possibility of being a contemplative, you will probably understand what I am saying; for it's likely some of the things I have said will already have happened to you. But what actually has happened to you is beyond your words or mine to express. No amount of verbalization can ever capture the experience of contemplation and make it intelligible to one who has not had it. "One who does not actually know, in his own life, the nature of this breakthrough and this awakening to a new level of reality cannot help being misled by most of the things that are said about it" (6).

New Thoughts on the True Self [22]

The discovery of one's true identity is a major theme in Merton's writings on contemplation. We have seen in *Seeds* and in *The Inner Experience* how he develops this theme and sees contemplative spirituality in terms of the disappearance of the false, external self, which is ultimately illusory, and the emergence of the true self—the self we are before God. [23]

In *New Seeds*, Merton identifies the external self with the "individual" or the "ego," and the true self with the "person." He quotes Maritain's *Scholasticism and Politics*, which discusses at some length the difference between the individual and the person, Maritain writes: "Pascal tells us that 'the ego is hateful.... [This] is a commonplace expression of Pascalian literature.... As a counterpart of the word of Pascal, we must remember the words of Saint Thomas: 'The person is that which is noblest in the whole of nature.'" [24]

This contrast between the "ego as hateful" and the person as that which is "noblest in nature" strikes responsive chords in *New Seeds*. Thus, Merton writes:

"The person must be rescued from the individual. The free son of God must be saved from the conformist slave of fantasy, passion and convention. The creative and mysterious inner self must be delivered from the wasteful, hedonistic and destructive ego that seeks only to cover itself with disguises." (38)[25]

Merton is telling us that reality resides and freedom is found, not in the individual, but in the person. Insofar as we are individuals, we are not free: We are "slaves," in bondage to our illusions and fantasies and victimized by our self-seeking, hedonistic and ultimately destructive drives and desires. Indeed we are not just "slaves," but "conformist slaves," submitting blindly to material forces and to the conventions of the collective society in which we find ourselves. The individual cannot function in community; but instead escapes into "the great formless sea of irresponsibility which is the crowd" (54). The collectivity swallows the individual up in its "shapeless and faceless mass" (53). She may live in the midst of others, but is always apart from them, for she shares neither communion nor real communication but only "the common noise and the general distraction" (55). Even when she seeks solitude, it is for the wrong reason: She seeks to escape from other people. For she does not know that "reality is to be sought not in division but in unity" (47-48). Solitude, therefore, becomes simply a refuge, a retreat from others. "The man who lives in division is not a person, but only an 'individual'" (48).

This is the individual: the slave self, the self that lives by illusion and in separateness. How very different the person! For, insofar as one is a person, he is free. The person is a creative and mysterious center of freedom, unity and independence, with a reality that is inviolate, eternal and one with God. Persons act in community. They are able to share with others something that is truly personal and real, because they themselves are real. At times persons separate themselves from others by seeking solitude. But they do this not because they want to escape people, but because they need to find perspective—so that in interior silence they can learn to love not only God but also others and thus fulfill what is the noblest capacity of their nature as persons. Merton writes: "The person is constituted by a uniquely subsisting capacity to love—by a radical ability to care for all beings made by God and loved by Him. Such a capacity is destroyed by the loss of perspective" (53). Solitude gives that perspective. Whereas the individual seeks a false solitude that separates, the person seeks true solitude which unites in love. "True solitude is the home of the person, false solitude the refuge of the individualist" (53).

Merton warns us, however, that in distinguishing the individual from the person we must avoid the Platonic error of identifying the individual with the body and the person with the soul. He had already made a similar point in *The Inner Experience*. The person is not a part of ourselves: It is our whole reality. "Hence both body and soul belong to, or better, subsist in our real self, the person that we are. The ego, on the other hand, is a self-constructed illusion that "has" our body and part of our soul at its disposal, because it has "taken over" the functions of the inner self as a result of what we call man's fall'" (280).

While using the distinction between the individual and the person, Merton tends to move away from the neo-Scholastic approach. Rather than "individual and person," he becomes more comfortable with the contrast between the false self and the true self. Essential for understanding this distinction is an appreciation of the meaning he gives to the fall. (This was already mentioned earlier in Chapter Five.) The fall, as he sees it, is a fall from unity into disunity, from depths into superficiality, from union with God into a state of alienation from him. Because of the fall, our outer self masks our inner self, so that we do not know who we are. The only way we can return to unity in our own being and to communion with God is through contemplation. "[T]he deep, transcendent self...," Merton writes, "awakens only in contemplation" (67). Apart from contemplation, we can discover our true self only in heaven. This is the destiny of many. "Most of us," Merton says, never discover "that mysterious and unknown 'self'" until we are dead (7).

The return to God and the discovery of our identity in him demand a long journey; and we have to start from where we are: our fallen state, our condition of alienation. "We are prodigals in a distant country, 'the region of unlikeness,' and we must seem to travel far in that region before we seem to reach our own land (and yet secretly we are in our own land all the time!)" (280).

The parenthesis in the above quotation is significant. The true self is not something we have to create. It is there as God's gift to us. We have to awaken it, become aware of it. We have to discover that in the depths of our being we are contemplatives. In the meantime, accepting our existential situation as we are, we have to allow the "ego," the "outer self," to carry out the functions which our inner self cannot yet assume on its own. "We have to act, in our everyday life, as if we were what our outer self indicates us to be" (281). Yet at the same time we must remember that what for the moment seems to be most real in us is actually a mask that covers what is truly real. Though we must adapt ourselves to our alienated condition, we can never rest comfortable with it. Life's greatest task is to become aware of who we really are.

A Hindu Story

There is a delightful story, told by Ramakrishna about the tiger and the sheep. One day a female tiger who is pregnant and about to deliver comes upon a flock of sheep. Her tiger instincts come to the fore and she attacks the flock who scurry away. In her leaping attack, she gives birth to a baby tiger and dies in the pangs of giving birth. After a "safe" amount of time has passed, the sheep return and see the baby tiger. He is an orphan and they adopt him into their flock. They teach him how to bleat and eat grass. Though first he found these activities difficult, he did get used to them. For all intents and purposes he was now a sheep. Then one day, as the sheep were in the meadow, another tiger came along and attacked the flock. All fled except the little tiger. He stood his ground, looking fearlessly at the big tiger. He bleated and chewed on a piece of grass. The big tiger was quite disgusted with his un-tigerlike actions. He grabbed him by the ear, took him to a clear pool of water and made him look in to see that his image was the same as that of the big tiger. But he didn't get it! Thereupon the big tiger took him to his cave. The day before he had killed a deer. He took a piece of meat and offered it to the little tiger. Horrified, he refused. Finally, totally exasperated, the big tiger shoved the meat into the little fellow's mouth. At first he recoiled from it. Then, as he experienced the blood dripping down his throat, he began to chew. It was a whole new and exciting experience for him. Then all at once—he let out the roar of a tiger! At last he knew who he was. Under the direction of his guru, the big tiger, he came to an awareness of his own identity. He always was a tiger, but it was only in this breakthrough experience that he came to understand that what he had for so long a time thought himself to be was actually an illusion. He had arrived at self-awareness.

At this point in our discussion of Merton's understanding of the external self, an important qualification must be made. "[W]e must not," Merton says, "deal in too negative a fashion even with the 'external self'" (295). This is precisely what we have done thus far: for we have considered passages in which Merton views the external self in a pejorative way: It is the false self that alienates us from God and from our own inner unity: the "hateful ego" of Pascal; the self that ultimately is a lie. It is from this external self, considered as the false self, that we must be delivered.

But, paradoxically, this very external self may initiate our deliverance. For there is another way of viewing the external self. While Merton generally describes that self in pejorative terms, there are passages in *New Seeds* (and elsewhere in his writings) where his descriptions are more neutral than pejorative. The external self is presented at times not as false but simply as superficial. In other words, it would be a mistake to read false self in a moral sense, i.e., as untruthful, sinful, immoral. No doubt it can have such a meaning. But that meaning, it seems to me is derivative and does not catch the primary sense in which Merton uses the term "false self." If I understand him correctly, he means by "false" to convey the notion of insubstantiality, of lacking in the fullness of being. The false self, one might say, is deficient in being: deficient especially in the sense that it is impermanent, not enduring. It cannot survive death. It is, therefore, frail. It is feeble. Granted these are hardly words of praise; but neither are they words of condemnation. What is frail and feeble deserves, at the very least, our sympathy. What is superficial may be on the threshold of a breakthrough to what is below the surface. Merton speaks of such a breakthrough. When I consent to the will and mercy of God as it "'comes' to me in the events of life, appealing to my inner self and awakening my faith, I break through the superficial exterior appearances that form my routine vision of the world and of my own self, and I find myself in the presence of hidden majesty" (41). The superficial self is the self that lives at the level of appearances. While appearances are never a substitute for reality, "[t]hey can be transparent media in which we apprehend the presence of God in the world. It is possible to speak of the exterior self as a mask: to do so is not necessarily to reprove it. The mask that each man wears may well be a disguise not only for that man's inner self but for God, wandering as a pilgrim and exile in His own creation" (296).

Apprehending the Creator as a pilgrim in his own world may well be the door that opens the way to the contemplative experience, in which we move from a knowledge of God disguised in the world of things to an experience of God in her very divine Being. At this point, the inner self is at last able to assume its own function. Then "God confronts man not through the medium of things," but in God's own simplicity. "The union of the simple light of God with the simple light of man's spirit, in love, is contemplation.... In this meeting there is not so much a fusion of identities as a disappearance of identities" (291-292). God raises us above dualities and makes us one with Him. Our subjectivity becomes one with the subjectivity of God. "For in the depths of contemplative prayer there seems to be no division between subject and object, and there is no reason to make any statement either about God or about oneself. He is and this reality absorbs everything else" (267).

New Thoughts on Faith

In *The Ascent to Truth*, Merton has made it clear that faith is more than intellectual assent to propositions and concepts about God. For faith not only attains to God as God is revealed in the articles of faith, it attains to God in the divine Self, that is, to God as God really is, but known in the darkness of unknowing.

In *New Seeds* Merton reiterates this perspective on faith and expands it. Faith is intellectual assent, but it is more; it is the whole person assenting not merely to truths about God but also, and especially, to God in his own true reality. In faith, we not only "hear" God, we "receive" God. For the propositions which faith accepts on divine authority are media through which we grasp God, or, better still, are grasped by God. Faith, therefore, terminates, not in statements or formulas, but in God, the transcendent One. For this reason the formulas of faith are not ends in themselves; rather, they are means whereby God communicates divinity to us. While we must make every effort to express the content of faith in precise formulas, "we must not be so obsessed with verbal correctness that we never go beyond the words to the ineffable reality which they attempt to convey." For "faith is the opening of an inward eye, the eye of the heart, to be filled with the presence of Divine light" (129-130). This divine light, however, as Merton makes clear in *The Ascent to Truth*, is so dazzling that it is darkness for us: We apprehend God in "the darkness of faith."

Because faith is adherence to what we do not see, the act of faith, as Merton pointed out in *The Ascent to Truth*, is elicited under the impulse of the will. In the act of faith we submit to authority as it teaches us what God has revealed. Merton warns in *New Seeds* that submission to authority which proposes the truths of revelation must not be "so overemphasized that it seems to constitute the whole essence of faith" (133). Faith must not be reduced to an act of obedience. Such reductionism could lead to a credulity that revels in the unintelligible, as in the case of the person who said of the Trinity: "Wish there were four of them, so that I might believe in more of them." Reducing faith to obedience trivializes faith and strips it of any real content. It can lead also to "a forced suppression of doubt rather than an opening of the eye of the heart by deep belief" (137). Doubts about faith need to be faced and dealt with, not suppressed. Most often, they do not indicate an unwillingness or an inability on our part to accept the propositions of faith, but simply a sense of our weakness and helplessness in the presence of the wondrous mystery of God. We can never express the full reality of our experience of God. After we have spoken all the words we can, there is always so much more of the experience left over.

It's a lot easier to say "yes" to propositions about God than to say "yes" to God. I am writing this in the early days of 1999. Roman Catholics are living through an uncomfortable period in the life of the Catholic Church where safeguarding the correctness of the formulas of faith seems to be more important than experiencing the reality which these formulas attempt to embody. When this happens faith becomes a treasure that we must guard at all costs rather than an investment of self that we make. In such circumstances it is all too easy for faith to become an evasion rather than a commitment. When the disciples ask Jesus: "Increase our faith,"[26] they don't mean, "Tell us more things to believe in." What they do mean is: Deepen our commitment, strengthen the investment of our energies, our times, our selves, in your service. Faith is not yet vision. "Increase our faith" is not a prayer that there be no darkness, no doubt, but simply a prayer that—whether in light or in

173

darkness—we may experience the reality of a Presence and realize that the Holy Presence which grasps us is not a thing, but a person.

In faith I not only encounter God, I also encounter myself in the mystery of my life at a level beyond concepts and rationalization. Faith opens up new dimensions of our being, integrating in the unity of the person, the unknown that is below reason with the unknown that is above reason. That is to say, faith serves as a principle of integration, bringing together into one whole the unconscious (the realm of instinct and emotion that is below reason), the conscious (the realm of intelligence and thought), and the superconscious (the realm that is beyond reason's ken). The Greek Fathers used three terms to describe these dimensions of the human person: the unconscious they called "anima" (in Greek, *psyche*); the conscious principle, "animus" (in Greek, *nous*); and that which integrates both, "spiritus" (*pneuma*, in Greek). Anima, the feminine principle, is Eve; animus, the masculine principle, is Adam. The meaning of original sin is that Eve tempts Adam and he falls into a state in which reasoned activity continually yields to the movement of blind impulse and emotion. (I hesitate to use this analogy with its obvious sexist implications, but I decided that it could be useful, as it is actually mythological language. If we can just ignore the sexist overtones, it can be seen simply as a description of characteristics present in every man and woman. If, however, you find it bothersome, accept my apologies and ignore it.)

Faith restores the proper balance in one's life, not simply by achieving the submission of instinct to reason, but by transcending both and integrating them into a higher principle which is "above the division of masculine and feminine, active and passive, prudential and instinctive" (139). This higher principle is spiritus, or pneuma, of which Saint Paul writes: "Live by the Spirit, I say, and do not gratify the desires of the flesh."[27]

> The "spiritual life" is then the perfectly balanced life in which the body with its passions and instincts, the mind with its reasoning and its obedience to principle, and the

spirit with its passive illumination by the Light and Love of God form one complete man who is in God and with God and from God and for God. One man in whom God is all in all. One man in whom God carries out His own will without obstacle.(140)

Such a person, living by faith and united with God in the Spirit, is the true self. It is the contemplative person.

The General Dance

The reader may have noticed that up to now I have not quoted any reviews of *New Seeds*. This is not an oversight. I have not been able to locate any substantive reviews of this work. In one brief review a sister of St. Joseph, Sister Mary Vianney, writing in *Ave Maria*, draws special attention to the final chapter of the book, whose title is "The General Dance." She describes this chapter as "prime Merton."[28] I agree with her completely. This chapter is one of those unique pieces of Merton writing that belongs in the same special category as "The Fire Watch"[29] in *The Sign of Jonas* or the little book, *Day of a Stranger*.[30]

Merton was doing this extensive revision of *Seeds* in 1961. In January of that year, he wrote to Edward Deming Andrews, a well-known scholar on the Shakers. In his letter he refers to an article by a Hindu scholar, Ananda Coomaraswamy, in which Coomaraswamy had made reference to an ancient English Christmas carol. In the carol, the Lord speaks of his coming (at Christmas, in his earthly life and finally in his Resurrection) in the words: "Tomorrow is my dancing day." Each stanza concludes with a call to dance ("To call my true love to my dance") and the refrain following each stanza is an invitation to sing ("Sing, O my love...").

Of special interest is the fact that in ten of the eleven stanzas the Lord speaks of the dance as "the dance" or "my dance," but in the final stanza the dance becomes the "general dance." Thus in Stanza Eleven the risen Lord ascends into heaven:

Then up to heaven I did ascend,
Where now I dwell in sure substance
On the right hand of God, that man
May come unto the general dance.

"The General Dance" is the title Merton gives to the final
chapter of *New Seeds*. The chapter is about God's presence in
the universe, drawing us out of life's seeming dualities by
enabling us to discover our true reality by finding our
oneness in God. It is only in the last three paragraphs that
Merton talks explicitly about the dance, but its movement
inescapably gambols through the whole chapter. On the
second last page Merton urges us to forget ourselves in order
to see God playing and diverting himself in the garden of
creation. We are invited to do this—to forget our cares, our
concerns, our very selves, in order that "we might be able to
hear His call and follow Him in His mysterious, cosmic
dance" (296). It is difficult not to see in these words of Merton
the language of the ancient carol.

In the concluding paragraphs of this final chapter there
are two more references to the "cosmic dance." In one Merton
writes that, when there is stillness and awakedness and true
emptiness in our lives, we have a purity of vision that gives
us "a glimpse of the cosmic dance." In the other reference he
makes clear that, however much we may misunderstand the
true realities of life, we cannot alter those realities or "stain
the joy of the cosmic dance, which is always there." He goes
on "Indeed, we are in the midst of it and it is in the midst of
us, for it beats in our very blood, whether we want it to or
not" (297).

The concluding sentence of *New Seeds* switches adjectives
and the cosmic dance becomes the general dance. "[W]e are
invited," he tells us, "to forget ourselves on purpose, cast our
awful solemnities to the winds and join in the general dance"
(297). It is hardly a coincidence that Merton's final chapter,
and indeed, his book, ends with the same words that form
the conclusion of the carol "My Dancing Day," namely "the
general dance."

What is meant by the "general dance" or the "cosmic

dance?" It is the universe, the cosmos that God made, moving and swirling in perfect harmony with the Creator. This harmonious oneness with God was God's gift to creation, especially God's gift to the man and woman. The point of the early chapters of Genesis, Merton writes, is "that God made the world as a garden in which He himself took delight" (291). God also made the man and the woman in the divine image, so that, through the light of reason, they might know all the other creatures and give them their names.

But that was not all. God also gave them a higher light that goes beyond names and forms, a light by which God's human creatures are able to meet God, not through the medium of things, but in God's own divine simplicity. In a sentence that gives us a strong hint of what he means by the general dance, Merton writes: "The union of the simple light of God with the simple light of man's spirit, in love, is contemplation" (291-292). He continues:

> The two simplicities are one. They form, as it were, an emptiness in which there is no addition, but rather the taking away of names, of forms, of content, of subject matter, of identities. In this meeting there is not so much a fusion of entities as a disappearance of entities. (292)

Making the link once more with the early chapters of Genesis, Merton tells us:

> The Bible speaks of this very simply: "In the breeze after noon, God came to walk with Adam [and Eve] in Paradise." ...In the free emptiness of the breeze...God and man are together, not speaking in words, or syllables or forms. And that was the meaning of creation, and of Paradise. (292)

In that emptiness that knows no dualities, but only the oneness of simplicity, the walk of God with God's human creatures in unison and tranquil accord is poetry, not prose, which is to say: It is the dance. For what is dance but harmonious movement in perfect oneness, beyond all dualities and multiplicities? In the dance there are not many movements, but one movement. The dancers forget themselves. They lose themselves in the dance and thus are emptied of a separate self. "The world and time," Merton adds, "are the dance of the Lord in emptiness" (297). They are our dance, too, as long as we allow God to raise us above all dualities by making us one with God.

But we were created free. We can refuse to lose ourselves in the dance, unwilling to rise above the dualities that illusion projects on reality. Or we can be a self aware of its oneness with all of reality and with its divine source. And when we are aware of this true self—that is, emptiness, for it is only in God—then, in all truth, we belong to the dance.

> [I]f we could let go of our obsession with what we think is the meaning of it all, we might be able to hear His call and follow Him in his mysterious, cosmic dance. We do not have to go far to catch echoes...of that dancing. When we are alone on a starlit night; when by chance we see the migrating birds in autumn descending on a grove of junipers to rest and eat; when we see children in a moment when they are really children; when we know love in our hearts; or when, like the Japanese poet Basho we hear an old frog land in a quiet pond with a solitary splash—at such times the awakening, the turning inside out of all values, the "newness," the emptiness and the purity of vision that make themselves evident, provide a glimpse of the cosmic dance." (296-297)

So, Merton invites us, let us forget ourselves on purpose. Let us cast our awful solemnity to the wind and join in the general dance!

New Seeds ends on this wonderful upswing, this crescendo of song and dance—Merton at his best. I confess that whenever I read it I recall his fondness for Dante. I remember *The Seven Storey Mountain* and its governing metaphor taken from the *Purgatorio*. *The Seven Storey Mountain* narrated Merton's journey to Gethsemani. I wonder: is Merton, in writing *New Seeds* twenty years later, telling us that, after the arduous purifying climb to the top of the mountain, it is in contemplation that we return to the earthly paradise from which the first humans were expelled?

Is *New Seeds*, especially in its final chapter, Merton's "version" of the *Paradiso*?

Notes

[1] The December, 1949, edition made minor changes in content. Here or there a word was changed. The chief change in contents is really a change in chapter organization. The 1949 revision has 28 chapters to the initial edition's 27. The added chapter was not primarily new material. Rather, Chapter Thirteen, while retaining its title, "Through a Glass," broke off into a new chapter on Mary, entitled "Electa Ut Sol." Three new paragraphs (amounting to a page and a half) have been added to this new chapter. The pagination is different in the two editions. The publisher used lowercase roman numerals for the introductory materials of the 1949 revision, whereas in the initial edition Arabic numbers were used for the introductory materials as well as for the rest of the text. Thus, the initial edition has 201 pages, while the 1949 revision has 191 pages and pages i to xvi.

[2] Donald Grayston has clarified the differences among the three editions in this way: "*Seeds* and *Seeds Revised* share a common framework, but differ in tone; *Seeds Revised* and *New Seeds* differ in both tone and framework." (Donald Grayston, "The Making of a Spiritual Classic: Thomas Merton's Seeds of Contemplation and New Seeds of Contemplation," *Sciences Religieuses/Studies in Religion* (1973-1974), p. 339. Donald Grayston has done remarkable research on the different versions of *Seeds*. See his *Thomas Merton: The Development of a Spiritual Theologian* (New York: Edwin Mellen Press, 1985) and his excellent comparative study of the various versions, *Thomas Merton Rewritings: The Five Versions of Seeds/ New Seeds of Contemplation as a Key to the Development of His Thought* (New York: Edwin Mellen, 1989).

[3] Chinese, Danish, Dutch, French, German, Italian, Japanese, Korean, Polish, Portuguese, Spanish, Swedish and Vietnamese. *New Seeds* has been translated into French, German, Italian, Portuguese and Spanish.

[4] "Is the World a Problem?", *Commonweal*, 84 (3 June 1966) p. 305. Also in the posthumously published *Contemplation in a World of*

Action (New York: Doubleday, 1971), p. 159.

[5] *Seeds*, p. 147; rev. ed., p. 142.

[6] Grayston, "The Making of a Spiritual Classic," p. 353.

[7] Merton was master of scholastics (monks studying for the priesthood) from 1951 to 1955 and master of novices from 1955 to 1965.

[8] *Seeds*, p. 60.

[9] *Seeds*, rev. ed., p. 46.

[10] This book, begun in December, 1948, as *The Cloud and the Fire*, was finally completed in 1951 as *The Ascent to Truth*. In February of 1949 he had described it to Sister Therese Lentfoehr as a book on the theology of contemplation. See Chapter Four.

[11] Existentialism is a system of thought that concentrates on the existence of the individual, emphasizing the radical singularity of the individual existent person. Our essence is not so much something we are given (which would be essentialism), but something we bring into being through our actions and our encounter with the culture of the time.

[12] Personalism is a way of thought that emphasizes the dignity and value of each individual person. It sees dialogue as necessary for the creation of community among persons.

[13] Zen is a blending of Indian Buddhism with Chinese Taoism. It flourishes especially in Japan. The goal of Zen is enlightenment (*sunyata*). Enlightenment is the non-mediated experience of reality. By "non-mediated," I mean experiencing reality simply as it is, without the mediation of words or ideas. Zen is radically non-dualistic.

[14] The writings of French philosopher Rene Descartes (1596-1650), exercised a strong influence on philosophical thought even to our own time. In his *Discourse on Method* he begins doubting everything he had received from sense experience or tradition. But he could not doubt that he was thinking about the fact that he doubted. Hence his famous dictum: "*Cogito, ergo sum.*" ("I think, therefore I am.") Where he began with thought, existentialism would begin with "being." Hence Merton's "no cogito, only sum."

[15] Etienne H. Gilson, *The Spirit of Medieval Philosophy* (Notre Dame,

Ind.: University of Notre Dame Press, 1936).

[16] Aldhelm Cameron-Brown, "Seeking the Rhinoceros: A Tribute to Thomas Merton," *Monastic Studies*, 1969, p. 68.

[17] Preface to the Japanese edition of *Seeds of Contemplation* (March, 1965), in *Honorable Reader*, p. 87.

[18] The new material on contemplation may be found in Chapters One and Two, which are completely new, as also is the wonderful concluding Chapter Thirty-Nine. Besides there are major additions and corrections throughout the book. Donald Grayston has indicated the variations in the different versions in his book, *Thomas Merton's Rewritings*, to which I have already referred.

[19] *Hidden Ground of Love*, p. 115.

[20] See unpublished letter to Marie Tadie, 22 November 1962. Merton Center, Louisville, Kentucky.

[21] Evelyn Underhill, *Mysticism* (New York: New American Library, 1955), p. 63.

[22] The new material on the self may be found in Chapters Two, Four, Six, Thirty-Eight and Thirty-Nine, as well as in scattered additions and corrections throughout the text.

[23] See my article "Original Blessing: the Gift of the True Self," in *The Way* (January, 1990), pp. 37-46.

[24] Jacques Maritain, *Scholasticism and Politics* (Manchester, N.H.: Ayers Co. Publishers, 1977) p. 46.

[25] In a letter to Jacques Maritain, dated May 24, 1964, Merton comments on the Buddhist doctrine of *anatta*, which is generally taken to mean a denial of person. He suggests that it may actually offer us new insights into the meaning of person. "I think that one of the most crucially important subjects to investigate today is the Buddhist metaphysic of the person which claims to be non-personal (*anatta*), but as a matter of fact might well be something completely unique and challenging. The anatta idea is simply a 'no' to the Hindu atman as a pseudo-object of thought. If once one can find that, on this crucial point where Buddhism and Christianity are completely opposed, they are in fact perhaps united.... Today is the feast of the Holy Trinity, Person but not individual nature..." (*Courage for Truth*, p. 45).

[26] Luke 17:5.

[27] Galatians 5:16.

[28] *Ave Maria*, 95 (March 3, 1962), p. 27.

[29] "Fire Watch," July 4, 1952, *The Sign of Jonas*, pp. 349-362.

[30] *Hudson Review*, 20 (Summer, 1967), pp. 211-218.

7

The Climate of Monastic Prayer

(*a.k.a.* Contemplative Prayer)

Our knowledge of God is paradoxically a knowledge not of Him as the object of our scrutiny, but of ourselves as utterly dependent on His saving and merciful knowledge of us.

In the summer of 1979, while working on the manuscript of *Thomas Merton's Dark Path*, I went to the Thomas Merton Studies Center at Bellarmine College in Louisville to do further research. The week before I left I had been reading Merton's *The Climate of Monastic Prayer*—a reading that was to prove important as I continued my research. One of the first things I did at the center was to look at some of Merton's unpublished manuscripts. There was one that particularly interested me. Titled *Prayer as Worship and Experience*, it was a manuscript that Merton had offered to Macmillan Publishing Company in 1963 and for which Macmillan had paid an advance of ten thousand dollars. There was one problem: At that time Merton was under contract with Farrar, Straus and Giroux to deliver his next book to them. When news leaked out about the Macmillan deal, Farrar, Straus and Giroux threatened a suit against the monastery. Merton with his minimal understanding of finances was bewildered by the whole thing and wondered why there was such a fuss. Fortunately, his agent Naomi Stone stepped in and worked out a compromise whereby the monastery returned the advance and Macmillan gave up the manuscript with the stipulation that it was not to be published elsewhere. Naomi warned Merton that he was not to touch this manuscript again.

It was this very manuscript, withdrawn in 1963, that I was reading in the summer of 1979. As I read, I was at first puzzled by the fact that the text seemed quite familiar to me. I thought to myself: "I'm sure I have read this before, but I can't remember where." Suddenly the light dawned. I remembered where I had read it. I got up from the desk where I was working, went to the bookcase where the Merton books were kept and found a copy of *The Climate of Monastic Prayer*. Sure enough, whole sections of the "forbidden" manuscript were scattered throughout *The Climate of Monastic Prayer*! With some excitement at this discovery, I compared the manuscript with the book and was eventually able to piece together what Merton had done. This is the story that unfolded.

In 1964 Merton had written a brief article called *"The Climate of Monastic Prayer."* First circulated privately, it was published in 1965 in *Collectanea Cisterciensia*. That same year Merton enlarged the article, originally fifteen pages, into a 58-page booklet that was completed in October, 1965. This booklet, carrying the same title as the original article, was also privately circulated.

Merton evidently wanted to publish this material, but 58 pages did not constitute a publishable book. He conceived a plan that would enable him, in a brief time and in a painless way, to expand this booklet into a book, which also carried the title *The Climate of Monastic Prayer*. This was the plan: Instead of writing new material, he inserted (one is tempted to say "intruded"), in various places in the booklet verbatim excerpts from the unpublished manuscript, *Prayer as Worship and Experience*—a manuscript which, remember, just a couple of years earlier, he had agreed to put aside for good.

The resulting manuscript was published by Cistercian Publications under the title *The Climate of Monastic Prayer*. Yet another sleight of hand, the identical text, though with different page numbering, was published the same year by Herder and Herder under a different title, *Contemplative Prayer*. (*Climate* is 154 pages, *Contemplative Prayer*, 144.) The book has a preface of fifteen pages written by Merton's Quaker friend, Dr. Douglas V. Steere.

An intelligent reading of this book requires some understanding of the maneuvering Merton did when he expanded the booklet of October, 1965, into a book. The manuscript that had been offered to Macmillan and then withdrawn, is made up of four sections: "The Life of Prayer"; "Prayer as Worship"; "Prayer as Experience"; and "Epilogue: Wisdom or Evasion." It was the last two sections of this unpublished manuscript that Merton had used to create the book. Diagram C on page 292 in the Appendix shows how Merton combined what I will call the primary material of the book (the booklet of October, 1965) with what I see as the secondary material (the third and fourth sections of *Prayer as Worship and Experience*).

This diagram is no idle exercise in "source criticism." I consider it an essential tool for an enlightened reading of *The Climate of Monastic Prayer*. It is necessary, for example, for the reader to know that there is a continuity between Chapter V of the book, which concludes with some remarks on the "purpose of monastic prayer...in the sense of prayer of the heart" (45),[1] and Chapter XI, which begins with the question: "What is the purpose of meditation, in the sense of 'the prayer of the heart'?" (67). Between these two chapters there is a huge parenthesis—five chapters and twenty-seven pages long—which discusses the history of private prayer in the Benedictine tradition from the time of Saint Benedict to the Counter-Reformation and after. Following this parenthetical intrusion, Merton returns in Chapter XI to the topic he had been discussing in Chapter V. To understand what Merton is doing, it is necessary for the reader to know that the long historical digression which he inserts at this point actually comes from *Prayer as Worship and Experience* which of course was not written with this book in mind at all.

The same may be said about Chapters XII and XIII and Chapter XV: They are insertions into the text and they do not blend harmoniously with the original material of the book. Chapter XIX is also from the "intruding" work.

Two Books in One

From the diagram and my brief remarks about it, it can readily be seen that *The Climate of Monastic Prayer* is actually two quite different books, one within the other, or, perhaps more accurately, the second scattered throughout the first. The "primary material," taken from the October, 1965, booklet, comprises 102 pages of the text. The "book within the book," the "secondary material" from *Prayer as Worship and Experience*, makes up the other 52 pages and therefore approximately one-third of the book. The reader would be well advised to read the text as two separate books. This would mean reading ten chapters plus Merton's Introduction (102 pages) as *The Climate of Monastic Prayer* and nine chapters (52 pages) as a totally different work. This is the approach to the text that I intend to follow. I shall deal first with the "primary material" and then the "secondary material."[2] This dual path through the text will make the study of the book much more intelligible.

As I have mentioned, the book under discussion was published under two different titles: *The Climate of Monastic Prayer* (Cistercian Publications edition) and *Contemplative Prayer* (the Herder and Herder edition). The choice of the title *Contemplative Prayer* for the Herder and Herder publication was obviously intended to open the book to a wider readership by suggesting through the new title that the book would be of interest to people who were not monks. Merton states in his Introduction:

> What is written about prayer in these pages is written primarily for monks. However...a practical, non-academic

> study of monastic prayer should be of interest to all
> Christians, since every Christian is bound to be in some
> sense a man of prayer. (19)

Merton's words make a great deal of sense. Those of us who live with the pressures of modern urban life often experience the need for some sort of interior silence, if we are to maintain a sense of unity in our lives as well as a realization of our own human dignity and freedom. Should Merton have made a greater effort to adapt his book to readers who did not live in monasteries? The answer is surely yes. In fact, it was something he intended to do. In a letter to Naomi Stone, he expressed his concern that some revisions in the book were called for to make it more appealing to a general readership. For, on March 8, 1966, Stone, not realizing that he had "smuggled" parts of the forbidden manuscript into the book, wrote to him: "I have nearly finished reading *The Climate of Monastic Prayer* and think it's terrific! Obviously, as you say, it will need more revision for the general public, but I think that the general public can get a great deal out of it."[3]

Actually, very little revision was made in the original text to accommodate the book to the needs of the "general public." Apart from the change in title in the Herder and Herder edition and the occasional substitution of "prayer" for "monastic prayer," the book remains in its original form. Merton may have considered the insertion of the "secondary material" from the unpublished manuscript as an accommodation to a more general public; but in view of the confusion which this material introduced into the book, as well as the largely "monastic" character of the insertions themselves, it can be doubted that this secondary material actually helped in any way to make the book appeal to a wider readership. This means that we, the non-monastic readers, have to make our own adaptation.

The book remains, in other words, what it was originally intended to be: a book for monks. This is not to say that it has nothing to offer to the rest of us. Much that Merton says about monastic prayer can be adapted with great profit to the life of the lay Christian; but Merton has pretty much left us on our own to make that adaptation.[4] He has made only token gestures in that direction. The book remains *The Climate of* Monastic *Prayer*. In fact, one might seriously question whether the substitution of *Contemplative Prayer* for the original title is accurate or justifiable. The term "contemplative prayer" occurs only six times in the text: five times in the "secondary material" and only once in the "primary material." (Even the word "contemplation" is used only sparingly in the "primary material.) The word Merton seems to prefer in this book to describe monastic prayer is, curiously, the word "meditation." (Interestingly, on page 150, in the midst of a section from the "secondary material," Merton substitutes the word "meditation" for what was "prayer" in the original text of the unpublished manuscript.) He frequently uses "prayer of the heart" as a synonym for "meditation." Either of these two terms would have reflected the book's terminology more accurately than *Contemplative Prayer*.

The Primary Material

What is the climate of monastic prayer? Merton identifies it as the desert.

> The climate in which monastic prayer flowers is that of the desert, where the comfort of man is absent, where the secure routines of man's city offer no support, and where prayer must be sustained by God in the purity of faith. (27)

That the desert is the climate of monastic prayer can be demonstrated both historically and existentially. Historically, the desert is the place where monastic prayer originated. Specifically, it is the Egyptian desert where Saint Anthony went to give up all things for the love and service of God, where others followed him in great numbers. The desert is the place where John Cassian (c. 360-435) came to drink from its source the wisdom that these Desert Fathers had come to experience in their prayer and to bring an understanding of that experience to western Christians.

Merton always had a deep affection for the Desert Fathers, "those men of fabulous originality"[5] who "sought a way to God that was uncharted and freely chosen, not inherited from others who have mapped it out beforehand. They sought a God whom they alone could find, not one who was 'given' in a set stereotyped form by somebody else."[6] They "did not imagine themselves to be mystics," Merton says, "though in fact they often were."[7]

The key that opens the door to the spirituality of the Desert Fathers is the "heart." Their prayer was the "prayer of the heart." It was, first of all, the Bible in the heart. Their lives were rooted in the Scriptures, especially in the psalms. They were not biblical scholars: They did not analyze biblical texts. They put the Bible in their hearts by memorizing its words and repeating them with deep and simple concentration. The Psalter was especially their book of prayer, for in the psalms they saw "revealed the secret movements of the heart in its struggle against the forces of darkness. The 'battle psalms' were all interpreted as referring to the inner war with passion and with the demons."[8]

Their prayer was also "Jesus in the heart." "The Prayer of Jesus," so popular in the Eastern Church, originated in the Egyptian desert. It "consisted in interior recollection, the abandonment of distracting thoughts and the humble invocation of the Lord Jesus with words from the Bible in a spirit of intense faith."[9] Keeping the name of Jesus in the ground of their being was for them the secret of the control of thoughts and of victory over temptation. It was the way of keeping themselves in the presence of God and in touch with the reality of their own inner truth. They could find God in their lives only if they were in touch with their own inner truth; and they could experience their own true selves only if they were truly in the presence of God. This was the reason they had come into the desert: "to be themselves, their ordinary selves, and to forget a world that divided them from themselves"[10] and separated them from God.

The ultimate goal of their lives was the kingdom of God and union with God; but the proximate goal to which they directed all their energies was "purity of heart," which is the aim of "prayer of the heart." Purity of heart meant for them much more than moral or even ascetical perfection. It was the culmination of a long process of spiritual transformation whereby, detached from all creatures and freed from all movement of inordinate passion, they were able to live "absorbed in God." Purity of heart meant "to keep their minds and hearts empty of care and concern, so that they might altogether forget themselves and apply themselves entirely to the love and service of God" (20).

They did not talk a great deal about purity of heart. They lived and experienced it; and from their experience they distilled a very practical and unassuming wisdom that shines through the words they spoke that have been preserved for us. This wisdom represents a discovery of the reality of the human person in the course of an inner and spiritual journey that, as Merton says, "is far more crucial and infinitely more important than any journey to the moon." He asks, "What can we gain by sailing to the moon if we are not able to cross the abyss that separates us from ourselves?"[11]

As we non-monastics reflect on what Merton is saying, there is much with which we can identify. More and more of us are turning to the Bible, striving to locate it within our hearts, so that its words become the source and motivation of our actions. We try also to keep Jesus in our hearts and to live more fully in awareness of the presence of God. Over the course of time we go through many purifying conversion experiences, which we can surely identify as movements toward that purity of heart of which Merton writes.

So, historically the climate of monastic prayer is without question the desert and for us who are not monks the desert has to be of our own making: finding solitude in our lives when and where we can. Merton makes clear that the place of prayer is also the desert in an existential sense. It is the solitude in which we seek the ground of our own being, searching our own hearts. It also means plunging into the heart of the world, of which we are very much a part, in order that we may listen more attentively to the deepest and more neglected voices that proceed from the depths of what is most truly real. "The monk," Merton says, "is bound to explore the inner waste of his own being as a solitary" (28), with an ever-deepening realization of the life he is called to live in Christ. This means for today's monk (and today's Christian) what it meant for the early Desert Fathers: breaking with the familiar and established and secure norms to travel off into the unknown toward a freedom rooted not in social approval but in a profound sense of dependence on God in pure faith. To achieve this freedom, the monk (and the Christian) must first endure the questioning and the doubt and the sense of dread that will force him to confront his false self with its illusions, its masks, and its role playing. As Merton puts it:

> [T]he dimensions of prayer in solitude are those of man's ordinary anguish, his self-searching, his moments of nausea at his own vanity, falsity and capacity for betrayal. Far from establishing one in unassailable narcissistic security, the way of prayer brings us face to face with the sham and indignity of the false self that seeks to live for itself alone and to enjoy the "consolation of prayer" for its own sake. This "self" is pure illusion, and ultimately he who lives for and by such an illusion must end either in disgust or in madness. (24)

In earlier chapters we have already reflected on the false self, but what Merton makes clear is that it is only by unmasking this false self in the solitude of prayer that we can be delivered from the bondage of an inauthentic existence and hope to recover a sense of our own true self firmly rooted in our own inner truth. "The monk [the Christian] confronts his own humanity and that of his world at the deepest and most central point where the void seems to open out into black despair" (25). He or she faces the serious possibility that despair may be the only answer to life's ambiguities. They face it and reject it. For in the darkness the firm stand they have taken, beyond falsity and illusion, in the ground of their being, opens to them the light of God. In this divine light they can perceive, however dimly, the mysterious workings of the Spirit of God who makes all things new and creates a new humanity in Christ.

This, then, is the climate of true prayer: the desert of Egypt and the lonely waste of one's own solitude. Both are "places" where we come to realize that we are not fully at home in the world and that the world by itself can offer us no ultimate meaning for the life we live in it. Something of ourselves seems to be elsewhere. Life's ultimate meaning, which the world cannot give, is something that we discover only when we transcend our own humanity and that of the world by a freedom that turns despair into hope and a life of illusion into a life of authentic existence. At last aware of God, we let our hearts go out in gratitude, obedient love and service to the one who has enabled us to know our inner truth. "The climate of this prayer is, then, one of awareness, gratitude and a totally obedient love which seeks nothing but to please God." (33)

This book is about prayer. But in it Merton discusses prayer in its very nature rather than its techniques. Hence his reflections can be helpful to anyone who seeks to make prayer a necessary element in her life. While he draws occasionally on ancient texts, the whole development, Merton states, is "essentially modern" (23). For a contemporary understanding of meditation (i.e., "prayer in the heart," or prayer in the ground of one's being), Merton turns not only to the Egyptian Fathers but also to modern existentialists, who emphasize freedom and the human need for authenticity and spiritual liberation. They insist on exploring the dark side of the human psyche in terms of the ineluctable fact of death and the sense of dread in the face of the apparent meaninglessness of life. Merton makes explicit references to the existential philosophers, Heidegger (23) and Marcel (109) and implicit references to Kierkegaard's important work, *The Concept of Anxiety* (96-102).

Merton's study of prayer is concerned especially with personal prayer, although in the "secondary material" of the book he does discuss the relationship of personal prayer to liturgy and to a life of action. His special concern, in discussing prayer, is "the monk's [the Christian's] own deepening existential grasp of his call to life in Christ, as it progressively reveals itself to him in the solitude where he is alone with God" (28).

Our prayer life is richer than any particular "spiritual exercise." Meditation, psalmody, prayerful reading of the Scriptures (*lectio divina*), and contemplation are all part of a unified and integrated life in which we turn ourselves toward God. Prayer is, therefore, the ensemble of these varied ways of finding God and resting in His presence. If it sometimes means "turning from the world, that turning is not a goal that terminates the spiritual quest, but rather points to a "returning to the world" with clearer eyes and a better perspective on what matters in human life.

Though he uses in his title the words "monastic prayer," Merton's emphasis throughout the book is on "meditation." He makes it clear that he wants to understand meditation in its close relation to psalmody, reading, prayer and contemplation, yet he scarcely touches on meditation's relationship to these other important aspects of monastic prayer.

Meditation or Contemplation?

Merton's concentration in this book on "meditation" is, to say the least, curious. One would expect, in the light of his previous books, that in writing about the central exercise of prayer he would have chosen to discuss "contemplation." Yet, as I have pointed out, in the "primary material" of the book, the word "contemplation" occurs only infrequently and the words "contemplative prayer" only once. Why does he use the word "meditation," when his preferred term for the life of prayer, as evidenced by his earlier works, is "contemplation"?

At the time he was writing (the mid-sixties), meditation as a practice borrowed from Hinduism and Buddhism was enjoying a wide popularity in the West among Christians and non-Christians alike. To those who were embracing this practice in large numbers, he wanted to point out that meditation is more than a psychological exercise that may bring a measure of quiet and a power of concentration into a person's life. It is more than a way of relaxing from life's pressures. Furthermore, it should not be viewed as an import from the East, previously unknown in the West. On the contrary, it is a practice deeply rooted in the Christian tradition of prayer. What he calls "meditation" in this book, therefore, is what he calls "contemplation" in his earlier works. Whatever name one gives it, it is a deeply spiritual experience that can change the whole orientation of a person's life.

It should be clear, then, that by meditation Merton does not mean "mental prayer," which, he says, "is totally misleading.... We rarely pray with the 'mind' alone" (30). Mental prayer suggests a cleavage between prayer in the mind and vocal prayer—something totally foreign to any understanding of the life of prayer. Nor does he mean "discursive meditation," which consists of "busy discursive acts, complex logical reasoning, active imagining, and the deliberate stirring up of the affections."[12] Meditation, in this sense of discursive reflection, Merton believed, tends to conflict with our receptivity to the inner working of the Holy Spirit. We become too intent on what we are doing. This is not to say that discursive meditation cannot serve a valid purpose in the Christian life. But one needs to know, as Merton has pointed out in other works, when its usefulness for spiritual growth has come to an end and, therefore, when it should be abandoned for a simpler way of prayer that, even though it may be more obscure, will be more fruitful.

By meditation, Merton means a type of prayer that has some kinship with authentic Zen meditation in that it seeks an intuition of being beyond the dualities of life. Like Zen it is an integrating prayer in which one finds the center of his life; the "original self" (as Zen practitioners would put it). It differs, however, from Zen in that Merton would see that center as rooted in God.

Perhaps the best way of understanding what Merton wants to express by the term "meditation" is to link it with the prayer of the early Desert Fathers. In fact, Merton explicitly does this. He says:

> In these pages, then, meditation will be used as more or less equivalent to what mystics of the Eastern Church have called "prayer of the heart"—at least in the general sense of a prayer that seeks its roots in the very ground of our being, not merely in our mind or our affections" (30).

Again he writes:

> Monastic [Christian] prayer begins not so much with "considerations" as with a "return to the heart," finding one's deepest center, awakening the profound depths of our being in the presence of God who is the source of our being and our life (30).

Merton clarifies what he means by the "heart" and "the return to the heart." The heart, he says, is

> ...the deepest psychological ground of one's personality, the inner sanctuary where self-awareness goes beyond analytical reflection and opens out into metaphysical and theological confrontation with the Abyss of the unknown yet present one who is "more intimate to us than we are to ourselves" (33).

"Return to the heart" means that "purity of heart"—so important to the Desert Fathers—which is the only atmosphere in which the "prayer of the heart" can grow and flourish. "Purity of heart" involves total surrender to God as the source and ground of our being and an unconditional acceptance of our situation as willed by him. It is an existential acceptance of the whole of reality, seen at once in its depths and in its concreteness. It is not a flight into a world of abstractions, but rather embraces the everyday realities of one's life.

Some people have a spontaneous gift for meditation; others enter upon the experience only with difficulty. Most of us have to learn how to meditate. Yet, learning how to meditate means not so much looking for a "method" or a "system" as cultivating an "outlook," an "attitude": faith, submission, attention, expectation, supplication, trust and joy. Such attitudes will permeate our being with love and living faith that will help us to experience the presence of God, seeing God without "seeing," knowing God without "knowing."

We need to realize, too, that there is a movement in prayer. It is the rhythm of the paschal mystery: the passage from life to death, the alternation of darkness and light. Sometimes meditation is death and darkness; a descent into our nothingness, a recognition of our helplessness, our dependency, our sinfulness. But at other times we pierce through the darkness, as God leads us by the light of faith into new realms. Here we become increasingly receptive to the hidden action of the Holy Spirit and begin to realize that God is All.

At times the darkness we experience in our prayer may be God's work in our lives, calling us to greater detachment and to a more obedient and cooperative submission to grace. It may be God's grace emptying our minds and hearts "in order to fill them with a higher and purer light which is 'darkness' to sense and to reason" (44). This is the "dark night" of which John of the Cross speaks—a night in which God darkens the mind only in order to give a more perfect light. It is excessive light that causes the darkness.

Yet we must not overlook the possibility that the darkness we encounter in meditation may be of our own making. It may be brought on by the false dichotomy we set up between the world of inner truth and the world of external realities—a dichotomy that prevents us from accepting the whole of reality for what it is. For meditation is not an exploration of abstract ideals; it must respect the concrete realities of everyday life—nature, the body, one's work, one's friends, one's surroundings. In a passage which suggests the influence of Zen and its "pointing" to the concrete realities of ordinary life as the way to enlightenment, Merton writes:

A false supernaturalism which imagines that the
"Supernatural" is a kind of Platonic realm of abstract
essences totally apart from and opposed to the concrete
world of nature offers no real support to a genuine life of
meditation and prayer. Meditation has no point and no
reality unless it is firmly rooted in life. (39)

Meditation cannot be a "privatized" experience. We are not
really progressing in meditation if we wall ourselves up
inside ourselves in order to cherish our thoughts and
experiences as a kind of private treasure. Love for others and
openness to them remains "the condition for a living and
fruitful inner life of thought and love. The love of others is a
stimulus to interior life, not a danger to it, as some
mistakenly believe" (40).

This definite, though not always unambiguous, concern
for the ordinary realities of life and for an openness to other
people as necessary conditions for a genuine interior life
represents a shift of emphasis in Merton's writings. One
might want to suggest that such concern is at least latent in
his earlier books; but there can scarcely be any doubt that his
explicit articulation of it in this book bears the mark of his
contact with Zen Buddhism.

The Purpose of Meditation

The Discovery of Who We Are

One of the goals of meditation is to answer the question: Who
are we? Meditation seeks for the deepest ground of our
identity in God's truth and in the realization of our total
dependence on God. Its goal is that purity of heart whereby
we surrender ourselves to God and His purposes for us and
in the process come to understand our own identity. We are,
Merton says, "a word spoken by God" (68). God's words
always have meaning; our task, therefore, is to discover the
meaning that we are. What is the word God speaks in us?

What is our identity? It is not an identity foisted upon us. The "word" (*logos*), as Merton understands it, is not the notion of stoic philosophy of a meaning imposed on a person from within by a static natural law; much less is it a meaning imposed on a person from without by custom, routine or social forces. It is, rather, a meaning that one is called by God to construct. "My true identity lies hidden in God's call to my freedom and my response to Him" (68).

> This means I must use my freedom in order to love, with full responsibility and authenticity, not merely receiving a form imposed on me by external forces or forming my own life according to an approved social pattern, but directing my love to the personal reality of my brother [and sister], and embracing God's will in its naked, often impenetrable mystery. (68)

But we cannot discover our meaning in God till we realize how utterly void of meaning we are without God. This experience of life's meaninglessness is dread. Hence Merton says: "I cannot discover my 'meaning' if I try to evade the dread which comes from first experiencing my meaninglessness!" (68). Our descent into the center of our being where we experience our nothingness before God must be authentic; that is to say, it must be genuinely lived by us. We cannot simply play a religious role. It is one thing to know our nothingness in a speculative way, quite another actually to experience that nothingness. It is not enough for us to "believe" that we are grounded in God; we must experience it. We must let ourselves "be brought naked and defenceless into the center of that dread where we stand alone before God in our nothingness, without explanation, without theories, completely dependent upon his providential care, in dire need of the gift of his grace, his mercy and the light of faith" (69).

This confrontation with our nothingness and helplessness is an experience of dread; yet this same confrontation in the presence of God is an experience of joy. For it puts us in "direct contact with the source of all joy and all life" (70). In God we find our meaning. In God we find our "heart." At the

same time we unmask the false identity we had been living:
We recognize that the external, everyday self we seem to be is
to a great extent a mask and a fabrication. In hiddenness and
obscurity we come to know the true self that we are at our
center. It is only then that we truly begin to meditate: for
meditation cannot be the action of a false self.

The Discovery of God as God Is

The goal of meditation is not only to know ourselves as we
really are but also to know God as God is. As Merton repeats
over and over, to know God as God is can never mean
knowing God as an object that submits to our scrutiny. For
God is not an "object" or a "thing." God's infinity, as the very
word implies, knows no boundaries; hence we cannot
"define" God as we define things in the world. "His presence
cannot be verified as we would verify a laboratory
experiment" (79). As soon as we try to verify God's presence
as an object of exact knowledge, God eludes us.

The only knowledge of God of which we are capable is
knowledge about God—through analogies, images and
symbols. We must not underestimate the value of this kind of
knowledge of God. The Bible and our culture offer us rich
imagery and symbols that help us to speak about God. The
richer this imagery, the more deeply we will be able to
penetrate into the presence of God in creation and the better
prepared our inner self will be for the experience of God in
faith. More than that, this imagery will enable those who
have had the experience of God to reflect on that experience
and articulate it for others.

But the true experience of God can never be achieved
through our conceptual knowledge of God. If we are to know
God in the divine Self, we must transcend our analogies and
"grasp" God in the general awareness of loving faith,
knowing God by "unknowing." Indeed, we must not only
transcend our analogies, we must also transcend our
ordinary ways of knowing. "[W]e must forget the familiar
subject-object relationship" and "become aware of ourselves

as known through and through by him" (83). Those who have persevered in reading this book up to this point will understand what Merton means by transcending the images and symbols that enable us to say something about God and moving toward experiencing the divine reality beyond words and concepts. Once again we are talking about the apophatic way. To quote Merton:

> [T]he aim of meditation, in the context of Christian faith, is not to arrive at an objective and apparently "scientific" knowledge about God, but to come to know him through the realization that our very being is penetrated with his knowledge and love for us. Our knowledge of God is paradoxically a knowledge not of him as the object of our scrutiny, but of ourselves as utterly dependent on his saving and merciful knowledge of us. (83)

Thus, coming to know God in the divine Self and coming to know our real selves converge in a single intuition—our awareness of our total dependence on God. When we know God, we know ourselves; when we know ourselves, we know God. The goal of meditation is well summed up in the prayer of Saint Augustine: *"Noverim te, noverim me"* ("May I know you, may I know myself").

The Meaning of Dread

Dread, or anxiety, is a condition of human existence that has been analyzed at great length by contemporary existentialists. Those who have written about it are careful to distinguish dread from fear. Fear always has some specific thing in the world as its object. When I fear, I know precisely what it is that I fear. If, for instance, I am speeding on a highway (which would be very, very wrong of me) and spot a police car as I pass, I know exactly what I fear, as I quickly try to lower the speed of my car. I know even more definitely when I suddenly see a car behind with lights flashing and an officer signaling me to pull off to the side of the road. Dread, on the other hand, has no such specificity. It is the awakening of a person to the reality of an existence in which his freedom is poised over an abyss of nothingness. In his important book, *The Concept of Anxiety*, Søren Kierkegaard likens anxiety (also sometimes translated as "dread") to the experience of dizziness. "He whose eye chances to look down into the yawning abyss becomes dizzy.... Thus dread is the dizziness of freedom which occurs...when freedom gazes down into its own possibility, grasping at finiteness to sustain itself."[13]

It is only through experiencing this dread and coming to realize that finiteness cannot sustain us that we are able to break the bondage and the forgetfulness that bind us so relentlessly to things in this world. Then we can begin to live an authentic life.

Merton links the existentialist's concept of dread with the "fear of the Lord" of the early Fathers and with the "dark nights" of John of the Cross. But he sees dread as more than a perception of our contingency, our finiteness, our ultimate "nothingness." For the poverty of our creatureliness is compounded by the fact that we are sinners alienated from God. We are not only creatures, we are creatures in rebellion. In our depths there is not only nothingness, there is also falsity. We have failed to measure up to the existential demands of our lives. We have failed to meet the challenge of our meaning as "words of God." And the price of this failure is guilt—a guilt[14] that is real and not just a neurotic anxiety. *"It is the sense of defection and defeat that afflicts a man who is not facing his own inner truth and is not giving back to life, to God and to his fellow man a fair return for all that has been given him"* (97, emphasis original).

Dread is not simply a feeling of being out of favor with God. For estrangement from God can be juridically regained through receiving the sacraments of the Church with the proper dispositions. Indeed, one may do so and feel himself fully restored to the divine favor; "[b]ut this will not liberate him from 'dread' and 'night,' as long as he tends to cling to the empty illusion of a separate self, inclined to resist God" (97). For dread, Merton says, is "the deep, confused metaphysical awareness of a *basic antagonism between the self and God* due to estrangement from him by perverse attachment to a 'self' which is mysterious and illusory" (97, emphasis original). It is something that cannot be assigned to a definite cause or attributed to a specific action. It is not something we can repent of, but an experience we must face and struggle with.

Meditation is the scene of that struggle. The struggle ends at the moment we learn that we can find our authentic existence only when we are lost in God. It ends when we come to realize that we have no hope but in God. In the struggle we prove "the seriousness of our love for God and prayer," and in the peace that follows the struggle we come to realize that the experience of dread was not a punishment but a purification and a grace. Though the experience of it may have seemed a kind of hell, it turns out to be, in the curious words of the twelfth-century Cistercian, Isaac of Stella, "a hell of mercy and not of wrath." As Merton described it:

> To be in a "hell of mercy" is to fully experience one's nothingness, but in a spirit of repentance and surrender to God with desire to accept and do his will.... It is in this "hell of mercy" that in finally relaxing our determined grasp of our empty self, we find ourselves lost and liberated in the infinite fullness of God's love. We escape from the cage of emptiness, despair, dread and sin into the infinite space and freedom of grace and mercy. (102)

Secondary Material

A substantive portion of the "secondary material" in *The Climate of Monastic Prayer* deals with the role of action and contemplation in the life of the monk. Merton presents in Chapters VI to X a historical perspective in which to place the discussion of these two aspects of monastic life.

Before Saint Benedict

Out of the earliest monastic experience there emerged two divergent concepts of prayer: that of Saint Anthony (251?-356) in the Egyptian desert and that of Saint Basil (c. 330-379) at Annesi near Constantinople. Saint Anthony represents an understanding of prayer that is essentially contemplative; Saint Basil, one that is essentially active. For the Egyptian monks who followed Anthony, prayer meant resting as far as possible from exterior activity and seeking God in solitude. For the monastic communities founded by Basil, prayer is that which accompanies work and sanctifies it. Whereas the Egyptian monks saw contemplation in solitude as the heart of monastic prayer, Basil felt that such prayer was to be discouraged. He organized the prayer life of his monks according to the pattern of the canonical hours, leaving private prayer to be carried out by the monks while they were busy at the tasks assigned to them. "In the midst of our work," he said, "we can fulfill the duty of prayer."

The Rule of Saint Benedict

The Rule of Saint Benedict (c. 480-550) provides for a balance of both liturgical prayer and contemplative prayer. Influenced by John Cassian (c. 360-435), the Rule expresses "the classical monastic belief that secret and contemplative prayer should be inspired by liturgical prayer and should be the normal crown of that prayer" (47). In the early Benedictine tradition and in the spiritual writers of the Middle Ages, there is no conflict between "public" and "private" prayer or between liturgy and contemplation. This is a modern problem, or, as Merton suggests, a pseudo-problem. The Benedictine ideal was that "[l]iturgy by its very nature tends to prolong itself in individual contemplative prayer, and mental prayer in its turn disposes us for and seeks fulfillment in liturgical worship" (46).

Saint Gregory the Great

The problem that does arise in the Benedictine tradition is the problem of the relationship of the life of contemplation to the active life. Gregory the Great (c. 540-604) wrestled with the problem, and his treatment of it has had a profound influence on Benedictine life in subsequent ages. Gregory's solution is that "the contemplative life is theoretically superior to and better than the active, and should be preferred to the active whenever possible," however, "there are times when activity must supplant contemplation" (52). Hence, what is theoretically better may not necessarily be the choice one should make in a given situation. Gregory makes it clear, however, that the monk who is required by strict duty to leave contemplation for action should do so only with regret. "The vocation of the monk was to stay in his monastery and pray, and when he was called forth from the cloister, as he often was, to engage in church affairs, he was expected to go forth with weeping and lamentation" (53).

Saint Bernard of Clairvaux

Saint Bernard of Clairvaux (1090-1153) takes up the same question and reaches much the same conclusion as Saint Gregory. In the monastic life, according to Bernard, there are three vocations: that of Lazarus the penitent; that of Martha, the active servant of the monastic household; and that of Mary, the contemplative. Mary's portion is the best of the three, and therefore she should never leave her contemplation unasked to share in the labors of Martha. Yet the monastery needs administrators who will care for the temporal needs of the monks. Martha's portion, therefore, should not be looked down upon. Indeed, Saint Bernard suggests that Mary and Martha supplement one another. "[A]fter all, Mary and Martha are sisters and they should dwell together in the same household in peace" (54). In fact, for Saint Bernard, true monastic perfection consists in "the union of all three vocations: that of the penitent, the active worker (in the care of souls above all) and the contemplative" (54).[15]

When the monasteries of the Middle Ages lost their fervor, the last observance that ceased to be carried out was the choral office. Hence, those who attempted to reform the monasteries in the Counter-Reformation period did not turn their attention to the liturgy, because, though the soul may have gone out of it, it was still functioning in fairly good order; rather, they turned their reforming zeal to the sphere of personal prayer and piety, drawing on the *Devotio Moderna*,[16] with its insistence on personal devotion to the humanity of Christ and on affective prayer. The subjective element of prayer was emphasized and given primacy of importance over "objective" liturgical worship. The conclusion eventually arrived at was that, if you really wanted to pray, you waited till the liturgical office was over. Then, "spontaneous and subjective prayer can be given free rein" (64). This mentality has survived in monasteries and also among clergy bound to the recitation of the office. In this context it is worth recalling the story of the three priests on a fishing trip. They take time out on the boat to say their breviary together. When a sudden storm arose, one of them said: "We had better stop saying the office and start praying." The story is not atypical of the unhealthy attitude that prevails when the subjective experience of the individual at prayer becomes the sole criterion for judging the value and validity of all forms of prayer. The contemporary liturgical movement—especially with the more recent emphasis on the contemplative dimension of liturgical prayer—has restored a much-needed perspective to this all too narrow understanding of Christian prayer.

Dom Augustine Baker

Merton concludes his brief history of personal prayer in the Benedictine tradition with a short evaluation of the interesting and unusual "case" of Dom Augustine Baker (1575-1641), the English Benedictine who fought a lifelong battle to restore contemplation to the monastic life as the sole and only legitimate reason for its existence.[17] His stance represents a significant departure from the traditional teaching on action and contemplation as we have seen it expressed in the writings of Gregory the Great and Bernard of Clairvaux. Dom Augustine Baker saw action and contemplation as separated by a great gulf, with no possibility of bridging the gap between them. "For Dom Augustine, both liturgy and meditation were on the wrong side of the gulf. The real prayer was simple contemplative introversion" (66).

The terms he used to describe conflicting groups in monasteries sounds a bit hilarious in American English. He describes them as either "active livers" or "internal livers." He is not speaking about anatomy, but of a way of living! To quote Merton:

> He found himself in a life-long conflict with those of his brethren for whom he coined the caustic and ambiguous expression "the active livers."... [He] goes so far as to say that the trouble with monasteries is that they are usually run by "active livers" who destroy the life of prayer by frustrating the lives of the contemplatives ["the internal livers"]. (65-66)

His stance was extreme and one that can scarcely be expected to appeal to modern Benedictines, who have espoused with enthusiasm the cause of the liturgical movement. His overemphasis of one aspect of the monastic life to the exclusion of all else created a false problem. "The true vocation of the monks of the Benedictine family," Merton says, "is not to fight for contemplation against action, but to restore the ancient, harmonious and organic balance between the two. Both are necessary. Martha and Mary are sisters" (66).

Notes

[1] *Contemplative Prayer*, p. 45. Page citations are from *Contemplative Prayer*. Page numbers in *Climate* will be slightly different.

[2] By primary material I intend to designate the contents of the booklet of 1965; by secondary material the excerpts from *Prayer as Worship and Experience*.

[3] Thomas Merton/Naomi Burton Stone correspondence, unpublished, in the Thomas Merton Center, Bellarmine College, Louisville, Kentucky.

[4] This kind of adaptation is something that Merton readers are used to doing and do it with great spiritual profit.

[5] Thomas Merton, *The Wisdom of the Desert* (New York: New Directions, 1960), p. 10.

[6] *Wisdom of the Desert*, p. 6.

[7] *Wisdom of the Desert*, p. 20.

[8] *Wisdom of the Desert*, p. 20.

[9] *Wisdom of the Desert*, p. 20. The "Jesus Prayer" is usually expressed as follows: "Lord Jesus Christ, Son of God, have mercy on me, a sinner."

[10] *Wisdom of the Desert*, p. 23.

[11] *Wisdom of the Desert*, p. 11.

[12] This is what many people thought was the meaning of meditation. It was a meaning that brought frustration to the prayer life of many.

[13] Søren Kierkegaard, *The Concept of Anxiety: A Simple Psychologically Orienting Deliberation on the Dogmatic Issue of Hereditary Sin* (Princeton, N.J.: Princeton University Press, 1980), p. 59.

[14] The reader might want to compare what Merton says about "guilt" here with the way he discussed it in *The Inner Experience* (pp. 136-137).

[15] In *Thomas Merton on St. Bernard* (Kalamazoo, Mich.: Cistercian Publications, 1980), Merton develops in detail Saint Bernard's understanding of the three vocations in the Cistercian life. "Commenting on the Gospel of the feast [of the Assumption of the Blessed Virgin Mary], St. Bernard compares the monastery to the family which Jesus used to visit at Bethany. In the monastic community we find Lazarus, the penitent, Martha engaged in administration, and Mary the contemplative. All these three are

necessary to make the monastery what it ought to be, not only materially, but above all spiritually. They are the effect of the good order of charity in the monastery. It would be a distortion and a caricature of monastic life to demand that a community consist exclusively of one or the other of 'these orders.' It is a corruption of the Cistercian ideal to insist that everyone confine himself exclusively to the vocation of Lazarus. It is a further distortion of the Cistercian ideal when in actual practice, the house becomes a collection of querulous and somewhat excitable Marthas. Mary has chosen the best part. And yet not even Mary has a monopoly on the Cistercian ideal. The monastery is not expected to consist exclusively of Marys sitting at the feet of Jesus. If St. Bernard makes this last qualification, it is certainly not because he regretfully accepts it as inescapable. We are not to believe that the monastery ought to be peopled entirely by Marys, but that, since human nature is what it is, we must be content to let two-thirds live below the level of our true vocation. This is by no means the case. It is better that the community should live on these different levels, and all who live on their own level within the community are in fact fulfilling the Cistercian ideal" (pages 30-31).

"The Abbot of Clairvaux has shown us that the contemplative life is to be sought and preferred to the active life, but that the 'mixed life,' composed of action and contemplation together, is in a certain sense more necessary to the Church than contemplation alone and therefore it has a higher dignity than the life of pure or unmixed contemplation.... A very high degree of Christian perfection is necessary for the 'mixed' life, according to St. Bernard. He says that the most perfect souls combine in themselves the vocations of Martha, Mary and Lazarus. They excel at the same time in apostolic action, in contemplation and in works of penance" (page 106).

[16] *Devotio Moderna* was a revival of spirituality that originated in Holland in the fourteenth century. It stressed the inner life of the individual and the methodical practice of meditation.

[17] *Sancta Sophia* (Holy Wisdom) is a posthumous collection of his ascetical writings that expounds his teaching on the way of contemplation.

8

Zen and the Birds of Appetite

(With Some Reflections on Merton's Asian Journey)

When I raise the hand thus, there is Zen. But when I assert I have raised the hand, Zen is no longer there.

—D. T. Suzuki

The taste for Zen in the West is in part a healthy reaction of people exasperated with the heritage of four centuries of Cartesianism: the reification of concepts, idolization of the reflexive consciousness, flight from being into verbalism....

In 1931 Merton as a young lad of 16, staying the summer with his maternal grandparents in Douglaston, Long Island, spent a good bit of his time reading contemporary writers, among them one of his favorite novelists, Aldous Huxley. Little did he realize then that six years later, as a student at Columbia, he would be reading Huxley again, but a transformed Huxley. The man he had admired as a novelist had become a writer on mystical experience. One day in November of 1937 Merton and his friend Robert Lax were riding downtown on a New York City bus. Lax spoke eloquently about a book of Huxley's he had been reading. It was called *Ways and Means*. Merton bought the book. It opened a new vision of life to him. Huxley spoke of experiences of reality that put one in touch with a whole new world—a world beyond and above the superficial and ephemeral realities with which most people were content to live. The human problem, as he saw it, was that many people were so blinded by selfish interests, violence and ill-will, that they failed to use the means that could lead them to these higher experiences. The way Huxley proposed to reach this new dimension of reality was self-discipline, prayer and asceticism. This fascinated the young Merton. His heart as well as his mind was touched. He sought out the mystical writers of which Huxley had written. It seemed evident to Merton that, though he quoted people like John of the Cross and Teresa of Avila, Huxley was clearly more comfortable with Oriental mystics. With the enthusiasm he never ceased to bring to an issue that caught his interest, the twenty-two-year-old Columbia student set about searching the university library for books on Eastern mysticism. He spent long hours pouring over Weiger's French translations of Oriental texts. He was baffled, unable to make sense of them. It was this initial confusing encounter with the East which led to the rather sweeping conclusion he drew in *The Seven Storey Mountain* that Oriental mysticism, while "not evil *per se*..." was "simply more or less useless."[1]

By an interesting turn of events his thoughts about the mystical life were turned in a different direction by a Hindu monk, Bramachari. Merton met this monk from the East for the first time in 1938 at Grand Central Station in New York. Merton describes him as a "shy little man, very happy, with a huge smile, all teeth, in the midst of his brown face. And on the top of his head was a yellow turban with Hindu prayers written all over it in red. And on his feet, sure enough: sneakers."[2] Merton and this Eastern monk became good friends; indeed, on his Asian journey in 1968 he tried, though without success, to contact his Hindu friend in Calcutta.

Bramachari seemed to sense from the beginning that his young friend was feeling his way toward some settled religious conviction and toward some kind of life centered in God. He made no attempt, however, to change the young Merton's attitude toward the religions of the East; instead, he said to him: "There are many beautiful mystical books written by the Christians. You should read St. Augustine's *Confessions* and *The Imitation of Christ*."[3] Merton later reflected on Bramachari's advice:

> Now that I look back on those days it seems to be very probable that one of the reasons why God had brought him all the way from India was that he might say just that.... After all, it is rather ironical that I had turned, spontaneously to the east, in reading about mysticism, as if there were little or nothing in the Christian tradition.... So now I was told that I ought to turn to the Christian tradition, to St. Augustine—and told by a Hindu monk![4]

Five months after his meeting with Bramachari, Merton was received into the Roman Catholic Church. Three years later, on December 10, 1941, he entered the Abbey of Gethsemani to become a Trappist monk. As a monk, he read deeply in the "many beautiful mystical books written by the Christians." He steeped himself in the writings of the early Church writers, the Fathers and Mothers of the Desert, the great Cistercian writers of the twelfth century, the fourteenth- and sixteenth-century mystics. His reading—and writing—firmly established him in the apophatic tradition that stemmed from Gregory of Nyssa and Pseudo-Dionysius down to the Rhenish mystics of the fourteenth century and Saint John of the Cross in the sixteenth century. Over and over again, as we have seen in earlier chapters, Merton describes the contemplative experience as one of "self-naughting," darkness and negation that is beyond verbalization, beyond rationalization. More and more, he attempts to describe the contemplative life—as he said he would in the preface to the revised edition of *Seeds of Contemplation*—in terms of experience rather than in precise dogmatic statements.

This emphasis on experience beyond concepts and verbalization inevitably led Merton back to Eastern thought. Thus it was his study of his own Christian tradition that enabled him in the late fifties and the sixties to look once again at Eastern thought. He did so with a new sympathy and openness, as well as with a mind-set, formed by his immersion in his own religious tradition, that enabled him to understand and appreciate what had been simply puzzlement to him as a young university student. As I have said elsewhere: "He had to find the East in the West before he could find the East in itself."[5] He wrote about Hinduism, Buddhism, Confucianism, Taoism,[6] but I think it fair to say that his special interest was in Zen. Not Zen Buddhism, which can be discussed as a religious system, but simply "Zen," as pure consciousness, not necessarily related to any particular religious system. Zen can "work" with any particular system or religion. "It can," Merton writes, "shine through this or that system, religious or irreligious, just as light can shine through glass that is blue, or green, or red, or yellow. If Zen has any preference it is for glass that is plain, has no color, and is 'just glass'" (4). Zen is about experience, not about words that tell you about experience. This is something that students of Zen need to learn. The story is told of a Zen master named Sekito (700-790) whose students repeatedly asked him to tell them what Zen was. After many refusals on his part, he finally appeared to consent. He told them to gather in an auditorium. When they were all assembled, he walked in, went to the lectern and said: "For the clarification of the sutras, there are sutra scholars. For philosophical explanations, there are philosophers. I, however, am a Zen master and you need to realize it." With that he stepped off the rostrum and left the room—leaving students puzzled, but perhaps closer to the Zen experience than they had been before. He wanted them to realize that philosophical explanations would not bring them any closer to enlightenment. For one can never get to the real experience itself by logical interpretations.

When Merton wrote "The whole aim of Zen is not to make foolproof statements about experience but to come to direct grips with reality without the mediation of logical verbalizing" (37), he was accurately summing up the meaning of Zen. But more than that, he was also summing up what for so many years he had been saying about Christian contemplation.

If it was a Hindu monk who encouraged Merton to study Christian mystical writing, it was a Japanese Zen master, the late Daisetz T. Suzuki, who gave him an insight into Zen that enabled him to become one of its most authentic interpreters to the Western world. Merton began reading Suzuki's writings in the late fifties. His admiration for this Zen master was profound. In *Zen and the Birds of Appetite* he calls the Japanese scholar a remarkable man who "contributed no little to the spiritual and intellectual revolution of our time" and who brought "the active leaven of Zen insight" "into the already bubbling ferment of Western thinking" (59). "Speaking for myself," Merton wrote, "I can venture to say that in Dr. Suzuki, Buddhism finally became for me completely comprehensible, whereas before it had been a very mysterious and confusing jumble of words, images, doctrines, legends, rituals, buildings, and so forth" (59).

Merton's contact with Suzuki was threefold: in his many works in English on Buddhism and Zen that had been translated into English (which Merton read in the late 1950's), in a written dialogue with him published in 1961, and in a face-to-face dialogue at Columbia University in 1964. Merton was much impressed with Suzuki's writings, which he considered "the most complete and authentic presentation of an Asian tradition and experience" available to English-speaking readers. "The uniqueness of Dr. Suzuki's work," he wrote, "lies in the directness with which an Asian thinker has been able to communicate his own experience of a profound and ancient tradition in a Western language" (62-63).

Dialogue With Suzuki

The written dialogue between them, which comprises Part Two of *Zen and the Birds of Appetite*, grew out of Merton's *The Wisdom of the Desert*. The book was a translation of selected "sayings" of the Desert Fathers. In translating the *Verba Seniorum*, Merton had been struck by the fact that the "words" of the Desert Fathers bore a remarkable resemblance to some of the stories told of the Japanese Zen masters. "There are countless Zen stories that almost exactly reproduce the *Verba Seniorum*—incidents which are obviously likely to occur whenever men seek and realize the same kind of poverty, solitude and emptiness" (100).

Merton sent the text of his translation to Suzuki with the suggestion that they engage in a dialogue about the "wisdom" of the Desert Fathers and the Zen masters. Suzuki accepted the invitation. But Dom Gabriel Sortais, the French Abbot General of the Cistercians, refused his approval for publication of *The Wisdom of the Fathers*, if it included Suzuki's text. Catholics, he feared, might be misled by the inclusion of a Zen master's reflections in a book about early Catholic monastics. He did say, however, that the Merton-Suzuki dialogue might be published in some American journal. This happened in 1961, when "Wisdom in Emptiness: A Dialogue by Daisetz Suzuki and Thomas Merton" was published.[7] In 1968 it was reprinted as Part Two of *Zen and the Birds of Appetite* (pages 99-138).

Significantly, for his part of this dialogue, Suzuki chose as the common ground for this dialogue between East and West, not the ascetical and meditative practices of the desert spirituality, but what Merton calls "the most primitive and most archetypal fact of all Judaeo-Christian spirituality: the narrative of the Creation and Fall of man in the Book of Genesis" (103).

Suzuki equates the original state before the fall with innocence—the state of undifferentiated unity, above the distinction of good and evil, in which everything one does is good. Doing what was good was the natural thing to do. This was the state of true consciousness. All this was changed by the "fall." Human persons became morally "concerned," Suzuki states, only after they fell from the state of innocence into the state of knowledge: the knowledge of good and evil. Knowledge begets "moral" consciousness, for it "differentiates just from unjust, good from evil, right from wrong, foes from friends" (106). In such a condition a person no longer chose the good or the just or the right naturally. There was an inner struggle because the natural attraction to the good (which belonged to the state of innocence) was gone. To be in a state where evil could be as attractive as good was to be in a state of illusion (unreality). Thus, knowledge, with its pair of discriminating eyes, sees no longer unity but difference. Since it is not seeing what really is, Suzuki identifies it with ignorance. Ignorance thus creates the unrealistic world of dualism, a world of "either-or": contemplation or action, God or the world, love of God or self-love.

Human life must involve keeping innocence (wisdom, *prajna*) and knowledge (ignorance) in proper balance—a difficult thing to do in a world where "the growth of Knowledge is everywhere encouraged in a thousand and one ways" (115). The human task is to regain, or, better, to recognize that one already possesses in a hidden way that primitive mindedness, that undifferentiated consciousness, which in the Genesis story is symbolized by innocence and in Zen by emptiness. The mind must be emptied of all that pollutes it. What is it that pollutes the mind? It is the egocentric consciousness; namely, the ignorance (knowledge) that distinguishes ego from non-ego. Once the mind realizes the truth of emptiness (innocence), then it knows that there is no self, no ego, no *atman*.[8] One is reminded here of Paul's words, which also speak of emptiness: "[I]t is no longer I [*ego*] who live, but it is Christ who lives in me."[9] Emptiness is a state of zero in which all good is performed and all evil is avoided. This is "zero," not as a mathematical symbol but as the infinite—the storehouse of all possible good or values. Zero, Suzuki says, equals infinity and infinity equals zero.

Suzuki finds a parallel to this idea of emptiness in the writings of the Rhenish mystic, Meister Eckhart, who speaks of the "most intimate poverty" whereby a person is emptied of things, creatures, himself and even God. If a person leaves in himself a place for God to act, he is not yet truly empty.

For God himself must be the place where God acts.

> If God once found a person as poor as this [i.e., without
> even a place for God], he would take the responsibility of
> his own action and would himself be the scene of action,
> for God is one who acts within Himself. It is here, in this
> poverty, that man regains the eternal being that once he
> was, now is and evermore shall be. (110)

It is only in this "most intimate poverty" of total selflessness,
Dr. Suzuki tells us, that "we find ourselves to be the ordinary
Toms, Dicks and Harrys we had been all along" (114). For the
experience of emptiness is not only metaphysical and
ontological, it is existential and empirical, too.

In his reply to Suzuki, called "The Recovery of
Innocence," Merton writes that the Desert Fathers went into
the desert to seek the "lost innocence, the emptiness and
purity of heart that had belonged to Adam and Eve in
Eden"(117). The paradise they sought was not an outward
one but a paradise within themselves. They strove for "purity
of heart," that primal unity that had been shattered by the
"knowledge of good and evil" that resulted from the fall.
Humanity, once a unity in Adam, but divided into a
"multitude" by the fall, recovers unity, innocence and purity
in Christ, the New Adam. The individual dies with Christ to
the "old man," [fallen humanity] that is his exterior,
egotistical self, and rises in Christ to the "new man"
[humanity redeemed]: "a selfless and divine being, who is
the one Christ, the same who is 'all in all'" (117).

Merton sees the difference between Christianity and
Buddhism in the fact that "emptiness" for the Buddhist
seems to be a complete negation of personality, whereas
"purity of heart" for the Christian means a supreme and
transcendent fulfillment of personality. The problem, as he
sees it, is that Christian thought and Zen thought often
appear at opposite poles which actually fail to represent their
true positions. Thus, Christian thought all too often seems to
identify personality with the illusory, exterior ego-self, which
is by no means the true Christian person. Buddhist thought,
on the other hand, appears to deny any positive value to

personality, yet this is not in fact Buddhist practice. For, as Suzuki stated, as noted above, when people become "absolutely naked," they find themselves to be the ordinary Tom, Dick or Harry that they had been all along. The difference, in part at least, is one of language: the Zen language of "emptiness" being more radical, austere and ruthless, and the Christian language of "purity of heart" expressing itself more in metaphorical terms and concrete imagery, though always with the realization that one must penetrate the surface and reach the inner depths. "In any case," Merton says, "The 'death of the old man' is not the destruction of personality, but the dissipation of an illusion, and the discovery of the new man is the realization of what was there all along, at least as a radical possibility, by reason of the fact that man is the image of God" (118). Merton believes that Suzuki's formula, zero equals infinity, can be equated with the basic Christian intuition of divine mercy, which is grace considered not "as a reified substance given to us by God from without," but "precisely as emptiness, as freedom, as liberality, as gift" (136-137). In Christian thought, emptiness and nakedness, because they are pure gift, equal fullness.

> But lest the idea of gift be interpreted in a divisive "dualistic" sense, let us remember that God is his own gift and that the gift of the Spirit is the gift of freedom and emptiness. His giving emerges from his Godhead, and as Ruysbroeck says, it is through the Spirit that we plunge back into the essential nakedness of the Godhead where "the depths themselves remain uncomprehended. This is the dark silence in which all lovers are lost." (137)

The Merton-Suzuki dialogue is sometimes difficult to follow—and still more difficult to summarize—as each tries to use the language of the other to clarify his own tradition. The fact that, despite differences of vocabulary, they were able to communicate in depth is at once a sign of the unique ability of each of them to interpenetrate the thoughts of the other and a model of what interreligious dialogue can accomplish when one tradition opens its eyes to the reality of another. The exchange was possible only because each had penetrated to the depths of his own tradition. The "innocence" of Thomas Merton encountered the "emptiness" of Daisetz Suzuki and they found that in many respects they were in the same "place," or, if one prefers, the same "no-place."

Meeting With Suzuki[10]

Having met Suzuki in his works and in written dialogue, Merton had the pleasure of meeting him in person when the Japanese scholar made his last visit to the United States. On June 12, 1964, Merton received a letter from Suzuki's secretary, Miss Okamura, saying that he would be in New York City and that, while he definitely could not come to Gethsemani, he would be pleased to have Merton come to meet him in New York. The abbot gave permission for the trip and on June 15 Merton flew out of Louisville. He recalled the thrill he experienced when the hostess asked him his destination and he said "New York" and realized that he was "going home."

The Trappist monk and the Zen scholar had two long talks.[11] Suzuki had read several of Merton's books and commended him for what he had written on Zen. Merton left the talks profoundly impressed at the deep understanding that existed between himself and this frail but alert scholar, then ninety-four years of age, whose writings he had read for so long.

> One had to meet this man in order fully to appreciate him. He seemed to me to embody all the indefinable qualities of the "Superior Man" of the ancient Asian, Taoist, Confucian and Buddhist traditions. Or, rather, in meeting him, one seemed to meet that "True Man of No Title" that Chuang Tzu and the Zen Masters speak of. And of course this is the man one really wants to meet. Who else is there? In meeting Dr. Suzuki and drinking a cup of tea with him, I felt I had met this one man. It was like finally arriving at one's own home. (60-61)

Merton felt, too, that in meeting Suzuki he had come to understand Buddhism as never before, not because they had talked about abstract doctrinal matters (for they had not), but because he had come face to face with a man who lived what he had written about. "One cannot understand Buddhism," Merton wrote, "until one meets it in this existential manner, in a person in whom it is alive" (62). Perhaps this may be something of a comfort for readers who have struggled through the previous pages of this chapter!

Merton's encounters with Suzuki bore fruit not only in his own life but in a series of articles written after the New York City visit that were published in various places and eventually gathered together in Part One of *Zen and the Birds of Appetite*.

This section brings together some nine articles on Zen, all of which were published in the last three years of Merton's life. The first, called "The Study of Zen" was originally published in the *Cimarron Review* of Oklahoma State University in June, 1968. Next is "The New Consciousness," which appeared in a journal of McGill University.[12] The third article is actually a preface which Merton contributed to *The Golden Age of Zen*, written by his friend John C. H. Wu. The book was published in 1967, though Merton wrote the article in July, 1966. Article four is about his mentor in the study of Zen, "D. T. Suzuki: the Man and his Works," first published in *The Eastern Buddhist*.[13] The fifth article is about a Japanese scholar of Zen Buddhism who died in 1945 (when Merton was only four years at Gethsemani and had not yet made any deep connection with Zen). The article is called "Nishida: A Zen Philosopher," and is actually a review of a book by Kitaro Nishida (*A Study of Good*) which Merton wrote for the Cistercian journal, *Collectanea Cisterciensia*.[14] Article six "Transcendent Experience," appeared in the *R. M. Bucke Memorial Society's Newsletter*.[15] Article seven, titled simply "Nirvana" was first written as a foreword to a dissertation by a Smith College student, Sally Donnelly. The dissertation was called "Marcel and Buddha: A Metaphysics of Enlightenment." Merton's essay was published in *The Journal of Religious*

Thought.[16] The final article, called "Zen in Japanese Art" was a review of a book by that name written by Totshimitsu, translated from the German by John Petrie in 1962. Merton's review was published in *The Catholic Worker*.[17]

Clearly it is not possible for me to attempt to summarize all these articles individually. I shall try to touch on what I think are fundamental insights that can be gleaned from them, as a way of understanding Zen. Before discussing these themes, I want to quote from two brief, but insightful reviews of *Zen and the Birds of Appetite*. One reviewer, Francis Sweeney, English professor at Boston College, points to a quality of Merton that we considered in the Introduction. The book, he says, "shows Merton's flair for synthesis (his noble mind was essentially French) and his openness to the entelechies[18] of other cultures."[19] The other reviewer notes how the essays in this collection move back and forth in the period before 1968—Part Two, in fact, going back to 1961. The reviewer suggests that the book shows "the growth of the poet to a new clear eye and calmer center." He continues:

> When the reader is finished he realizes that Merton meant to show that he started writing about Zen with unwieldy words and twisty theologizing. In this way the book is dramatic and revelatory; its mode is partly autobiography, partly confession, and partly and humbly a song of Merton's self. As the essays approach the present, Merton's sentence structure, argumentation, diction and tone relax; parenthetical awkwardness, debate-class rhetoric, latinate diction, and half-recognized biases change into progressively clearer and better-humored prose. And so the book escapes the word-idea-style traps of Merton's earlier *Mystics and Zen Masters*.... Like a haiku the book demonstrates Merton's final vision, and like a koan it challenges the reader's. As a look into the style and thinking and writing and living of a Catholic monk who knew at last his Zen-nature, too, it is unique in English.[20]

I quote these perceptive reviews as a help to the reader in dealing with a book that is not easy to read unless one has a reasonably good understanding of Eastern thought. I offer them also as an encouragement to the reader. They offer, I believe, some assurance that, despite the difficulties the book may raise, it will be worth the effort to struggle with it; indeed it will be rewarding to spend some time with *Zen and the Birds of Appetite*. I hope that the comments that follow, which represent my attempt to synthesize what Merton has written, will make the reader's journey through this book a bit easier and—even more than that—a truly rewarding experience.

Toward an Understanding of Zen

The first instinct of one who may have a superficial acquaintance with Zen is to study it as a religion. As a religion, it may be placed in the context of Chinese and Japanese history and seen as "a product of the meeting of speculative Indian Buddhism with practical Chinese Taoism." One may read books about Zen and make the assumption that, in doing so, he is learning the "doctrines" of Zen. He may then compare these with the doctrines of Christianity and perhaps reach the conclusion that, apart from the fact that both have something to do with meditation,[21] they are otherwise utterly alien to one another.

One could do this and perhaps find some justification in the history of religions for doing so; yet he would miss the point of Zen. For, whatever historical studies may have to say, responsible practitioners of Zen deny that it is a religion. They deny that it is a sect or school or that it is confined to Buddhism and its religious structure. "Zen is outside all structures and forms" (5). It is not a worldview or an ideology that attempts to explain the meaning of reality; indeed, Zen does not attempt to explain anything. It is not a philosophy; it refuses to make statements about the metaphysical structure of being and existence. It is not a theology; it is not concerned with God. It neither denies nor affirms a Supreme Being, though it is possible "to discover sophisticated analogies between the Zen experience of the

Void (Sunyata) and the experience of God in the 'unknowing' of apophatic Christian mysticism" (35). Zen is not a doctrine constructed to explain the Buddha's experience of enlightenment in order to propose it as a matter of "faith": rather, it seeks "an existential and empirical participation in that enlightenment experience" (36).

Zen as Transformed Consciousness

Zen is about consciousness, but a consciousness that is transformed. As such, it is beyond any system, structure or religion that would try to categorize or classify it. "But," as I quoted Merton earlier, "it can shine through this or that system, religious or irreligious, just as light can shine through glass that is blue, or green, or red, or yellow. If Zen has any preference, it is for glass that is plain, has no color, and is 'just' glass."[22] This transformed consciousness or superconsciousness has been compared by a modern Zen writer to a mirror.

The mirror is thoroughly egoless and mindless. If a flower comes it reflects a flower, if a bird comes it reflects a bird. It shows a beautiful object as beautiful, an ugly object as ugly. Everything is revealed as it is. There is no discriminating mind or self-consciousness on the part of the mirror. If something comes, the mirror reflects; if it disappears the mirror just lets it disappear.[23]

The meaning is that Zen consciousness does not try to fit things into artificially conceived *a priori* structures. It is simple attentiveness to reality. It "simply *sees* what is right there and does not add any comment, any interpretation, any judgment, any conclusion. It just *sees*" (53). This freedom from categorizing and classifying is exemplified in Zen language, which seems at times an anti-language, and in Zen logic, which often appears to be a reversal of philosophical logic. Zen does not have the habit of verbalization and rationalization, so common in the West, whereby we tend to falsify even our ordinary experiences. As Merton puts it:

> The convenient tools of language enable us to decide

beforehand what we think things mean, and tempt us all too easily to see things only in a way that fits our logical preconceptions and our verbal formulas. (48)

We do not see things as they are; we manipulate them to fit our prejudices.

Zen uses language against itself to blast out these preconceptions and to destroy the specious "reality" in our minds, so that we can see directly. Zen is saying, as Wittgenstein said: "Don't think: Look!" (49).

Zen is interested in the real, not the verbal. "When I raise the hand thus, there is Zen," says Daisetz T. Suzuki. "But when I assert I have raised the hand, Zen is no more there" (4).[24] As soon as you conceptualize an experience, you objectify it, and there is danger of confusing the concept with the experience itself, of forgetting that it is the experience which is real, not the description of it. "The whole aim of Zen," as I have quoted Merton earlier, "is not to make foolproof statements about experience, but to come to direct grips with reality without the mediation of logical verbalizing" (37). Zen involves attentiveness and receptivity to what is.

The awareness of Zen, therefore, is not the self-conscious awareness of a reflecting, knowing, talking ego, but pure awareness—an awareness that is immediately present to itself. It is not the experience of an ego-subject; it is experience pure and simple. "It just sees. Sees what? Not an Absolute Object, but Absolute Seeing" (54).

Zen is a direct experience of life, seized bare-handed, with no gloves on (as Suzuki puts it), that is at once an experience of undifferentiated unity (a non-dualistic experience) and at the same time of existential concreteness. It is not an abstract grasp of pure being: not an idealism that lays hold of invisible realities that lie beyond the visible, of noumena that are above phenomena. Rather, the invisible is grasped as imbedded in the visible; the noumena, in the phenomena. *Nirvana* (enlightenment) is *samsara* (the flow of everyday life).[25] Enlightenment, transformed consciousness, is to be found in the realities of one's daily life, in the flow of life with which one is identified. "There is certainly," Merton says, "a kind of living and nonverbal dialectic in Zen between the ordinary everyday experience of the senses (which is by no means arbitrarily repudiated) and the experience of enlightenment" (37). Enlightenment is the attainment of the "Buddha mind," yet an attainment that is no attainment, for the "Buddha mind" is not something esoteric that is "not there" which has to be put there. "The Buddha is your everyday mind" (7). Hence, the Zen saying that going to a monastery to seek enlightenment is like a man riding on an ass in search of an ass.

Zen Is Not Kerygma

Zen, therefore, is not, like Christianity, a revelation of life's meaning (though Christianity, too, when properly understood, is more than that); rather, it is a direct grasp of life in its unity and concreteness, in its pure, inarticulated ground—a grasp of what was always there, but not perceived, because an ego-subject cannot perceive it.

> [Zen] does not bring "news" which the receiver does not already have, about something the one informed did not yet know. What Zen communicates is an awareness that is potentially already there but is not conscious of itself. Zen is, then, not Kerygma[26] but realization, not revelation but consciousness, not news from the Father Who sends His Son into this world, but awareness of the ontological ground of our own being here and now, right in the midst of the world. (47)

Since Zen is a direct grasp of what was always there, right in the midst of the world, it is perfectly logical to say with Suzuki that "Zen teaches nothing": It merely enables one to wake up and become aware. True wisdom (Prajna) is not a replacement of old knowledge with new knowledge; it is a transformation whereby one knows what was always potentially knowable. Hence, the Zen master, when asked "What is knowledge?" could answer: "It is no knowledge." For, with enlightenment, nothing new is added from the outside. Or, as the Zen saying puts it: "When enlightenment is achieved, nothing is known, nothing is unknown." "Nothing is known," for no new knowledge has been acquired (it was already there). "Nothing is unknown," for the phenomenal world is simply a manifestation of "the primordial emptiness in which all things are one" (68).

Merton believed that modern persons, so fragmented in their own lives, so divided from other people, so caught up in their own prejudices that they live more often with illusion than with reality, have much to learn from Zen. For "it is nondoctrinal, concrete, direct, existential, and seeks above all to come to grips with life itself, not with ideas about life" (32). It is so much easier to talk about spirituality and spiritual awareness than to live it.

Christianity and Zen

Dom Aelred Graham's *Zen Catholicism* and William Johnston's *Christian Zen* suggest by their very titles the possibility of a dialogue between Christianity and Zen. Yet Merton, initially at least, seems to be dubious about such a possibility. He points out: "You can hardly set Christianity and Zen side by side and compare them. This would almost be like trying to compare mathematics and tennis" (33). What he seems to be saying is that it would be better to treat each by itself, without attempting any rapprochement between them. Yet this is clearly not Merton's intent, for the obvious purpose of his dialogue with Suzuki, as also of the other chapters in *Zen and the Birds of Appetite*, is precisely to show the points of intersection between these two approaches to reality.

The point that Merton is intending to make is, I believe, that you cannot compare Christianity and Zen as religions, that is to say, you cannot compare them at the level of doctrine. As he puts it: "To approach the subject [of Zen] with an intellectual or theological chip on the shoulder would end only in confusion" (33). For Zen is neither an intellectual approach to reality nor a theological explanation of human existence. Christianity, on the other hand, seems at first sight to be both. Zen is realization; it is not doctrine. Christianity is revelation; and through the centuries that revelation has been formulated into an elaborate system of doctrinal statements. Christianity is verbal: Much ink has been spilled in expounding its doctrines. Zen is, as far as possible, nonverbal. To compare the two at the level of doctrine, therefore, would be futile. For Christianity, doctrine is of primary importance; in Zen, it is accidental.

But there is a possible point of meeting for the two; namely, at the level of experience. Zen gives priority to experience; but so does Christianity, if it is properly understood. It is true that Christianity, unlike Zen, begins with revelation. But it is a mistake to think of this revelation simply as doctrine; it is the self-revelation of God calling the Christian to experience God in Christ. Granted, this revelation is communicated in words and statements, and Christians have always been profoundly concerned with the exact meaning of these statements and their precise formulation. Nonetheless, Christian theologians, at least in their better moments, have always understood that no conceptual formulation can adequately embody God's self-revelation. We must admit, however, the fact, to which history testifies all too well, that obsession with correct doctrinal formulas has often made people forget that the heart of Christianity "is a living experience of unity in Christ which far transcends all conceptual formulations" (39).

This was clearly the realization of the Apostolic Church. The kerygma of the early Church was not simply an announcement of certain propositions about Jesus Christ dead and risen; it was a summons to participate in the reality of his death and rising. It was a call to taste and experience eternal life. "[W]e declare to you the eternal life that was with the Father and was revealed to us—we declare to you what we have seen and heard so that you also may have fellowship with us; and truly our fellowship is with the Father and with his Son Jesus Christ."[27]

> Too often the Catholic has imagined himself obliged to stop
> short at a mere correct and external belief expressed in
> good moral behavior, instead of entering fully into the life
> of hope and love consummated by union with the invisible
> God "in Christ and in the Spirit," thus fully sharing in the
> Divine Nature. (40)

Christianity, as I have already pointed out, means much more than a change in behavior; it means a change in consciousness. And if it is understood in this way, it involves, just as truly as Zen, an experience that is transforming, an experience that can never be adequately grasped in verbal formulations.

It is worth noting that the early Church writers understood theology not so much as reflection on doctrine as the experience of the realities that doctrines attempt to express. This is still true to a large extent in the Christian East, where the theologian is not thought of primarily as one who writes books or gives lectures on theology but as one who has had the experience of God. The theologian is the saint who has something to say about God because he has experienced God.

With the rise of Scholasticism in the West, theology came more and more to be separated from experience. Initially a reflection on experience, it came to be a reflection on reflections, as it tended to move farther and farther from the experience. We need, therefore, to ask the question that Merton puts:

> To what extent does the theology of a theologian without
> experience claim to interpret correctly the "experienced
> theology" of the mystic who is perhaps not able to
> articulate the meaning of his experience in a satisfactory
> way? (45).

The question is an important one, for Christianity is much more than the intellectual acceptance of a religious message by a blind faith that understands the message only in terms of the authoritative interpretations handed down by Church experts.

> On the contrary, faith is the door to the full inner life of the
> Church. [It means] "access not only to an authoritative

teaching but above all to a deep personal experience which is at once unique and yet shared by the whole Body of Christ, in the Spirit of Christ.... [The] Holy Spirit is given to us in such a way that God knows Himself in us and this experience is utterly real, though it cannot be communicated in terms understandable to those who do not share it. (56-57)

Saint Paul calls this experience having "the mind of Christ."

Now, when we see that for Buddhism *Prajna* is describable as "having the Buddha mind," we understand that there must surely be some possibility of finding an analogy somewhere between Buddhist and Christian experience. (57)

Indeed, quoting the words of Eckhart: "In giving us His love God has given us the Holy Ghost so that we can love Him with the love wherewith He loves Himself," Suzuki calls them an exact expression of what Zen means by *Prajna* (wisdom). Further, Merton points out, Suzuki also equates with *Prajna* Eckhart's words: "The eye wherein I see God is the same eye wherein God sees me" (57).

It would seem clear that despite his initial reluctance to compare Christianity and Zen on theological grounds, Merton ultimately reaches the conclusion that theology may well be the most fruitful meeting place of Christian-Zen dialogue, so long as it is "theology as experienced in Christian contemplation" and "not the speculative theology of textbooks and disputations" (58).

Thomas Merton was much occupied with the problem of human consciousness: the need of a human person to arrive at an awareness of his true identity. The modern person, he believed, has open to him two approaches to consciousness. One begins with the thinking, self-aware subject; the other, with being ontologically perceived as beyond and prior to any subject-object distinction. The first approach is the Cartesian reflexive awareness by which one is preoccupied with his ego-self and sees himself as a subject over against objects in the world. This is clearly a dualism and a system of thought that denies or ignores the relatedness of all reality. The second approach is a consciousness in which one transcends his ego-self and achieves an immediate experience of undifferentiated being. The first involves a flight from being into verbalism and rationalization; the second, a discovery of the unity of being. The first (as I have suggested earlier) has dominated Western thought since Descartes (1596-1650). The second approach to consciousness is that which is characteristic of the Zen perception of reality.

The Cartesian person is "a subject for whom his own self-awareness as a thinking, observing, measuring and estimating 'self' is absolutely primary" (22). His stance in the world, Merton says, is characterized by self-consciousness, separateness and spectatorship. His self-awareness involves no consciousness of unity with what is real but of separateness from it as other. With this self-awareness swirling about his own limited subjectivity, he gazes out upon a world of objects and other subjects without ever experiencing reality from within itself. Such a person is a spectator, an outsider. This Cartesian alienation from reality in a "solipsistic bubble" is well expressed in Rilke's verse:

> And we, spectators, always, everywhere,
> Looking at, never out of, everything![28]

For this Cartesian thinking self, even God becomes an object that can be reached only by concepts. This perhaps is why an age that glorifies the ego-self is the age of "the death of God."

> Cartesian thought began with an attempt to reach God as object by starting from the thinking self. But when God becomes object, he sooner or later "dies," because God as object is ultimately unthinkable. God as object is not only a mere abstract concept, but one which contains so many internal contradictions that it becomes entirely nonnegotiable except when it is hardened into an idol that is maintained in existence by a sheer act of will. (23)

Willie Yaryan has expressed the Cartesian problem with God:

> As inheritors of the Cartesian point of view, we cannot conceive of a subject other than as an object looked at

subjectively.... The subject/object structure of our language lures us into thinking it reflects reality, while, in fact, it constructs reality in its own image, a false reality because it excludes God.[29]

Elsewhere in this book, I have already indicated how central to Merton's thought is the realization that God cannot be turned into an object. When one attempts to do this, the object thus conceived is not God, but an idol.

Many Christians today, exhausted by the effort to preserve a contradiction in existence, "have let go the 'God-object' which their fathers and grandfathers still hoped to manipulate for their own ends" (23). Yet liberation from the strain of maintaining an "idol" in existence has not left the Cartesian consciousness any less imprisoned within itself. Hence, it feels the need to break out of itself and somehow to meet the "other" in "encounter," "openness," "fellowship," "communion." These are "in-words" for today's Cartesian person struggling in vain to escape the ego-prison. "I-Thou" relationships with the "other" have become the desirable goal. "Yet the great problem is that for the Cartesian consciousness, the 'other,' too, is object." Hence, it is legitimate to ask, as Merton does: "Is a genuine I-Thou relationship possible at all to a purely Cartesian subject?" (23).

It is the bankruptcy of the Cartesian approach to reality that has led many people, including Merton, to seek another model for approaching reality. And many have found the Zen model a congenial one—a model that not only suits the needs of modern people but also squares well with the Christian contemplative experience of reality. Merton writes in *Conjectures of a Guilty Bystander*:

> The taste for Zen in the West is in part a healthy reaction of people exasperated with the heritage of four centuries of Cartesianism: the reification of concepts, idolization of the reflexive consciousness, flight from being into verbalism, mathematics and rationalization. Descartes made a fetish out of the mirror in which the self finds itself. Zen shatters it.[30]

Merton, therefore, reminds his readers that another model of consciousness—a metaphysical one—is available to a modern person. This model starts "not from the thinking and self-aware subject but from Being, ontologically seen to be beyond and prior to the subject-object division" (23). Being is understood not as an object of empirical observation that a subject comes to know by a process of rationalization; rather, there is an immediate intuitive experience that goes beyond reflexive awareness. What is experienced in the kind of consciousness Merton is speaking about is not an idea of being as something abstract and objective but rather a concrete non-objective intuition of what really is. (By "non-objective" Merton means that I do not turn "being" into an object apart from me of which I become aware.) It is not "consciousness of something," but pure consciousness, "in which the subject as such 'disappears'" (24).

The experience is, therefore, a unitive one in which the "other" is perceived not in separation but in oneness. It is a transcendent experience in which the ego-consciousness is left behind, so that the self is not its own center, around which all else orbits. Rather, its center is God, the one center of all, who is everywhere and nowhere, from whom all proceed and in whom all are encountered. Thus, from the very start, this consciousness is disposed to encounter the 'other' with whom it is already united anyway "in God."

To say that "the ego-consciousness is left behind" is not to deny the pragmatic psychological reality of the ego's self-awareness; it is simply to say that "once there has been an inner illumination of pure reality, an awareness of the Divine, the empirical self is seen by comparison to be 'nothing'"(26). This is to say that "it is contingent, evanescent, relatively unreal, real only in its relation to its source and end in God, considered not as an object but as the free ontological source of one's own existence and subjectivity."

Such a transcendent experience liberates a person from inordinate self-consciousness and from obsession with self-affirmation, thus leaving a person free simply to be himself or herself and to accept things as they are. For in this experience one lets go of one's own superficial thoughts and preoccupations in order to gain a deeper life in an unimpeded unself-conscious looking at reality. This deeper life is for the Christian a new and liberated life "in the Spirit." Zen calls it *Prajna*, which is "[t]he mature grasp of the primordial emptiness in which all things are one" (68).

It should be evident that, if the ego-consciousness is "left behind" in the transcendent experience, the empirical ego cannot be the subject of that experience. This forces a radical questioning of the whole nature of the experience precisely as experience. How can we speak of "consciousness" when the conscious subject can no longer be aware of itself as separate and unique?

In attempting to answer this question, Merton returns to the personalist vocabulary that he used in *The Inner Experience* and in *New Seeds of Contemplation*.

> The subject of this transcendent consciousness is not the ego as isolated and contingent, but the person as 'found' and 'actualized' in union with Christ. In other words, in Christian mystical tradition the identity of the mystic is never purely and simply the mere empirical ego—still less the neurotic and narcissistic self—but the "person" who is identified with Christ, one with Christ. "I live now, not I, but Christ lives in me" (75).

This "finding," "actualizing," which is an "awakening" of the transcendent self or the person, Merton describes in different ways. In the preface to the Japanese edition of *The New Man*, he calls it "spiritual rebirth."

> This deep consciousness to which we are initiated by spiritual rebirth is an awareness that we are not merely our everyday selves, but we are also one with One Who is beyond all human and individual self-limitation.[31]

In *Zen and the Birds of Appetite* he calls it a participation in "the mind of Christ." Quoting Saint Paul's words to the Philippians: "Let this mind be in you which was also in Christ Jesus...*who emptied himself*...obedient unto death. Therefore God raised him and conferred upon him a name above all names,"[32] Merton comments:

> This dynamic of emptying and of transcendence accurately defines the transformation of the Christian consciousness in Christ. It is a kenotic[33] transformation, an emptying of all the contents of the ego-consciousness to become a void in which the light of God or the glory of God, the full radiation of the infinite reality of His Being and Love are manifested. (75)

As Eckhart expresses it with his characteristic directness: "We love God with His own love; awareness of it deifies us" (75).

Similar to this kenotic experience of the Christian is the Buddhist experience of sunyata. The individual ego is completely emptied and takes on the mind of the Buddha.

> Thus the Buddhist enters into the self-emptying and enlightenment of Buddha as the Christian enters into the self-emptying (crucifixion) and glorification (resurrection and ascension) of Christ. The chief difference between the two is that the former is existential and ontological, the latter is theological and personal. (76)

But, Merton reminds us, when we speak of the Christian transformation of consciousness as being "personal," we must be careful to distinguish the person from the individual empirical ego.

What has been said of Christianity and Buddhism is actually true also in other higher religions: The path to transcendent realization is the path of self-emptying rather than self-fulfillment. The ego-self, instead of being realized in its limited selfhood, is described as simply vanishing out of the picture altogether. The reason for this seemingly negative terminology is "not that the person loses his metaphysical or even physical status, or regresses into non-identity, but rather that his *real* status is quite other than what appears empirically to us to be his status" (76).

Hence it becomes overwhelmingly important for us *to become detached from our everyday conception of ourselves as potential subjects for special and unique experiences, or as candidates for realization, attainment and fulfillment....* That is why a St. John of the Cross is so hostile to visions, ecstasies and all forms of "special experience." That is why the Zen masters say: "If you meet the Buddha, kill him" (76-77).[34]

Merton suggests that the difference between the "ego-self" and the "person" is a crucial area of dialogue between Eastern and Western religions. Is the transcendent consciousness achieved by the Buddhist the same as that achieved by the Christian? Do all religions meet "at the top," beyond their differing creeds and doctrines? Is having the Buddha mind the same "experience" as having the mind of Christ? Merton believes that we have not yet learned enough about different states of consciousness and their implications to be able to answer these questions in a definitive way. They are, nonetheless, questions that must be discussed, if there is to be fruitful ongoing dialogue between the East and the West. In an interesting letter to Erich Fromm on February 7, 1966, Merton speaks of a conversation he had with Ivan Illich:

> We had some discussion on the question of a non-theistic religious experience. The point I was trying to convey was that religious experience in the Jewish, Christian, Zen Buddhist, or in a general mystical human way, is an experience that may not be different as a human experience in the case of a theist or a non-believer. I am not denying the significance of various conceptual frames of reference, but I do believe that when it comes down to the phenomenon of the religious experience itself, the theological frame of reference is not as crucial as it may appear to be."[35]

Merton's Journey to the East

It was to further this interreligious dialogue that Merton journeyed to the East in 1968. (One cannot help but feel that after *Zen and the Birds of Appetite* this journey had to be the next step.) He went as a Christian monk, deeply grounded by years of study in his own tradition and totally committed to it, yet at the same time deeply convinced that there was much he could learn from firsthand experience of Eastern monasticism. In the notes he had prepared for a talk at the Temple of Understanding Conference[36] in Calcutta on October 23, 1968, he had written:

> I think we have now reached a stage of (long-overdue) religious maturity at which it may be possible for someone to remain perfectly faithful to a Christian and Western monastic commitment and yet to learn in depth from, say, a Buddhist or Hindu discipline and experience. I believe that some of us need to do this in order to improve the quality of our own monastic life and even to help in the task of monastic renewal which has been undertaken within the Western Church.[37]

Some might question the optimism with which Merton approached the East-West dialogue and the hopes he had for its success. No one can question the enthusiasm with which he entered into the dialogue. In reading *The Asian Journal*, one is amazed at the untiring eagerness with which he recorded subtle and often esoteric Hindu and Buddhist texts in his notebooks[38] and at the ease with which he seemed to establish instant rapport with the Dalai Lama and the many other holy persons whom he met on his journey.

Even if it be conceded that he was overly optimistic about the possible fruits of East-West contemplative dialogue (a concession that one need by no means necessarily make), he was in no sense "naive" about the "rules" that must guide the dialogue. He spelled them out most clearly in the notes he prepared for the Calcutta talk:

> (1) The dialogue must be reserved for those who have been seriously disciplined by years of silence and by a long habit of meditation. (2) It must avoid a facile syncretism, by (3) scrupulously respecting important differences that exist between religious traditions. (4) It must concentrate, not on secondary matters (such as institutional structure, monastic rules, and suchlike), but on what is essential to the monastic quest: namely, the meaning and experience of self-transcendence and enlightenment achieved through transformation of consciousness.[39]

Monastic dialogue between East and West, following such guidelines, was of crucial importance, Merton felt, for today's world. For the monk has something important to say to modern men and women, and he needs to say it with utmost clarity. Dialogue with other monastic traditions can help prepare him for the task.

> It is the peculiar office of the monk in the modern world to keep alive the contemplative experience and to keep the way open for modern technological man to recover the integrity of his inner depths.[40]

But, ultimately, communication through dialogue is not enough. Communication with words must yield place to communion without words: communion which, while it cannot dissolve differences, can in a certain way surmount them. For "communication takes place between subject and object; but communion is beyond the division: it is a sharing in basic unity."[41] This is what Merton was talking about when he concluded his Calcutta talk with these words:

> If [all] are faithful to their own calling...and to their own message from God, communication on the deepest level is possible. And the deepest level of communication is not communication, but communion. It is wordless. It is beyond words, and it is beyond speech, and it is beyond concept. Not that we discover a new unity. We discover an older unity. My dear brothers, we are already one. But we imagine that we are not. And what we have to recover is our original unity. What we have to be is what we are.[42]

On November 16, 1968, Merton met Chatral Rimpoche,[43] "the greatest rimpoche I have met so far," he said, "and a very impressive person." They talked for two hours, discussing points of Christian and Buddhist doctrine: the Risen Christ, *dharmakaya*,[44] suffering, compassion for all creatures. Chatral told Merton that he had meditated in solitude for thirty years and had not attained to perfect emptiness; Merton agreed that he hadn't either. "The unspoken or half-spoken message of the talk was our complete understanding of each other as people who were somehow on the edge of great realization and were trying, somehow or other, to go out and get lost in it."[45]

Did that realization come to Merton on December 2, 1968, when he visited Polonnaruwa in Ceylon and saw the Buddha figures there—the huge seated Buddha beside a cave, and a reclining Buddha on the right, with Ananda standing at attention? He describes the experience:

> Looking at these figures, I was suddenly almost forcibly jerked clean out of the habitual, half-tied vision of things, and an inner clearness, clarity, as if exploding from the rocks themselves, became evident and obvious.... I do not know when in my life I have ever had such a sense of beauty and spiritual validity running together in one aesthetic illumination.... My Asian pilgrimage has come clear and purified itself. I mean, I know I have seen what I was obscurely looking for. I do not know what else remains, but I have now seen and have pierced through the surface and have got beyond the shadow and the disguise.[46]

What was the "surface" he had pierced through? Was it that of Asia or of himself? Though the words seem to mean the first, they could also mean the second. Had Merton come halfway across the world to realize at last the experience of emptiness and that total transformation of consciousness that were the goal of his life? Had he, in the presence of the Buddha figures, at long last entered fully into the kenotic experience of the paschal mystery and put on the mind of Christ? We cannot answer these questions; and perhaps we have no right to ask them. But this much we can say: His conversation with Chatral Rimpoche and his experience at Polonnaruwa give a special poignancy to the words he spoke on the last day of his earthly existence. In Bangkok on December 10, 1968, he said to a gathering of Christian monks and nuns from various parts of Asia:

> The monk is a man who has attained or is about to attain, or seeks to attain, full realization. He dwells in the center of society as one who has attained realization—he knows the score. Not that he has acquired unusual or esoteric

information, but he has come to experience the ground of his own being in such a way that he knows the secret of liberation and can somehow or other communicate this to others....

The whole purpose of the monastic life is to teach men to live by love. The simple formula, which was so popular in the West, was the Augustinian formula of the translation of *cupiditas* into *caritas*, of self-centered love into an outgoing, other-centered love. In the process of this change the individual ego was seen to be illusory and dissolved itself, and in place of this self-centered ego came the Christian person, who was no longer just the individual but was Christ dwelling in each one.[47]

These are words he might have spoken to the monks at Gethsemani. It is indeed a paradox of Divine Providence that this "pilgrim of the Absolute," who had insisted that his monastery was not a "home," spoke these words thousands of miles away from his monastery; and then, in solitude, joined the company of "the burnt men."[48]

Notes

[1] See *Seven Storey Mountain*, p. 188.

[2] *Seven Storey Mountain*, p. 195.

[3] *Seven Storey Mountain*, p. 198.

[4] *Seven Storey Mountain*, p. 198.

[5] William H. Shannon, *Silent Lamp: The Thomas Merton Story* (New York: Crossroad, 1994), p. 279.

[6] In the last years of his life Merton developed an interest in the Muslim mystics, the Sufis, and lectured on them at Gethsemani. Unfortunately he never got to write in any detailed way about Sufism.

[7] *New Directions*, No. 17, pp. 65-101.

[8] *Atman* is the Hindu term for the self or the soul. In Hinduism *atman* is one with Brahman (God). But a transformation of consciousness is necessary before one can realize this truth.

[9] Galatians 2:20.

[10] The story of Merton's meeting with Suzuki, as well as the letters they exchanged, have been published in *Encounter: Thomas Merton & D. T. Suzuki*, ed. and intro. by Robert E. Daggy (Monterey, Ky.: Larkspur Press, 1988).

[11] Appropriately, their visit took place at Columbia University, where Merton had studied and in New York City and where, twenty-six years earlier to the very month, he made met under very different circumstances with the Hindu monk, Bramachari.

[12] *The R. M. Bucke Memorial Society's Newsletter*, Vol. II, No. 1, April, 1967.

[13] (New Series), Vol. II, No. 1, August, 1967.

[14] Vol. 29, 1967.

[15] Vol. I, No. 2, 1966.

[16] Vol. 24 (1967/1968).

[17] July-August, 1967.

[18] This is not exactly a household word. It means a condition in which one's full being has been actualized or it may mean the vital force that leads to such actualization and completeness.

[19] Francis Sweeney, review of *Zen and the Birds of Appetite*, *New York Times Book Review*, March 30, 1969.

[20] *Choice*, Vol. 6, May, 1969, p. 382.

[21] The term *Zen* is the Japanese equivalent of *Ch'an* which, in turn, is the Chinese equivalent of the Sanskrit word *dhyana* which means "meditation."

[22] Thus, Dom Aelred Graham has written a book called *Zen Catholicism* and William Johnston one called *Christian Zen*.

[23] In *Zen and the Birds of Appetite*, p. 6, quoting Zenkei Shibayama, *A Flower Does Not Talk: Zen Essays* (Tuttle: Kyoto, 1967).

[24] Quoted in *Zen Catholicism* (New York: Crossroad, 1994), p. 19.

[25] *Nirvana* means "enlightenment." *Samsara* refers to the ongoing flow of everyday life. One achieves enlightenment in the very living of everyday life, rather than by going out of it.

[26] *Kerygma* in the New Testament is the announcement of the Good News that God has saved us in Jesus Christ. But it should be remembered that the kerygma does not call us to be something we were at first not intended to be. It is rather a call to realize what God from the beginning willed us to be. The kerygma is the announcement of the mystery hidden in God for all eternity: the divine will to make all one with God in Christ. See Ephesians 1:10.

[27] 1 John 1: 2-3.

[28] From *The Duino Elegies* (New York: Norton, 1978). Quoted in Thomas Merton, *Mystics and Zen Masters* (New York: Farrar, Straus, Giroux, 1967), p. 245.

[29] Willie Yaryan, "Seeing Through Language: Merton's Contemplation of Hidden Wholeness," *The Merton Seasonal*, Vol. 11, No. 4 (Autumn, 1986), p. 3.

[30] *Conjectures of a Guilty Bystander*, p. 285.

[31] *Honorable Reader*, p. 133.

[32] Philippians 2:5-10.

[33] The Greek word *kenosis* means "an emptying." In Philippians 2:6, we are told of Jesus that "he emptied himself, taking the form of a slave." Kenotic theology stresses the radical humanness of Jesus in the Incarnation.

[34] William Johnston comments on this iconoclastic Zen statement. It means, he suggests, that "if you see the Buddha, what you see is not the Buddha, so slay him." Johnston believes that a Christian, too, could say: "If you meet the Christ, slay him"—the meaning being that what you see is not the Christ. See William Johnston, *Christian Zen* (New York: Harper and Row, 1971), pp. 50-51.

[35] Unpublished in the archives of the Thomas Merton Center, Bellarmine College. This letter was apparently overlooked in the publication of *The Hidden Ground of Love*.

[36] The Temple of Understanding is a world-wide organization of religious leaders established to foster communication and understanding among the religions of the world. Established in 1960, it held its first Spiritual Summit Conference in Calcutta in 1968. Merton was invited to participate in this conference.

[37] Thomas Merton, *The Asian Journal of Thomas Merton* (New York:

New Directions, 1973), p. 313. In the talk he actually gave at the conference, Merton did not speak from his prepared notes.

[38] On October 22, 1968, Merton recorded in his journal: "I've had the idea of editing a collection of pieces by various Buddhists on meditation, etc. with an introduction of my own" (*Asian Journal*, p. 31).

[39] These guidelines from *Asian Journal* systematize what Merton had said earlier about religious dialogue: "I will be a better Catholic, not if I can refute every shade of Protestantism, but if I can affirm the truth in it and still go further. So too with the Muslims, the Hindus, the Buddhists, etc. This does not mean syncretism, indifferentism, the vapid and careless friendliness that accepts everything by thinking of nothing. There is much that one cannot 'affirm' and 'accept,' but first one must say 'yes' where one really can. If I affirm myself as a Catholic merely by denying all that is Muslim, Jewish, Protestant, Hindu, Buddhist, etc., in the end I will find that there is not much left for me to affirm as a Catholic: and certainly no breath of the Spirit with which to affirm it" (*Conjectures of a Guilty Bystander*, p. 144).

[40] *Asian Journal*, p. 317.

[41] Thomas Merton, *Love and Living*, Naomi Stone and Patrick Hart, eds. (New York: Harcourt Brace, 1985), p. 73. Merton continues: "[T]he higher religions all point to this deep unity, because they all strive after the experience of this unity. They differ, sometimes widely, in ways of explaining what this unity is, and how one may attain to it. Christianity sees this unity as a special gift of God. The religions of Asia tend to see this unity in an ontological and natural principle in which all beings are metaphysically one. The experience of unity for the Christian is 'unity in the Holy Spirit.' For Asian religions it is unity in Absolute Being (*Atman*) or in the Void (*Sunyata*)."

[42] *Asian Journal*, p. 308.

[43] *Rimpoche*, meaning "the precious one," is a name given to spiritual masters in Tibetan Buddhism.

[44] *Dharmakaya* means the cosmic body of the Buddha or the Buddha as Absolute Being.

[45] *Asian Journal*, p. 143.

[46] *Asian Journal*, pp. 233-236.

[47] *Asian Journal*, pp. 333-334.

[48] See *Seven Storey Mountain*, p. 423; also *Sign of Jonas*, p. 224.

PART FOUR

The Outer Landscape
of Contemplation:
The World

9

Is the World a Problem?[1]

A contemplative who has no sense of history, no sense of historical responsibility, is not fully a Christian contemplative.

It does us no good to make fantastic progress, if we do not know how to live with it, if we cannot make good use of it, and if, in fact, our technology becomes nothing more than an expensive and complicated way of cultural disintegration.

In 1987, as I mentioned in the Introduction, I wrote a new preface for *Thomas Merton's Dark Path*. That preface grew out of an uneasiness on my part about the first edition of that book. My good fortune in having the time and the opportunity to immerse myself deeply in Merton's writings had brought me to an awareness that a significant piece of Merton's understanding of contemplation was missing from the first edition of that book. What I had tried to answer then was the question: What did contemplation mean for Thomas Merton? What I had failed to do was even to broach the question: "Where did contemplation lead him?" To put it in other words, I had discussed contemplation in terms of its inner landscape (silence and solitude), but had largely ignored its outer landscape (the world). In the time that has elapsed since then, I have come to an awareness that it is inadequate, even inaccurate, to isolate what Merton had to say about contemplation from the deep need he experienced, especially in the late fifties and in the sixties, of assuming his share of responsibility for the social problems of the world in which he lived.

What I have come to realize is that the man who had left the world in order to become a contemplative had "returned to the world" precisely because he had become a contemplative. He "returned to the world" not by leaving the monastery but by becoming involved in his own way in the social issues that occupy American society. Such involvement, he came to understand, was not a betrayal of his monastic and contemplative vocation, but rather its fulfillment.

I am quite willing, then, to confess that in the first edition of *Thomas Merton's Dark Path*, I failed to lead the reader to a full understanding of all that contemplation involves. I am not willing, however, to assume all the blame for this failure. I want to place at least some of it on Merton, for it was only gradually that he came to realize that contemplation of necessity summons one to action and social engagement. This was hardly his earliest understanding. When he first became a monk, he saw the world only as something from which he wanted to escape—an understandable attitude, considering the mess he had made of so much of his life "in the world" up to that time.

Thus it was that in the best tradition of the elders of the desert, he was, in his monastic journey, fleeing from the world that he might give his whole life to the search for God. Early in his monastic life he writes: "Never since I have entered religion have I ever had the slightest desire to go back to the world."[2] In that striking prayer that brings *The Seven Storey Mountain* to so soaring a conclusion, he bemoans the distance he sees between himself and God and pours out his heart: "That is the only reason why I desire solitude: to be lost to all created things, to die to them and to the knowledge of them, for they remind me of my distance from You."[3] These are the words of a young man in deadly earnest. He does not want to belong to the world. He wants nothing that the world can offer. He wants only God; and to find him, it was necessary—so he thought at the time—that he completely abandon the world.

Fourteen years later (October, 1961) in the pages of *The Catholic Worker*, the same man is writing with passion and a sense of indignation that the one task God imposes on us in our day is to work for the total abolition of war. Christians, he says, must become active, with every ounce of concern, in leading the way toward a non-violent solution to international conflicts: They must mobilize all their resources for the struggle against war. Every other responsibility to which we are called is secondary in importance.

This sense of social responsibility, so clearly expressed in 1961 but whose roots are considerably earlier than that date, continued to grow. Writing three months later to a cloistered Brazilian nun, he expresses the need for human solidarity with people all over the world in facing not just our own problems but those of the entire world:

> The problems of our times are very great.... People seem exhausted with the labor of coping with the complications of this world in which we live. Yet it is absolutely necessary that we do so. We have got to take responsibility for it, we have got to solve the problems of our own countries, while at the same time recognizing our higher responsibility to the whole human race.[4]

Yet Merton makes clear that he writes as a contemplative who in his solitude had come to the conviction that at least some contemplatives "must try to understand the providential events of the day....

> God, works in history, therefore a contemplative who has no sense of history, no sense of historical responsibility, is not fully a Christian contemplative: he is gazing at God as a static essence, or an intellectual light, or a nameless ground of being. But we are faced with the Lord of history, and with Christ, the King and Savior, the Light of the world.... We must confront him in the awful paradoxes of our day, in which we see that our society is being judged.[5]

What happened during those fourteen years to change Thomas Merton from a world-denying ascetic to a man well ahead of his times in grasping the responsibility of Christians to grapple with the social issues of the day? The answer, of course, is that quite a number of things happened to him. The most important, I believe, is that he became a true contemplative. The more deeply he entered into the contemplative experience, the more he was pushed in a direction he could never have dreamed of when he "left the world behind" and entered the monastery of Our Lady of Gethsemani.

The author of the Letter to the Hebrews says: "It is a dreadful thing to fall into the hands of the living God."[6] So often, people seem content to live with a God who is an abstraction or even perhaps a projection of their own needs, fears or desires. In genuine contemplation one meets the living God "bare-handed, without gloves on," so to speak. The experience can be fearful, even dangerous. For it turns our world inside out and upside down. Contemplation transforms our consciousness and forces us to see reality in a new and totally different light. It gives a sense of oneness not only with God but with the whole of reality that exists only because it is grounded in God. That sense of oneness begets all sorts of responsibilities. Life is irrevocably changed. It can never be the same again.

Merton's contemplative experience taught him that one cannot find God apart from the rest of reality. For the world that God made—especially the world of people—while distinct from God, is nevertheless not separate from God. God is the hidden ground of love in all things. How could anything or anyone be separate from that in which it is grounded? Thus, in finding the One, Merton found the many. He found his sisters and brothers, and he found them in God. He realized that he was not in the monastery to escape people but to be there for them.

What did it mean to be there for them? Merton spent much of the last years of his life pondering the answers to that question. Probably he never answered it fully to his own satisfaction, but he knew that for him it was the right question. For if one really listens to God in contemplation, one hears the cries of people. On June 25, 1963, Merton wrote to Daniel Berrigan:

> What is the contemplative life if one does not listen to God in it? What is the contemplative life if one becomes oblivious of the rights of men [and women] and the truth of God in the world and in His Church?[7]

That was 1963. By that time this sense of oneness begetting responsibility was an abiding, irreversible stance in his life. Obviously it was an intuition whose full implications dawned only gradually upon him, as his maturing prayer life continued to distance him from the over-exuberant flight from the world that had defined his initial entrance into the monastery. This ripening intuition was given classical expression in what has been described as "the Vision of Louisville."

On March 18, 1958, Merton was in Louisville on an errand in connection with the printing of a new postulants' guide. Standing at the corner of Fourth and Walnut Streets, he had an experience which may well be described as "mystical." He saw the crowd of people hurrying about the shopping district and was overwhelmed with a realization that he loved all these people and that they were neither alien to nor separate from him. The experience challenged the concept of a separate "holy" existence that made him, because he was a monk, different from all of them. He experienced the glorious destiny that comes simply from being a human person and from being united with, not separated from, the rest of the human race.

Merton wrote about this experience twice: first in his journal on March 19 (Saint Joseph's feast), the day after it occurred, and second on September 20, 1965, as part of *Conjectures of a Guilty Bystander*. The *Conjectures* passage, written more than seven years later, was a considerable expansion of, and an enthusiastic reflection on, the much more sober journal entry. In his biography of Merton[8] Michael

Mott suggests that the journal entry[9] captures the experience more concretely, whereas the *"Conjectures* version" seems to distance Merton from the people he is writing about. Yet there is, I think, another way of looking at these two "versions." We do not always understand fully the significance in our lives of an experience, as we are undergoing it or even immediately afterwards. Hence, while the passage in *Conjectures* is indeed a later reflection and even something of a flight of poetic fancy, it may also be read as drawing out the broader implications of an experience whose meaning and significance grew as Merton reflected upon it. After it, his life did move in new directions to which the experience pointed, even though such directions may not have been entirely clear at the time. Moreover, the year 1958 was, I believe, a decisive year in Merton's life (significant as, among other things, the year he wrote to Pasternak in Russia and Pablo Antonio Cuadra in Nicaragua, the year of many conversations with Ernesto Cardenal, Nicaraguan novice at Gethsemani, the year of early ecumenical encounters, and the year of the election of Pope John XXIII). The "Louisville Vision," therefore, was not an isolated experience, but may be seen as one event on a trajectory of experiences that were almost inevitably thrusting him toward greater involvement in the social needs of the world of this time in his life. I might add, in passing, that this movement toward deeper involvement in social issues may help to explain why Merton's efforts to revise *The Inner Experience* were not brought to successful completion in 1959 and why he never got back to it again in any intensive way. It is in this context of a growth toward maturity in grasping the social responsibility of a contemplative that I should like to quote the *Conjectures* passage, remembering that it postdates the experience by a number of years, yet seeing it as an interpretation that later insight brought to that experience.

It is noteworthy that it takes place not in his monastic cell or in the monastic church, not even in the woods on the monastery grounds, but in the center of a shopping district at the corner of Fourth and Walnut Streets in the city of

Louisville. (Occasionally, overly ardent disciples of Merton, when they are in Louisville, go in search of that corner in the hope that they, too, may have a mystical experience! Alas, they are doomed to disappointment: That corner is now Fourth and Muhammad Ali Streets! Visitors after March 18, 1998, at least have the satisfaction of knowing that they are at the correct corner. On that day, the fiftieth anniversary of Merton's "experience," a bronze commemorative plaque[10] from the Kentucky Historical Society was unveiled at this very corner.) Here are Merton's words as he describes people emerging from stores in a shopping district:

> I was suddenly overwhelmed with the realization that I loved all these people, that they were mine and I theirs.... It was like waking from a dream of separateness, of spurious self-isolation in a special world, the world of renunciation and supposed holiness. The whole illusion of a separate holy existence is a dream.
>
> This sense of liberation from an illusory difference was such a relief and such a joy that I almost laughed out loud. And I suppose my happiness could have taken form in the words: "Thank God that I am like other men [and women]."[11]

His reflection on the experience, whether explicit or not at the time, enabled him to see that in some mysterious way his monastic solitude belonged to all these people.

> I have a responsibility for it in their regard, not just in my own. It is because I am one with them that I owe it to them to be alone, and when I am alone they are not "they," but my own self. There are no strangers![12]

He continues his reflection on the splendor of it all:

> Then it was as if I suddenly saw the secret beauty of their hearts, the depths of their hearts, where neither sin nor desire nor self-knowledge can reach, the core of their reality, the person that each one is in God's eyes. If only they could see themselves as they really are. If only we could see each other that way all the time. There would be no more war, no more hatred, no more greed.[13]

Merton goes on in this passage to speak of that hidden core in each of us as the *point vierge*, the point of light that is at the center of our being and "is like a pure diamond blazing with the invisible light of heaven." It is in everybody, he says, and "if we could see it we would see these billions of points of light coming together in the face and blaze of a sun that would make all the darkness and cruelty of life vanish completely..."

This moving word-picture of billions of points of light coming together in a blazing fiery unity reminds me of an experience I had several years ago, while making a retreat at what had been Merton's hermitage in the woods of Gethsemani. One evening, as I sat for a long time on the porch of the hermitage, it grew dark and the fireflies, so it seemed, began putting on an entertainment for me. There seemed to be hundreds or even thousands of them in the valley. One would light up here, and then another there. The thought came to me: What if they all lit up at once? The whole valley would be a blaze of fiery light. And I remembered Merton's words about those points of light in each of us and how if they could all come together in unity the darkness and cruelty of life would vanish. And yet, even as I reflected, I realized that my parallel was not entirely apt, since it must be said that we do not really come together in unity. The unity is there: We just have to recognize it. As Merton said at Calcutta in October, 1968 (in words quoted earlier): "We are already one. But we imagine that we are not. And what we have to recover is our original unity. What we have to be is what we are."[14]

It is one thing to arrive at a new insight, another thing to translate that insight into action. If Merton's "return to the world" (his discovery of the outer landscape of contemplation) was rooted in his contemplative experience and in the sense of unity it begot, the manner of that "return" was shaped by the historical circumstances in which he found himself and also by the people who became, in one way or another, associated with his life. In other words, it was inner forces that expanded his consciousness and made him aware that he had responsibilities to the world. But it was external and historical forces (many of them seeming to converge in the late 1950's, and especially, as I have suggested, in the year 1958) that helped him to identify concretely where those responsibilities lay and what they called him to do.

The equation is something like this: Coming to know God means coming to know people and coming to know people means getting involved in history at a particular point in time. Each period of history has its own lights and shadows. Merton felt keenly that the period of history in which he lived was a time of gigantic shadows. He identifies the shadows of his own time in a statement which links awareness of responsibilities with the concreteness of historical reality. The statement, though written in 1966, articulates an insight that had been his at least since the late fifties:

> That I should have been born in 1915, that I should be the contemporary of Auschwitz, Hiroshima and the Watts riots, are things about which I was not first consulted. Yet they are also events in which, whether I like it or not, I am deeply and personally involved.[15]

What that deep and personal involvement called him to was not always immediately apparent to him. Of one thing he was sure: The social needs of the time and his duties toward them would no longer allow him, as he himself expressed it in a letter to Pope John XXIII, "to lock myself into solitude and lose all contact with the rest of the world.... This poor world," he continues, "has a right to a place in my solitude."[16] Yet he was equally certain, as he makes clear in his rapier-sharing correspondence with Rosemary Radford Ruether, that he was not called physically to leave the monastery to struggle with what she called, in one of her letters to him, "the dehumanizing forces in the city of man."[17] Whatever appealing arguments there might be to the contrary, Merton knew that the monastery was the place where God willed him to be. He wrote to Ruether of his "genuine realization that this is my vocation," even though he admits that as yet he had not quite found the way "of being really true to it."[18] Still, he is quite clear "about wanting to stay in the bushes, provided I can make some sort of noises that will reach my off-beat friends."[19] These words were written in May, 1967, but they articulated a commitment that had long been ripening within him. In fact, nine years earlier, in his congratulatory letter to Pope John XXIII on the occasion of the latter's election to the papal office, Merton had expressed the same conviction in less casual fashion to the Pope. In the letter to Pope John the "off-beat friends" became the "many intellectuals everywhere in the world"; and the "noises," his writings which expressed understanding and sympathy with "the terrible problems" these people have to face. "I have to think," he writes to the Pope, "in terms of a contemplative grasp of the political, intellectual, artistic and social movements in this world." While there is an apostolic value in prayer and penance, there is yet more required of him: "a sympathy for the honest aspirations of so many intellectuals everywhere in the world and the terrible problems they have to face."[20]

The "noises" that Merton uttered in his many writings on social issues and the contacts he made with a wide circle of intellectuals from various parts of the world are not the subject of this book.[21] What I want to maintain is that these "noises" and "contacts" must be seen as the fruit of Merton's contemplation. They form the outer landscape (his involvement as a monk in the affairs of the world of his time) to which his contemplative experience inevitably led him. For contemplation has not only an inner landscape; it has also an outer landscape: the world. Whatever brings a person to solitude, contemplation prepares her to return to the world with a wiser set of priorities, with a deeper sense of what really matters. And probably with the realization that she had never really left the world. She brought it with her into her solitude. It is simply that contemplation enabled her to see the world in a different light. It is still a place where there is sin and injustice, violence and war. But it is also a grace-filled world. The contemplative sees a world transfigured because in Christ God has entered our world. We meet God in the everyday realities of life.

In his last ten years, Merton was a monk who "rediscovered" the world. He returned to the landscape of his troubled youth, but it was transformed by his contemplative consciousness. The world was aflame with God's presence and filled with wonderful people who were often confused and mixed up, at times loving and at times self-seeking, sometimes movingly compassionate, sometimes terribly cruel. It was, as he put it, a world

> ...in which people suffer together and are sometimes utterly beautiful, at other times impossibly pathetic. In which there is much that is frightening, in which almost everything public is patently phony, and in which there is at the same time an immense ground of personal authenticity that is right there and so obvious that no one can talk about it and most cannot even believe that it is there.[22]

As we reflect on this conversion experience that so changed Merton's life, we need perhaps to consider our own relationship to the inner and outer landscapes of contemplation. At some point in our lives, in the midst of a harried, hurried, busy world, we come to see (which really means, we receive the grace to see) that we need some kind of withdrawal from the busyness of the world, if we are to live our lives in an authentic way.

The inner landscape of contemplation beckons us. This grace may come to us in a time of retreat or from a book we read, or from conversations with friends or from some other event in our lives that we could never foresee. We begin to look for opportunities in our overcrowded schedule for some peace and quiet: some time to be with God, to acquaint ourselves with the inner recesses of our being. The frustration of locating this inner landscape in our lives may move us to cast at least a momentary glance of envy at monasteries, where that inner landscape of contemplation is built into each day's horarium. Those of us who do not have this monastic "luxury," must be sufficiently convinced of the need for this dimension in our lives that we make it an essential element of a life that may already have too many "essentials." The more we are able to experience (often at great odds) a reasonable amount of solitude, the more we are going to return to "our world" with the awareness that that we can no longer continue to live simply on the surface of life. The inner landscape of contemplation changes the way we see our world: that world becomes for us the outer landscape of contemplation. It is the "place" where we live out the insights into reality arrived at in contemplation.

This discovery (or better, recovery) of a contemplative dimension of our lives brings with it the realization that we are called, not just to a change in behavior (by becoming better persons), but also to a change of consciousness (which means becoming new persons). For it means nothing less than a spiritual revolution that awakens deep levels of consciousness in us: We see reality differently. We experience our true self and experience that self in God. We are aware that we are nothing apart from the being of God. This is what the early Christian writers called the discovery of the heart: the heart not as a physical organ, but as the center of our being, the place where we are most truly ourselves, the place where we experience God, the place where we find our sisters and brothers in an entirely new way. We experience an intuition of the unity of all reality that carries us far beyond the surface dualism that normally characterizes our superficial consciousness.

When we come to this awareness of a transfigured world, in which people are one with each another (though so many fail to realize that they are), we begin to understand that our task in that outer landscape of contemplation is to work together with others to build community. For it is only in the community (whether that is the family, the church, the country, the world) that the highest human values, such as human dignity, human freedom and opportunities for solitude and contemplation, are able to flourish.

The community is the place of freedom. It is the home of the person, namely, the one who is linked with his sisters and brothers in the unity of everything that makes them human and in a sharing of all that makes them one in Christ. In the community there is an awareness that, though each of us is unique and distinct as persons, we are nevertheless not separate. For we are all one in that Hidden Ground of Love, whom we experience in contemplation and in whom we find our identity and our uniqueness. Christ, in whom, as Paul says, the fullness of the Godhead resides by God's design, is the archetype of the person living in community. For the Christian to be a person is "to be in Christ." It is in the context of community that persons experience the call to and the opportunity for contemplation. It is in community that compassion and out-reaching love are able to thrive and flourish.

The alternative to the community is the collectivity, "mass society," in which people live in isolation and alienation from one another.[23] People whose lives are shaped by the collectivity and by the mass media lose all sense of the transcendent. This means that they are deprived of their natural capacity for contemplation. In an essay that has been much anthologized, "Rain and the Rhinoceros"[24] Merton analyzes the sickness of such a society, which, following Eugene Ionesco's powerful play (*Rhinoceros*), he calls "rhinoceritis." This disease consists in conformity with whatever is the norm of the moment. In Ionesco's drama everyone in the world, except Beranger, becomes a rhinoceros. He is the last human being on earth. He feels the pull to give up his humanness and join the herd, but something deep within him prevents him from doing so. He persists in remaining human in what has become a nonhuman world.

In his own notes on the play Ionesco makes the point that only solitude can save people from succumbing to the slavery of unthinking conformity that characterizes the collectivity. He writes:

> Forms of rhinoceritis of every kind, from left and right, are there to threaten mankind when men have no time to think or collect themselves; and they lie in wait for mankind

today, because we have lost all feeling and taste for genuine solitude. For solitude is not separation but mediation. It would, of course, be a misunderstanding to think that either the community or the collectivity exists in pure form. There is a bit of each in all of us. Our task is to expose, in ourselves as well as in society, the fallacies and illusions that the collective lives by and to work to build up the community and its values.[25]

What is especially significant for us today is that the struggle between the values of the community and the priorities of the collectivity takes place within the context of an ever-escalating technology. I want to stress that the escalation of technology has been especially rapid in our time. For it has certainly been true since the Industrial Revolution, and probably to some extent throughout the whole of history, that technology has had a strong voice in determining whether it will be the values of the community or the priorities of the collectivity that will predominate in a particular society. I would venture to say that there has never been an age in which its voice has been so strong and its influence so all-pervasive as in our own. Today as never before the question must be asked: Is it possible to be a contemplative in a technological society? I want to put this question in the context of Merton's thoughts on technology.

At this point it might be appropriate to clarify what we mean by *technology*. It has been defined as "the ensemble of various practices by which humans use available resources to achieve values." Technology has benefited the human race in a number of ways: It has made for greatly increased production; it has reduced the amount of human labor that must be expended; it has made labor easier; it can give some people a higher standard of living. (Thus, computer technology has made Bill Gates, CEO of Microsoft, the richest person in the world.)

But there are also many undesirable effects that come from technology: It has brought about environmental pollution; it has often led to a depletion of irreplaceable natural resources; it has led to a enormous "downsizing," in industry, as mechanization and automation take away the need for many workers—even the workers who remain are reduced largely to a state of passivity in which they forego all creativity. They are no longer there to guide the machine: It works by itself. The workers are there to watch and then repair when necessary. As the social philosopher Jacques Ellul puts it: The worker "no more participates in production than a boxer's manager participates in a prize fight."[26] In the same vein, Merton writes: "It is by means of technology that man the person, the subject of qualified and perfectible freedom becomes quantified, that is, becomes part of a mass—mass man whose only function is to enter anonymously into the process of production and consumption."[27]

I think it can be said that technology and its relationship to a contemplative way of life became a problem for Merton soon after Dom James Fox became abbot and started to modernize the monastery and its operations. The noisy tractors, replacing horses and wagons, annoyed a Merton who had come to the monastery seeking silence and had suddenly found it becoming a place of noise and distraction. In volume three of his journals, I noticed a journal entry for July 23, 1956. Merton was participating in a conference at St. John's Abbey in Collegeville, Minnesota. He writes of his walk by the lake. It is a scene of beauty and serenity, abruptly spoiled by noise, as he sees a machine approaching, leveling a new lawn. Then he recalled how the night before he had walked alone in the pasture swatting mosquitoes when, in his words, I saw "the tracks of my enemy, the caterpillar tractor."[28]

In the fourth volume of the journals, I discovered a lone reference to technology. It is the journal's first entry. Merton writes that it is customary "to assume that technological progress is an unqualified good, as excellent as it is inevitable. But it becomes more and more passive, automatic—and the effects on 'backward people' more and more terrible."[29] This stinging statement is followed by a sarcastic remark about a notice on the monastery bulletin board: "Today they proudly posted on the bulletin board...the news about an intercontinental missile fired from Florida and landing in the Indian Ocean. Something to be proud of! Have we lost all sense of proportion along with our faith?"[30]

It is in volume five of the journals that more frequent references to technology are found. This is understandable because it is fair to say, I believe, that it was not till early 1964 that the problem of technology became a subject of serious reflection for Thomas Merton. His interest in technology was largely due to the influence of the late Wilbur Ferry, who was then vice president of the Center for the study of Democratic Institutions at Santa Barbara, California.

In March of 1964 Ferry sent him an important booklet published by the Santa Barbara Center and titled *The Triple Revolution*. The first revolution described in the booklet is the cybernation revolution, which meant a new era of production, whose principles of organization are as different from those of the industrial revolution, as those of the industrial era were from the agricultural revolution. The cybernation revolution is brought about by a combination of the computer (the "thinking" part) and the automated, self-regulating machine (the "doing" part). The result of this revolution is an almost unlimited productive capacity which requires less human labor. The second revolution is the "weaponry revolution," which has produced weapons which could obliterate the human race. Such weapons of mass destruction show the utter futility of war and the need to work for its abolition. And the third revolution spoken of in the booklet is the "human rights' revolution," which is a worldwide revolution directed toward the establishment of social and political regimes in which every person will feel valued and none will feel rejected on account of race.

The Triple Revolution together with the signature of a number of prominent scientists and other scholars was sent to President Lyndon B. Johnson on March 22, 1964. On April 6, 1964, the president replied through Lee C. White, Assistant Special Counsel to the President, in a letter that said "the President has asked the Congress to establish a presidential commission to study the impact of technological change on the economy and to recommend measures for assuring the full benefits of technology while minimizing any adverse effects."

Merton, who received the booklet at the same time as the President, was deeply impressed. He responded immediately. On March 23, 1964, he wrote to "Ping" Ferry:

> *Triple Revolution* is urgent and clear and if does not get the right reactions (it won't) people ought to have their heads examined (they won't). (Even if they did, it would not change anything.) We are in for a rough and dizzy ride, and though we have no good motive for hoping for a special and divine protection, that is about all we can look for. I have recently been accused again of pessimism because I refuse to equate hope in God with an unbounded trust in our economic structures. How is it that so-called Christians (and they are perfectly sincere, even devout, nay holy) are totally convinced that the promises of God to Abraham are now totally invested in our spiritually and mentally insolvent society? One cannot question this first and basic truth without being hustled at least spiritually toward the stake.[31]

Ferry also introduced Merton to the writings of several social philosophers. One was Lewis Mumford, an American and a passionate critic of technology, who deplored the dehumanizing effects of modern technological civilization. Another was the French social philosopher, Jacques Ellul. Actually, it was Ferry and the Center for the Study of Democratic Institutions who introduced Ellul, not only to Merton, but to American scholars in general. In 1961 the center had already been much occupied with the subject of technology. This interest prompted them to ask Aldous Huxley about European works on the subject. Huxley recommended, above all, Jacques Ellul's work, *La Technique*, which had been published in 1954. Ferry persuaded the publisher Alfred A. Knopf to put out an English translation which was published in 1964. Merton read it as soon as he was able to get a copy. In volume five of the journals, writing on October 30, 1964, Merton says that he is reading Ellul's book, titled in English *The Technological Society*. "Great, full of fire-crackers. A fine, provocative book and one that really makes sense." He wonders whether or not the fathers of the Second Vatican Council, who were then involved in drafting what became "The Constitution on the Church in the Modern World," "are aware of the implications of a technological society."[32]

The following month, Merton had invited a number of leaders in the peace movement (including A. J. Muste, Jim Forest, Daniel and Philip Berrigan, John Howard Yoder and others), to a meeting held at Gethsemani from November 18 to 20, 1964. Though the topic of discussion for the meeting had been announced as "Our Common Grounds for Religious Dissent in the Face of Injustice and Disorder," a good bit of the time was spent in discussing the nature of the technological society. Was such a society oriented by its very nature to self-destruction or could it become a source of hope for a new "sacral" order, a new millennial "city" in which God would be manifested and praised and people would become free and enlightened? The participants agreed that, whatever the eventual answer might be, "technology at present is not in a state that is morally or religiously promising."[33]

The reason the discussion was steered in this direction was Merton's excitement over Ellul's book. On December 28, 1964, he wrote to a French Franciscan priest in Bordeaux, Herve Chaigne, about that November meeting.

> There was much discussion of a book which I at the time had just read, Jacques Ellul's great work on technology. Do you know Ellul? You must, I am sure. I admire his work and find it entirely convincing and indeed it has the stamp of prophecy which so much Christian writing on that subject seems to lack.[34]

Commonweal carried Thomas Merton's review of Ellul's book. In his brief review, Merton calls the book:

> [O]ne of the most important of this mid-century. It should be required reading for anyone who wants to evaluate the

relation of the church with the contemporary world. To assume that our massive technology is fully under the rational control of human intelligence orienting it toward a flowering and fulfillment of [humankind] is not only naive, but perilous. Ellul does not say it cannot be brought under such control. But he thinks the situation is desperate and we have not yet begun to do anything serious about it. This book is a frank, hard-hitting and doubtless controversial, statement of our most crucial problem.[35]

One of the chief problems that Ellul finds in technology is that it tends to absorb, to subsume into itself, traditional values that pre-technological societies have always cherished. More than that, or as a part of that, it tends to absolutize its own values which are power, profit and, as a means to these, greater and greater efficiency. Merton puts it this way: "Technology has its own ethic of expediency and efficiency."[36]

Now great power and enormous profit tend to separate people rather than unite them; thus they move in a direction that reverses the unitive thrust that characterizes contemplation. Power, almost of necessity, tends to be concentrated in the hands of the few, often at the expense of the many; and profit-oriented endeavors tend to enrich even more the already wealthy and to increase the poverty of the already poor. All this suggests that the basic momentum of technology is away from such things as human dignity, neighborly love and compassion, which make for true community, but are unrelated to technology's all-consuming drive: for efficiency, power and profit.

It is this subversion of fundamental human values that Ellul sees as a result of a society that has turned itself over to technology and is willing to do its bidding for the sake of the benefits it hopes to achieve. This, I think, is what Ellul means when he speaks of technique as "the stake of the century."[37] Some one has said, in criticism of Ellul: "Technology opens doors. It does not compel us to enter." Is this really true? Can we escape *technique*, even if we choose? Merton thought he had made such a choice. Yet technology caught up with him in the monastery.

Technology, Ellul maintains, is so pervasive that we now live in a milieu created by technology rather than in the milieu given to us in nature. Throughout his book Ellul insists that he is not making value judgments, but simply reporting the facts as they are.

So, a first problem about technology that one discovers in Ellul's book is its subversion or absorption of traditional values that easily lead to the disintegration of human culture. To quote Merton:

> It does us no good to make fantastic progress, if we do not know how to live with it, if we cannot make good use of it, and if, in fact our technology becomes nothing more than an expensive and complicated way of cultural disintegration.[38]

A second problem Ellul discusses is especially germane to our question: Can one be a contemplative in a technological society? Technology, he says, "desacralizes the world" in which we live. It cannot tolerate mystery. It sees it only as a problem to be solved, with the confident assurance that the solution is somewhere down the line. Technology as technology knows no world of spirit or mystery. Theologians and sociologists, on the other hand, have always recognized that humans live not only in a material world, but in a spiritual world. In that spiritual world forces operate that are unknown, and perhaps even unknowable. There is in the universe what Rudolf Otto calls the *mysterium tremendum et fascinosum*, the mystery that produces awe and fear, yet at the same time infatuates and allures. We are drawn to it, but it always remains incomprehensible to us. It is always mystery. That is its fascination: We come to know something about it. We can experience its presence, but we never pierce through the mystery. It is there always inviting us to deeper insight. Yet no matter how deep our insight, there is always more. We can never plumb the depths of what Merton calls "the hidden ground of love for which there are no explanations." Never explanations, only awe and wonder! Contemplation revels in mystery, delights in mystery. In that booklet of prayers that he put together for the Gethsemani novices, Merton writes:

> Prayer is always shrouded in mystery. To pray is to enter
> into mystery, and when we do not enter into the unknown,
> we not pray. If we want everything in our prayer-life to be
> abundantly clear at all times, we will by that very fact
> defeat our prayer life.

But for technology there is no mystery. There are only
problems that we must solve. And technology has the
hubristic conviction that it will never meet a problem it
cannot solve. I use the adjective "hubristic" advisedly. For it
seems to me that, when one looks at the dark side of
technology, its overweening sin is hubris, which means
overbearing pride and presumption. McGeorge Bundy,
advisor to Presidents Kennedy and Johnson, though certainly
a believer in the importance of technology (he advised
increasing American commitment to the war in Vietnam), still
writes of the danger of a technology out of human control
and not subject to the critique of human values: "There is no
safety," he wrote, "in unlimited technological hubris."[39]

Against the background of these overarching concerns
voiced by Ellul—the tendency of technology to substitute its
own values for the traditional values of society and its efforts
to desacralize the world—I would like to suggest certain
faults which, I believe, have too often dogged the path of
technology.

First, technology provides us with a faulty choice of
goals. All too frequently technology is afflicted by a false
ethic that gives priority to material progress over moral
growth and to efficiency in getting things done over social
responsibility. The overriding imperative of technology
seems to be: What can be done, must be done. All too often it
ignores the wisdom that would teach us that the fact we are
able to do something does not mean we should do it or even
have a right to do it. Human values which technology as
technology cannot know may offer compelling reasons for
not doing something we have the power to do. The drive to
make the possible real can threaten the values of community

and help construct the illusions of the collectivity.

The second fault I would find with technology is actually a more specific form of the first, namely, a lack of proper balance or a sense of hierarchy in choosing its goals. There are many worthwhile goals technology may work toward. Granted that it cannot do everything—because time, energy and funds are limited—it must establish priorities among the possible goods it can work to accomplish. The temptation is always present to ignore human values for the sake of scientific accomplishments. Too often the exotic is preferred to the ordinary. It is all very exciting (though with repetition, the sense of excitement quickly begins to wear off) to put satellites in space, to build space stations, to send people to Mars. There is a subtle sense of acting like God when God made the stars and placed them in the heavens. Yet is peopling the heavens our most pressing problem? Do we have a greater responsibility to feed those who people the earth? In 1961 President John F. Kennedy promised that by the end of the decade the United States would put a man on the moon. On July 20, 1969, it happened: Neil Armstrong stepped out of his Apollo spacecraft onto the moon. A fantastic accomplishment! Science fiction come true.

Yet, we must ask: Was another scenario possible? Suppose that President Kennedy in 1961 had set a different priority, Suppose he had said: "By the end of this decade we shall eliminate starvation from the face of the earth"? Could we have done it? The answer is, of course, we do not know. But should we have tried? Did the choice to put people on the moon prevent us from making the choice to put food in the mouths of all the men, women and children on earth? Is technology, left to itself, unmediated by human wisdom, liable to choose scientific advancement over the service of people?

A third fault of technology is that it promotes a false activism that wants instantaneous results. Technology is geared toward speed, toward getting things done quickly. We have fast mail, as we put our correspondence into computers rather than envelopes. We have fast food, fast travel, speed reading (so destructive of that slow, meditative reading called *lectio divina*). Everything needs to be done as quickly as possible. Contemplation, on the other hand, is oriented toward leisurely moments of silence and quiet reflection. It realizes that just as you can't grow a plant in a hurry or make a friend in a hurry, so you cannot pray in haste.

Technology looks for instant results. It is full of overly zealous ambitions. It strives to outdo others in order to make it to the top. Contemplation, on the other hand, is content just to be. It sees the desire to achieve results as a goal that can be illusory. William Johnston, a Jesuit teaching at Sophia University in Tokyo, wrote to Merton in July, 1967, asking him what he thought about the desire of a colleague of his to achieve Zen enlightenment. Merton replied saying in effect, "I hope he gets there. I'm rooting for him. But perhaps," he suggests, "the desire to achieve enlightenment might itself be an obstacle to that achievement."[40] It is entirely within the Christian spiritual tradition that we don't seek for special gifts in prayer from God. We simply allow ourselves to be open to the divine largesse. To quote again from the novices' prayer book: "We should never seek to reach some supposed 'summit of prayer' out of spiritual ambition. For this would be a sure way to frustrate our own intentions. We should seek to enter deep into the life of prayer not in order that we may glory in it as in an 'achievement,' however spiritual, but because in this way we can come closer to the Lord who seeks to do us good, Who seeks to give us His mercy, and to surround us with His love. To love prayer is to love our own poverty and His mercy."

A fourth problem with technology is the fact that for vast numbers of people it has dulled the creativity of the human spirit. For all too often it makes work boring, routine, monotonous—so much so that workers' sense of their own worth and of their own creative powers has been diminished by the very work they do. Instead of enriching and energizing the human spirit, work becomes something to escape from as quickly and as often as possible. All too easily workers can be drawn into the vortex of the *divertissement* (which I have discussed earlier): mindless activities with little or no real human significance. The soap opera of television has become the stereotype of such soporific activity.

Fifth, by stressing competition and getting ahead of the "other," technology makes for separation. The "other" is seen as rival and even as a threat to one's achievement and well-being. The contemplative, on the other hand, believes, and in some ways experiences, that he is one with God and with all of God's creatures. Such an intuition necessarily sparks social responsibility. Once we let go of the illusion of separateness, we recognize the deepest possible reason for our responsibility to the needy, the poor, the oppressed, the homeless, the marginalized. They are our sisters and brothers. We must love them as ourselves, for in a very true sense they are our "other selves." True contemplation always issues in compassion.

Another matter on which I would take issue with technology is what I would call its sense of "omnipotence," the notion that, given the time, we can accomplish anything to which we set our minds and energies. We can run our universe; we have the technological skill to do so. The myth of the "omnipotence" of technology is the Pelagianism[41] of our time.

In 1967 in a small magazine called *Season* Merton published an article that appears to be whimsical enough, but actually is in deadly earnest. Entitled "The Angel and the Machine,"[42] it shows how the angels, once thought to be our helpers in carrying out God's plans, have been replaced by the machine. He writes, "Technological civilization is a civilization without angels...in which we have chosen the machine instead of the angel: that is to say we have placed the machine where the angel used to be: at the limits of our own strength, at the frontier of our natural capacity." More than that, Merton points out, "the machines are 'our angels.' We made them, not they themselves. They are, we think, entirely in our own power." They become extensions of our own intelligence, our own strength. "They form part of our own enclosed and comfortable world, they stand between us and nature. They form a 'room' in which we are isolated from the rest of material creation, and therefore all the more from spiritual beings." They create our weather for us and even abolish day and night, as we dwell in our windowless buildings "surrounded by angels of chromium and steel."

Merton goes on: "In our folly we have tried to convince ourselves our machinery is sufficient for all our needs and that there is nothing that science cannot do for us. It is in our anxiety to make our machine world completely self-sufficient and autonomous (something which is no fault of the innocent machine!) that we render it spiritually unlivable for ourselves." He suggests that we need the angels: not to replace our machines, but to teach us how to live with them. "For the angels come to us to teach us how to rest, to forget useless care, to relax, in silence, to 'let go,' to abandon ourselves, not in self-conscious fun but in self-forgetful faith. We need the angels to remind us that we can get along without so many superfluous goods and satisfactions which instead of lightening our existence weigh it down. May they come back into our world and deliver it from its massive boredom, its metaphysical fatigue."

Yet it would be wrong to see technology as the enemy. It can, when properly controlled and utilized, do much good for human persons and for the environment. The Second Vatican Council made this very clear in *Gaudium et Spes*. It says in Article 39 that while earthly progress must be carefully distinguished from the growth of Christ's kingdom; nevertheless the fact that the former can contribute to the better ordering of human society makes it of vital concern to the kingdom of God.

Or, as Merton put it:

Obviously I am not maintaining that we ought to get rid of matches and go back to making fires by rubbing sticks together.... Nor am I maintaining that modern transportation, medicine, methods of production and so on are "bad." I am glad to have a gas heater this winter since I can't cut wood. Yet I am not saying that I am a better human being this winter, when I have more "leisure," than

269

I was last winter when I did a lot of chopping. Nothing wrong with chopping either. What I question is the universal myth that technology infallibly makes everything in every way better for everybody. It does not.[43]

Merton believed that we can and must live in the world of the machine, the world of technology, and still build community. But we need the wisdom that comes from God: a wisdom that earlier ages personified in the form of superhuman beings. Without needing to explain what precisely earlier ages meant by these angelic beings, we need the wisdom they personified, the wisdom that was their message from God.

Almost all societies have recognized the "way of wisdom." It has been respected, not as a flight into illusion, but as a return to reality in its hidden ground and roots. Indeed special homage has been paid to those people who have attained to the inner meaning of life and being, who have expressed this meaning for their brothers and sisters and who have been able to unite in themselves the divisions and complications that confuse the lives of their fellow men and women. Such persons of "wisdom" can also be given a special place in a technological society, but only if it is ready to renounce its obsession with the triumph of the isolated individual and the collective will to power—in order to adopt a different view of reality. This calls for a readiness to listen to the way of wisdom—that insight into life's reality that springs from solitude and contemplation and constitutes the life of community.

Wisdom is understanding reality at the deepest possible level. Or, as the psalmist puts it: "I have wisdom you need to hear. / I see to the heart of things."[44] That is wisdom's task: to see to the heart of things. As Merton puts it in his prose-poem "*Hagia Sophia*" ("Holy Wisdom"): "There is in all visible things an invisible fecundity, a dimmed light, a meek namelessness, a hidden wholeness. This mysterious unity and integrity is Wisdom, the Mother of all."[45] The book of Proverbs suggests that wisdom has been in our world from the very beginning.

When he established the heavens, I was there,...
when he marked out the foundations of the earth,
then I was beside him, like a master worker;
and I was daily his delight, rejoicing before him always,
rejoicing in his inhabited world
and delighting in the human race.[46]

It is as if wisdom is in our world and it is for us to find it. The way to wisdom has been part of the culture of both the West and the East. Wisdom takes us beyond life's superficial realities and enables us to recognize the oneness of all that is. It calls us to the inner change of consciousness that recognizes the emptiness of a false self and knows the real self as one with God and with our sisters and brothers and with all that is.

We need to distinguish wisdom from information and knowledge. Information is simply raw, unconnected data. It involves facts that can be communicated. When information is organized into some kind of meaningful whole or pattern, we may speak of it as knowledge. Wisdom is knowledge of reality insofar as it is related to that which is most truly Real, to that which is the Source and Sustainer of all reality. Wisdom is grasping, or being grasped by, the *real* in all that is real. By the *real* here I mean that which alone is real in itself and is therefore the *real* in all else that is real. Another way of putting this is to say that wisdom calls us to keep alive within us a sense of the divine immanence. We have to deepen our awareness of God's presence everywhere and in all of reality as the source and ground of all. When we come in touch with God's creation, we come in touch with God.

The perceptive reader will notice that what I am saying about wisdom is not distinguishable from what I have said about contemplation. For a person of wisdom cannot help but be a person of contemplation.

We are perhaps the most knowledgeable of generations, pursuing knowledge to its utter limits and never satisfied, always searching for more. But we have to ask: Do we have the same drive to acquire wisdom without which knowledge alone can be dangerous?

It is worth remembering that a few generations ago, a person could not be heard beyond the range of his or her own voice. Now we can communicate with the entire globe. Given the fact that we can speak to the whole world, do we have anything that is worth saying? Do we have the wisdom to say the things that will be for the peace and betterment of the world? Henry David Thoreau, when told one day that inventors were on the verge of producing a technology that would eventually make it possible for people in New York City to speak with people in New Orleans, asked the pertinent question: "What if they don't have anything to say?"

His question remains valid today. The miracle of modern communication systems has brought people together so that their destinies are intertwined. But are we really speaking to one another? We have come to realize in our day that communication can mean two quite different things. It can mean the technical ability to be in touch with people or it can mean the ability to reach their minds and hearts. The first has little value without the second. There is little point in getting in touch with people all over the world if we cannot reach their inner spirits. And this we can do only if we accept the contemplative vision that all men and women are brothers and sisters, equal to one another and in communion with one another at the deepest possible level. We are united to one another in God. This is a reality that only wisdom can understand. Our greatest need today is not for technicians who can make faster computers or industries that can produce better televisions and ever more sophisticated weapons of war. Our greatest need is for men and women of wisdom who will have a sense of the real meaning of life and who can learn the ways of helping people to live authentic lives which put them in touch with the really real, with the wisdom which Scripture tells us has always been in the world.

Knowledge that points toward wisdom enhances the human spirit. Ralph Waldo Emerson once said: "Raphael paints wisdom. Handel sings it. Shakespeare writes it. Wren builds it." In a letter to Paul Tillich's secretary, Merton quotes with admiration a statement of Tillich that "one apple of Cezanne has more of ultimate reality in it than a Jesus by Hofmann."[47] Those who have achieved a measure of wisdom in their lives have a mission to help others go beyond the phony, the illusory, the superficial and to point them in the direction of what is most real and which touches on reality itself. Wisdom grows out of contemplation. Wisdom is of God. Wisdom builds community.

Notes

[1] This title is borrowed from an article Merton wrote for *Commonweal*, 84 (3 June 1966) also in *Contemplation in a World of Action*, pp. 143-156.

[2] *Seven Storey Mountain*, p. 383.

[3] *Seven Storey Mountain*, p. 421.

[4] *Hidden Ground of Love*, pp. 186-187.

[5] *Hidden Ground of Love*, pp. 186-187.

[6] Hebrews 10:31.

[7] *Hidden Ground of Love*, p. 79.

[8] Michael Mott, *The Seven Mountains of Thomas Merton* (New York: Houghton Mifflin, 1984), p. 311.

[9] *Search for Solitude*, pp. 181-182.

[10] The Thomas Merton Center Foundation provided financial support for this project. Side one of the marker reads: Thomas Merton (1915-68) Trappist monk, poet, social critic and spiritual writer. Born in Prades, France. After education at Cambridge and Columbia Univ., he entered Abbey of Gethsemani, Trappist, Ky., 1941; ordained as priest, 1949. His autobiography The Seven Storey Mountain (1948) earned international acclaim. He is buried in Abbey cemetery. Side two: A REVELATION Merton had a sudden insight at this corner Mar. 18, 1958, that led him to redefine his monastic identity with greater involvement in social justice issues. He was "suddenly overwhelmed with the realization that I

loved all these people..." He found them "walking around shining like the sun." *Conjectures of a Guilty Bystander.*

[11] *Conjectures of a Guilty Bystander*, p. 156.

[12] *Conjectures of a Guilty Bystander*, p. 158.

[13] *Conjectures of a Guilty Bystander*, p. 158.

[14] *Asian Journal*, p. 308.

[15] *Contemplation in a World of Action*, p. 161.

[16] *Hidden Ground of Love*, p. 582.

[17] Thomas Merton and Rosemary Radford Ruether, *At Home in the World: The Letters of Thomas Merton and Rosemary Radford Ruether*, Mary Tardiff, ed. (Maryknoll, N.Y.: Orbis, 1995), p. 41.

[18] *Hidden Ground of Love*, p. 509.

[19] *Hidden Ground of Love*, p. 511.

[20] *Hidden Ground of Love*, p. 482.

[21] Many of his essays on social issues may be found in *Thomas Merton, Passion for Peace: The Social Essays*, William H. Shannon, ed. (New York: Crossroad, 1995). See also *Faith and Violence* and *Hidden Ground of Love*.

[22] *Contemplation in a World of Action*, p. 160.

[23] Some of this material is taken from my book *Seeking the Face of God* which is presently out of print.

[24] Thomas Merton, *Raids on the Unspeakable* (New York: New Directions, 1964), pp. 9-23.

[25] Eugene Ionesco, *Notes and Counternotes: Writings on the Theater*, Donald Watson, trans. (New York: Grove, 1964), p. 151.

[26] Jacques Ellul, *The Technological Society* (New York: Alfred A. Knopf, 1964), p. 135.

[27] *Conjectures of a Guilty Bystander*, p. 76.

[28] *Search for Solitude*, p. 54.

[29] Thomas Merton, *Turning Toward the World: The Pivotal Years: The Journals of Thomas Merton, Vol. 4*, Victor A. Kramer, ed. (New York: HarperSanFrancisco, 1996), pp. 3-4.

[30] *Turning Toward the World*, p. 4.

[31] *Hidden Ground of Love*, p. 216.

[32] Thomas Merton, *Dancing in the Water of Life: Seeking Peace in the Hermitage: The Journals of Thomas Merton, Vol. 5*, Robert E. Daggy, ed. (New York, HarperSanFrancisco, 1997), pp. 159-60.

[33] Thomas Merton, *The Non-Violent Alternative*, Gordon Zahn, ed. (New York: Farrar, Straus, Giroux, 1980), p. 260.

[34] Thomas Merton, *Witness to Freedom: The Letters of Thomas Merton in Times of Crisis* (New York: Farrar, Straus, Giroux, 1994), p. 109.

[35] *Commonweal* 81 (4 December 1964).

[36] *Witness to Freedom*, p. 75.

[37] Ellul's book, *The Technological Society* (New York: Random House, 1967), has an interesting, even provocative, subtitle: *L'enjeu du siecle* (*The Stake of the Century*). It is something like Pascal's "wager": Pascal "wagered" about God, contemporary women and men wager about technology.

[38] *Witness to Freedom*, p. 73.

[39] Quoted in *The American Heritage Dictionary* (New York: Houghton Mifflin, 1992), under "hubris."

[40] *Hidden Ground of Love*, p. 443.

[41] Pelagianism was a doctrine proposed by an ascetic teacher named Pelagius (c. 350-c. 425). It appeared to overemphasize human freedom without the need for God's grace or Christ's redemption.

[42] Published originally in *Season*, Vol. 5, 1967, a small Dominican journal out of Berkeley that was short-lived. The essay was republished in *The Merton Seasonal*, Vol. 22, No. 1 (Spring 1997), pp. 3-6.

[43] *Road to Joy*, p. 98.

[44] Psalm 49:3 (ICEL translation).

[45] Thomas Merton, *Emblems of a Season of Fury* (New York: New Directions, 1961), p. 61.

[46] Proverbs 8:27-31.

[47] *Witness to Freedom*, p. 301.

Conclusion

The hen does not lay eggs in the marketplace.

You have to experience duality for a long time until you see it's not there.

Naomi Burton Stone has said: "Each one of us knows a different Thomas Merton." Though she was speaking of those who knew him personally, what she said is true also of those whose only acquaintance with him is through his writings. Some know him in his poetry; others, in his social criticism. Some find in his writings the road to solitude; others, the road to the East. He was many things for many people. His interests and concerns ranged far and wide. His reading was amazingly extensive—he was something of a literary gadabout. Though as a monk he had taken a vow of stability, he found it difficult to stay very long in one place. I don't mean geographically (though at times that was a problem, too) but spiritually and intellectually. There was a restlessness about him that showed in his spiritual search that never ceased and in his intellectual pursuits that kept broadening as time went on. He was constantly rethinking himself and revising his attitudes. There is a remarkably revelatory self-portrait in *A Vow of Conversation* under the date of January 20, 1964:

I am aware of the need for constant self-revision and growth, leaving behind the renunciations of yesterday yet in continuity with all my yesterdays. For to cling to the past is to lose one's continuity with the past, since this means clinging to what is no longer there.

My ideas are always changing, always moving around one center. And I am always seeing that center from somewhere else. Hence I will always be accused of inconsistency. But I will no longer be there to hear the accusation.[1]

Yes, there was a center. It was, I believe, his monastic commitment. Despite his seeming unsettledness, that center held. Somehow everything about him comes together, I would maintain, in the unity of his monastic vocation.

On November 16, 1938, at Corpus Christi Church in New York City Thomas Merton was baptized into the Roman Catholic Church. On December 13, 1941, he was officially accepted as a postulant in the Trappist Abbey of Gethsemani. From that day in 1941 till the day of his death twenty-seven years later, the monastic life defined the way in which he would live out his baptismal vocation. Thomas Merton lived as a monk, wrote as a monk, died as a monk. He saw the world through the eyes of a monk. Being a monk was, I firmly believe, at the heart of his life, his work, his spirituality. It is one thing, however, to make this assertion, quite another to realize that "being a monk" meant different things to Merton at different times in his life. His understanding of the monastic commitment was continually in process of revision. The man, who on his first visit to Gethsemani in the spring of 1941 described this monastery as the center of all vitality in America, is the same man who twenty-five years later wonders whether monastic life will survive or even deserves to survive, unless it is willing to undergo serious rethinking of that basic question: What does it mean to be a monk? The downcast eyes of a young monk's early flight from the world contrast sharply with the wide-open eyes of a more mature monk in later years looking out upon the world with love and compassion. The Merton who gave the final talk of his life at Bangkok on December 10, 1968, was a very different monk from the one who wrote *The Seven Storey Mountain* more than twenty years earlier.

Merton's commitment to a rethinking of the monastic vocation is, I am convinced, not sufficiently recognized. It is well known that during the sixties he expressed himself on many issues: war, racial justice, Latin America, Eastern religions. What is not so well known is that from 1964 till the end of his life, he reflected and wrote a great deal about the renewal of monastic life. On December 20, 1963 he wrote to Father Kilian McDonnell: "I am writing mostly monastic essays these days."[2] It is as if he is setting an agenda for himself: an agenda that will come to an end only with the final talk of his life "On Marxism and Monastic Perspectives."[3] In 1965 in the preface to the Japanese edition of *The Seven Storey Mountain*, he made clear that he was in the monastic life for good. "I have never for a moment thought of changing the definitive decisions taken in my life: to be a Christian, to be a monk, to be a priest. If anything the decision to depart from modern secular society, a decision repeated and reaffirmed many times has finally become irrevocable."[4] He adds, however, that the attitudes and assumptions behind this decision have changed in a number of ways over time.

In 1968, when he journeyed to the East, his purpose was monastic: to meet with Western monks who lived in Asia and to experience Buddhist monasticism at first hand. In the prepared notes for his talk at the Temple of Understanding meeting at Calcutta in October 1968, he identified himself.

> I speak as Western monk who is preeminently concerned with his own monastic calling and dedication. [I have] come here not just as a research scholar or even as an author.... I come as a pilgrim who is anxious to obtain not just information, not just "facts" about other monastic traditions, but to drink from ancient sources of monastic vision and experience.... I seek to become a better and more enlightened monk...."[5]

When death came suddenly to him at Bangkok on that fateful

day of December 10, 1968, it was at a gathering of monks. He died as he had lived: a monk among monks.

In August of 1967 Merton received a letter from Dom Francis Decrois, abbot of the Cistercian monastery of Frattocchie in Italy, informing him that Pope Paul VI had requested "a message of contemplatives to the world" and wanted Merton to be one of the contributors to that message. Dom Francis's letter, written on August 14, arrived on the twenty-first with a request for a response by the end of the month. This gave Merton little time to prepare a statement; nor was he in the mood to write such a letter, since at the time he was dealing with a severe bout of influenza. He did manage nonetheless to send a response to Dom Francis. He wrote a lengthy letter on August 21 and followed it with another shorter letter written the next day. The two were mailed together. [If only Merton had had e-mail!]

The first letter[6] is impressive, especially considering the fact that it had to be written quickly and spontaneously—and when he was ill. It is a remarkable letter from a monk to his fellow Christians outside the monastery. Merton began by apologizing to his brothers and sisters for addressing them when they had not asked him to do so. He apologized, too, for "being behind a high wall which you do not understand." If that high wall is a problem for them, he admits it may be a problem for him also. "Perhaps," he says, "you are no longer satisfied with the reply that if I stay behind this wall, I have quiet, recollection, tranquillity of heart. You may well ask me, by what right do I have the luxury of all this peace and tranquillity?" He has no ready answer, though he does quote an Islamic proverb: "The hen does not lay eggs in the marketplace."

He insists on his communion with all his sisters and brothers "in the world."

> My flight from the world is not a reproach to you who remain in the world, and I have no right to repudiate the world in a negative fashion, because if I do that, my flight will have taken me not to truth and to God, but to a private, though doubtless pious, illusion.

Does he have answers to the questions that torment people of his day? As a young monk he thought he did, but as he matured in the monastic life, he realized that he had only begun to learn the questions. The old pre-packaged answers seemed more and more like evasions instead of explanations. Perhaps it was his call to be an explorer for them, a searcher in realms that most people are unable to visit: a desert area of the human heart, in which explanations no longer suffice and in which one learns that only experience counts.

> In this area I have learned that one cannot truly know hope unless he has found how like despair hope is. The language of Christianity has said this for centuries in other less naked terms. But the language of Christianity has been so used and so misused that sometimes you distrust it; you do not know whether or not behind the word "Cross" there stands the experience of mercy and salvation, or only the threat of punishment.

He tells his readers what experience has taught him.

> If my word means anything to you, I can say to you that I have experienced the Cross to mean mercy and not cruelty, truth and not deception: that the news of the truth and love of Jesus is indeed the true good news, but in our time it speaks in strange places. And perhaps it speaks out in you more than it does in me. Perhaps Christ is nearer to you than He is to me. This I say without shame or guilt because I have learned to rejoice that Jesus is in the world in people who know Him not, that He is at work in them when they think themselves far from Him.

He calls people to hope even when they may think that hope for them is impossible. Hope not because of any goodness that may be in you, he says, but because God loves us irrespective of our merits. Indeed whatever is good in us comes not from our merits but from his love.

The statement is powerful and moving; yet it must be said that it betrays that ambiguity that so often seems to surface in Merton's writings on contemplation. He speaks as a contemplative about contemplation; but clearly his message is for non-contemplatives. Did Merton ever quite abandon the "elitist" view of contemplation that for all practical purposes restricted it to the monastic life? It appears that he himself sensed this ambiguity as he reread his letter to Dom Decrois. The next day he wrote a second letter in which he clearly disclaims such an elitist attitude. Thus he writes: "The contemplative life should not be regarded as the exclusive prerogative of those who dwell in monastic walls. All men [and women] can seek and find this intimate awareness which is a gift of love and a vivifying touch of creative and redemptive power."[7] And it is evident, especially after the Fourth and Walnut experience of 1958, that Merton took joy in identifying himself with ordinary, everyday people. Father Thomas Fidelis, O.C.S.O., a monk of the Abbey of the Holy Spirit in Conyers, Georgia, relates an anecdote, apparently current in the monastery at the time Merton was writing his "message" to Dom Decrois. Merton is supposed to have said of the Pope or perhaps of Dom Decrois: "He can play the Good Samaritan. As for me, I'm down here in the ditch with my neighbor and we are both struggling to get out together."[8]

A wonderfully disarming statement of Merton's desire to identify with people outside the monastery. Still when one reflects on the calm quiet his hermitage afforded him, it's a bit difficult to accept the "picture" of him down "in the ditch" with them. The peaceful solitude of his monastery is in stark contrast with the daily struggle of the very people for whom he writes. They are the ones in the "ditch," as they strive to find a measure of peace and quiet and seek to extricate themselves, if only for a short time, from that "ditch" of busyness and distractions so mercilessly thrust upon them by the world in which they live.

It is not that Merton thought that monks were superior people or that they loved God more than those who were not monks. It is simply that he seemed convinced (much of the time) that "life in the world" does not provide the atmosphere in which contemplation can flower. Yet he was not entirely consistent, for in book after book written for a general readership, he invites his readers to enter into the contemplative experience. As Father Fidelis remarked, he did not confuse contemplation with institutional monasticism. It was "his genius to open up the essence of what contemplation means to all people, not just monks and nuns."[9]

Whether or not this always represented Merton's position, it is my conviction that thousands of readers interpreted him in this way and have "translated" what he says about "monastic" contemplation into terms more congenial to their own way of life.

I believe it is fair to say that throughout his monastic life Merton grappled with the issue of dualism: a mentality deeply embedded in Western culture (especially since Descartes's time). Dualism sets up a dichotomy between the supernatural and the natural, the sacred and secular. Dealing with dualism was not a problem peculiar to Merton. It has a long history. One confronts it in almost all mystical literature. Indeed, it is a particular way of stating a more general problem that has engaged philosophers and theologians for centuries: Is reality one or many? Do we view reality in terms of dualism or non-dualism?

This is the unspoken question beneath much of what Merton wrote about contemplation. The training he received for the priesthood in neo-Scholasticism was heavily dualistic. Merton had to deal with this. He also had to deal with the censors who would review what he had written with an eye to its "Catholic orthodoxy." His writings after *The Seven Storey Mountain* (wherein his mind-set was clearly dualistic), show him moving rather quickly in the direction of the apophatic way and with it, toward a non-dualistic understanding of reality. Consistently, he presents the contemplative experience as a unitive one. In contemplation, one rises above the duality of subject and object: The subjectivity of the contemplative becomes one with the subjectivity of God. In contemplation, I, as a separate ego, vanish out of the picture and there is only God. In so early a book as *Seeds of Contemplation*, he had written: "Where contemplation becomes what it is really meant to be, it is no longer something poured out of God into a created subject, so much as God living in God and identifying a created life with His own Life so that there is nothing left of any significance but God living in God."[10] Yet, in *New Seeds of Contemplation*, written twelve years later, Merton speaks more guardedly: He writes of our true reality as being "in God" and "with Him"; yet (perhaps a lingering touch of his Scholastic training momentarily emerging or fear of a censor's pen seeming to threaten) he feels constrained to add: "Of course [this reality] is ontologically distinct from Him."[11]

It would seem that the non-dualism implicit, but not entirely unambiguous, in his earlier writings did finally become explicit in *Zen and the Birds of Appetite*. His discussion in that book of the "subject" of the transcendent experience makes sense only in the framework of non-dualism. If his preference for the apophatic way moved him toward non-dualism, it was his exposure to Zen that pushed him to take the final step in that direction.

Yet Merton was a practical man. He knew that life presents us with dualities and that we have to live with them until we are able to surmount them. Brother David Steindl-Rast records an interesting conversation with him at Our Lady of the Redwoods Abbey in Whitethorn, California, just before he left for his Asian journey. Merton was speaking about the prayer of intercession: "We are not rainmakers, but Christians. In our dealings with God he is free and so are we. It is simply a need for me to express my love by praying for my friends; it is like embracing them. If you love another person, it is God's love being realized. One and the same love is reaching your friend through you, and you through your friend."[12]

When Brother David asked him, "But isn't there still an implicit dualism in all this?" Merton answered:

> "Really there isn't, and yet there is. You have to see your
> will and God's will dualistically for a long time. You have
> to experience duality for a long time until you see it's not
> there. In this respect I am a Hindu. Ramakrishna has the
> solution. Don't consider dualistic prayer on a lower level.

The lower is higher. There are no levels. Any moment you can break through to the underlying unity which is God's gift in Christ. In the end, Praise praises. Thanksgiving gives thanks. Jesus prays. Openness is all."

"You have to experience duality for a long time until you see it's not there." These words have the ring of autobiography. What counts ultimately is not what you say or think but what you experience. No one understood this better than Merton. He wrote a great deal and (for a monk!) talked a great deal. But no one knew better than he that life is not a matter of concepts or of words. It is not a question of talking yourself out of duality or reasoning your way to unity. Life is opening yourself to experience—first to this experience and that; and finally to Experience Itself.

It was because Merton was attuned to experience that he was preeminently a theologian—a contemplative rather than a dogmatic theologian. His theology was not an expounding of the truths of revelation in order to offer an intellectual appreciation of them; rather, it was the theology of one who could talk about God because he had first walked with God. For him, God was the burning mystery of reality. God was the great experience beyond all experiences. No one in the twentieth century, I dare say, has articulated that experience with greater clarity of vision than Thomas Merton.

———

Notes

[1] Thomas Merton, *A Vow of Conversation: Journals 1964-65*, Naomi Burton Stone, ed. (New York: Farrar, Straus, Giroux, 1988), p. 19. The same text, slightly different, may be found in the fifth volume of Merton's journals, *Dancing in the Water of Life*, p. 67. I use the text from *Vow* because Merton had put this text together himself, though he sent it to Naomi Burton Stone for the final editing.

[2] *The School of Charity*, p. 190.

[3] *Asian Journal*, pp. 326-343.

[4] *Honorable Reader*, p. 63.

[5] *Asian Journal*, pp. 312-313.

[6] *Hidden Ground of Love*, pp. 154-158.

[7] *Hidden Ground of Love*, p. 159.

[8] Thomas Fidelis, O.C.S.O., "Contemplation in a World of Action: Is It Worthwhile in Today's America?", address at a conference held at Georgia State University, February 27, 1980.

[9] See note 8.

[10] *Seeds*, p. 196.

[11] *New Seeds*, p. 282.

[12] David Stendl-Rast, O.S.B., "Recollections of Thomas Merton's Last Days in the West," *Monastic Studies* reprint.

Appendix

Diagram A: THE INNER EXPERIENCE

FIRST DRAFT

The Inner Experience (Dark Path—crossed out):
Notes on Contemplation

I. A Preliminary Warning 1-5
(Originally: I. What Is Contemplation)
II. The Awakening of the Inner Self 5-15
An Example from Zen 7-11
The Christian Approach 11-15
III. Society and the Inner Self 15a-15j,11
IV. Christian Contemplation 16, 6, 21a
(Originally: II. Man the Contemplative)
1. Contemplation and Theology 12-16
2. Contemplation and the Gospels 16-18c, 16
Sacred and Secular 16-21a
IV. Kinds of Contemplation 22-23

Final Inserts

  5   XI.   Contemplation and Neurosis
10 XII. The Desire of Contemplation (Orig.: Conclusions)
12 XIII. The Sense of Sin
17 XIV. Problems of the Contemplative Life
            1. Contemplative Formation in Monasteries
18   2. Contemplation and Technology
21   3. Preparation for the Contemplative Life
27   4. Contemplative Life in the World
33 XV. Prospects and Conclusions

SECOND DRAFT

The Inner Experience:
Notes on Contemplation

I. A Preliminary Warning 1-5

II. The Awakening of the Inner Self 6-16
An Example from Zen 7-10
The Christian Approach 10-16
III. Society and the Inner Self 17-33
IV. Christian Contemplation

1. Contemplation and Theology 36-41
2. Contemplation and the Gospels 41-47
Sacred and Secular 48-54
IV. Kinds of Contemplation 55-56
* Five Texts on Contemplative prayer (7 pages—not
numbered)
* The Paradox of the Illuminative Way (5 pages)
X. Some Dangers 53-61

XI. Contemplation and Neurosis 62-66
XII. The Desire of Contemplation 67-69
XIII. The Sense of Sin 70-75
XIV. Problems of the Contemplative Life 75-95
1. Contemplative Formation in Monasteries 75-79
2. Contemplation and Technology 79-82
3. Preparation for the Contemplative Life 82-87
4. Contemplative Life in the World 87-95
XV. Prospects and Conclusions 96-108

* Added to the first draft.

288

Diagram A: **THE INNER EXPERIENCE**

	THIRD DRAFT		FOURTH DRAFT
I.	A Preliminary Warning	1-6	same as the third draft except:
II.	The Awakening of the Inner Self	6-16	
	An Example from Zen	7-10	
	The Christian Approach	10-16	has handwritten notes at various points in the text, including a detailed note on p.8.
III.	Society and the Inner Self	17-33	
IV.	Christian Contemplation	34-54	
	1. Contemplation and Theology	36-41	
	2. Contemplation and the Gospels	41-47	
	Sacred and Secular	48-54	
IV.	Kinds of Contemplation	55-69	
	* Liturgy	59-62	
	* Union with God in Activity	62-65	
	* Acquired and Infused Contemplation	65-66	
	* Natural Contemplation and Mystical Theology	66-69	
*VII	Infused Contemplation	70-78	VII. Infused Contemplation 70-77b
	Five Texts on Contemplation	79-85	
	The Paradox of the Illuminative way	86-90	The remaining pages are one number less than in the 3rd draft
*IX	What to Do—The Teaching of St. John of the Cross	91-95	
X.	Some Dangers	95-104	
XI.	Contemplation and Neurosis	105-9	
XII.	The Desire of Contemplation	110-12	
XIII.	The Sense of Sin	113-17	
XIV.	Problems of the Contemplative Life	118-38	
	1. Contemplative Formation in Monasteries	118-22	
	2. Contemplation and Technology	122-25	
	3. Preparation for the Contemplative Life	125-30	
	4. Contemplative Life in the World	130-38	
XV.	Prospects and Conclusions	139-51	XV. Prospects and Conclusions 138-50

*Added to the second draft.

Diagram B

THE INNER EXPERIENCE (4th draft-150 pages)	Common Material		WHAT IS CONTEMPLATION (1978 Templegate ed.- 79 small pages)
I. A Preliminary Warning p. 1-5			What is Contemplation p. 7-12
II. The Awakening of the Inner Self 6-17			
III. Society and the Inner Self 17-33			
IV. Christian Contemplation 34-54			
1. Contemplation and Theology 36-41			
2. Contemplation and the Gospels 41-47	45-46	14-18	The Promises of Christ 14-20
	46-47	21-24	St. Thomas Aquinas 21-26
Sacred and Secular 48-54	53-54	24	
IV. Kinds of Contemplation 55-69			Kinds of Contemplation 27-35
			Active Contemplation 27-29
Liturgy 59-62	62	30-33	Liturgy 29-33
Union with God in Activity 62-65	62-63	33-35	Union with God in Activity 33-35
Acquired and Infused Contemplation 65-66			
Natural Contemplation and Mystical Theology 66-69			
VII. Infused Contemplation 70-89	72-75	36-42	Infused Contemplation 35-44
			St. Bernard of Clairvaux 37-38
			"A Ray of Darkness" 38-44
Five Texts on Contemplative Prayer 78-84			The Test 45-54
The Paradox of the Illuminative Way 85-89	84-85	47-53	Peace, Recollection Desire 46-54

IX. What to do—   What to Do 55-68
     The Teachings of
     St. John of the Cross
     90-94   90-94 55-68
  X. Some Dangers   The Danger of Quietism
     95-103   95-97 69-77   69-78
 XI. Contemplation and Neurosis 104-8
 XII. The Desire of Contemplation 109-11
XIII. The Sense of Sin 112-16
XIV. Problems of the Contemplative Life 117-37
        1. Contemplative Formation in Monasteries 117-21
        2. Contemplation and Technology 121-24
        3. Preparation for the Contemplative Life 124-29
        4. Contemplative Life in the World 129-37
 XV. Prospects and Conclusions 138-50

291

Diagram C: **THE CLIMATE OF MONASTIC PRAYER**

THE BOOK	THE BOOKLET (OCT. 1965)	PRAYER AS WORSHIP AND EXPERIENCE
Introduction (pp. 29-38)	Introduction (pp. 1-6)	
Ch. I (39-41)		
Ch. II (42-48)	Ch. I (1-2)	
Ch. III (49-53)	Ch. II (1-4)	
Ch. IV (54-59)	Ch. III (1-4)	
	Ch. IV (1-8)	Part III Prayer as
Ch. V (60-64)		Experience
		1. Mental Prayer and
Ch. VI (65-69)		Contemplation
		Personal Prayer in the
		Benedictine Tradition
		(pp. 87-89)
Ch. VII (70-74)		St. Gregory the Great
		(89-92)
Ch. VIII (75-79)		St. Bernard of
		Clairvaux (92-95)
Ch. IX and initial		
paragraphs of Ch. X (80-85)		
Ch. X (remainder) (85-91)		Peter of Celles (95-98)
		Benedictine Prayer in
		the Counter-Refor-
		mation and After
Ch. XI (92-98)		(98-102)
Ch. XII (99-102)	Ch. V(1-6)	Ascetic Purification
Ch. XIII (103-107)		(106-108)
		Passive Purification
Ch. XIV (108-120)		(108-111)
Ch. XV (121-129)	Ch. VI(1-11)	
		2. The Way of
Ch. XVI (130-138)		Contemplative Prayer
Ch. XVII (139-140)	Ch. VII(1-8)	(111-116)
Ch. XVIII (141-148)	Ch. VIII(1-2)	
Ch. XIX	Ch. IX(1-7)	Part IV Epilogue:
		Wisdom or Evasion
		(117-122)

CLIMATE OF MONASTIC PRAYER

Douglas V. Steere: Foreword: 15 pp.

Total Merton Material: 126 pp.

(75 pp. from booklet of October 1965

51 pp.: excerpts from *Prayer as Worship and Experience*)

Works Cited

Primary Sources

Thomas Merton,

— *The Ascent to Truth*, Harcourt Brace, 1951.

— *The Climate of Monastic Prayer* or *Contemplative Prayer*, Herder and Herder, 1969.

— *The Inner Experience*, published serially in *Cistercian Studies*, Vols. 18 and 19.

— *New Seeds of Contemplation*, New Directions, 1962.

— "Notes for a Philosophy of Solitude" in *Disputed Questions*, Harcourt Brace, 1985.

— *Seeds of Contemplation*, New Directions, 1949.

— *Thoughts in Solitude*, Farrar, Straus, Giroux, 1998.

— *What Is Contemplation?*, Templegate, 1978.

— *Zen and the Birds of Appetite*, New Directions, 1968

Secondary Sources

Aldhelm Cameron-Brown, "Seeking the Rhinoceros: A Tribute to Thomas Merton, " *Monastic Studies*, 1969.

Jacques Ellul, *The Technological Society*, Random House, 1967.

Etienne H. Gilson, *The Spirit of Medieval Philosophy*, University of Notre Dame Press, 1936.

Aelred Graham, *Zen Catholicism*, Crossroad, 1994.

Donald Grayston, "The Making of a Spiritual Classic: Thomas Merton's Seeds of Contemplation and New Seeds of Contemplation," *Sciences Religieuses/Studies in Religion* (1973-1974).

John of the Cross, *The Dark Night of the Soul*, Image, 1990.

Søren Kierkegaard, *The Concept of Anxiety*, Princeton, 1981.

Vladimir Lossky, *The Mystical Theology of the Eastern Church*, James Clark and Co., 1957.

Jacques Maritain, *Scholasticism and Politics*, Ayers Co. Publishers, 1945.

Thomas Merton,

—*The Asian Journal of Thomas Merton*, New Directions, 1973.

—*The Collected Poems of Thomas Merton*, New Directions, 1980.

—*Conjectures of a Guilty Bystander*, Doubleday, 1966.

—*Contemplation in a World of Action*, Doubleday, 1971.

—*The Courage for Truth: The Letters of Thomas Merton to Writers*, Farrar, Straus, Giroux, 1993.

—*Dancing in the Water of Life: Seeking Peace in the Hermitage; The Journals of Thomas Merton, Vol. 5*, HarperSanFrancisco, 1997.

—*Emblems of a Season of Fury*, New Directions, 1961.

—*Entering the Silence: Becoming a Monk and Writer: The Journals of Thomas Merton, Vol. 2*, HarperSanFrancisco, 1996.

—*Faith and Violence: Christian Teaching and Christian Practice*, University of Notre Dame Press, 1968.

—*The Hidden Ground of Love: The Letters of Thomas Merton on Religious Experience and Social Concerns*, Farrar, Straus, Giroux, 1985.

—*Honorable Reader: Reflections on My Work*, Crossroad, 1989

—"Is the World a Problem?", *Commonweal*, 84 (3 June 1966).

—*Love and Living*, Harcourt Brace, 1985.

—*The Mystic Life*, Electronic Paperbacks, 1976.

—*Mystics and Zen Masters*, Farrar, Straus, Giroux, 1967.

—*The New Man*, Farrar, Straus, Giroux, 1961

—*No Man Is an Island*, Harcourt Brace, 1955.

—*The Non-Violent Alternative*, Farrar, Straus, Giroux, 1980.

—*Passion for Peace: The Social Essays*, Crossroad, 1995.

—*Raids on the Unspeakable*, New Directions, 1964

—*The Road to Joy: The Letters of Thomas Merton to New and Old Friends*, Farrar, Straus, Giroux, 1989.

—*Run to the Mountain: The Story of a Vocation: The Journals of Thomas Merton, Vol. 1*, HarperSanFrancisco, 1995.

—*The School of Charity: The Letters of Thomas Merton on Religious Renewal*, Harcourt Brace Jovanovich, 1993.

—*A Search for Solitude: Pursuing the Monk's True Life: The Journals of Thomas Merton, Vol. 3*, HarperSanFrancisco, 1996.

—*The Seven Storey Mountain*, Harcourt Brace Jovanovich, 1948.

—*The Sign of Jonas*, Harcourt Brace, 1953

—*The Silent Life*, Farrar, Straus, Giroux, 1975.

—*The Tears of the Blind Lions*, New Directions, 1949.

—*Thomas Merton on St. Bernard*, Cistercian Studies Series, No. 9. Cistercian Publications, 1980.

—*Turning Toward the World: The Pivotal Years: The Journals of Thomas Merton, Vol. 4*, HarperSanFrancisco, 1996.

—*A Vow of Conversation: Journals 1964-65*, Farrar, Straus, Giroux, 1988

—*The Wisdom of the Desert*, New Directions, 1960.

—*Witness to Freedom: The Letters of Thomas Merton in Times of Crisis*, Farrar, Straus, Giroux, 1994.

—and Rosemary Radford Ruether, *At Home in the World: The Letters of Thomas Merton and Rosemary Radford Ruether*, Orbis, 1995.

Michael Mott, *The Seven Mountains of Thomas Merton*, Houghton Mifflin, 1984.

William H. Shannon, *Silence on Fire*, Crossroad, 1991.

—*Silent Lamp: The Thomas Merton Story*, Crossroad, 1994.

Norman P. Tanner, *Decrees of the Ecumenical Councils, Vol. 1*, Georgetown University Press, 1990.

Evelyn Underhill, *Mysticism*, New American Library, 1955

Acknowledgments

The author expresses his gratitude for permission to quote material printed by the following publishers:

Reprinted by permission of Cistercian Publications, Inc.: *The Climate of Monastic Prayer* by Thomas Merton, copyright ©1969 by the Trustees of the Merton Legacy Trust. Reprinted by permission of The Crossroad Publishing Company: *Honorable Reader: Reflections on My Work*, ed. Robert E. Daggy, copyright ©1989; *Silence on Fire*, ed. William H. Shannon, copyright ©1991; *Silent Lamp: The Thomas Merton Story*, ed. William H. Shannon, copyright 1992; *Zen Catholicism* by Dom Aelred Graham, copyright ©1963. Reprinted by permission of Doubleday, a division of Random House, Inc.: *Conjectures of a Guilty Bystander* by Thomas Merton, copyright ©1966 by The Abbey of

Index

A

acceptance, existential, and
contemplation, 195, 231-232
acquired vs. infused
contemplation, 151n27
active contemplation
and affective prayer, 29, 32, 205
and infused contemplation,
131-133, 203-205, 207-208n15
vs. juridical contemplatives, 10
kataphatic tradition, 11-15, 76,
165-166
liturgy as, 29-30, 203
search for contemplative space
in world, 143-145
See also quasi-contemplatives
affective prayer, 29, 32, 205
alienation from true self/God, 7-8,
128-129
See also dualism (duality);
original sin
ambition and technological society,
266-267
Anthony, Saint, 188, 203
anxiety (dread), 138, 192, 198-202
apophatic tradition
and freedoms necessary to
experience God, 60-62
vs. kataphatic, 11-15, 76, 165-166
Merton's introduction to, 211
and self, 16-17, 121
See also darkness; union with
God; unity
Aquinas, Saint Thomas, 6, 27-28,
70, 76-77
Ascent to Truth, The (Merton),
65-71, 155, 159
asceticism of John of the Cross,
70-74
See also monastic life
Asian Journal, The (Merton),
235-238
attachments. *See* desire; diversion;
false self
attentiveness, contemplative, 161,
162-163, 222-223

See also awakening, soul
authority of the Church, 97-100,
105-106, 107-108, 227-228
awakening, soul
community's role in, 127-128
in contemplative experience, 35,
62, 121, 135-136, 160-161
and discovery of real self,
135-136, 166-170, 232, 233
in Zen, 223, 224
awareness
and Cartesian self, 228-229, 231
and contemplation, 161, 169-170
and God's immanence, 4
in Zen, 223
See also awakening, soul
awe, sense of, and function of
mystery, 264-265

B

Baptism, 9, 27
Benedict, Saint, 203-204
Benedictine Order, 203-204, 206
Bernard of Clairvaux, Saint, 33,
204-205, 207-208n15
Buddha figures and Merton's
insight, 237
"Buddha mind," 224, 228
Buddhism, 84n17, 163-164, 181n25,
219, 221
See also Zen path

C

Catholic tradition
authority of the Church, 97-100,
105-106, 107-108, 227-228
Merton's adherence to, 48, 67
Merton's expansion beyond,
154-155, 283
propositional vs. experiential
faith, 173-174
and technological impact on
society, 262

cenobitic vs. solitary monastic life, 5, 6, 97, 140-143, 259

censors, Church, 97-100, 105-106, 107-108

Christ, Jesus. *See* Jesus Christ

Christians
and call to contemplation, 26-27
types of, 27, 30-40
See also infused contemplation; quasi-contemplatives

Christian tradition
vs. Eastern tradition in contemplation, 124-125, 130
Merton's respect for, 48, 69, 154-155, 163
mysticism in, 67-68, 70, 72, 81-82, 84n15
personalism, 159-160, 180n12, 232-233
transformation of consciousness in, 47, 227
and Zen path, 194-195, 213-221, 224-236, 240n26, 241n41, 255
See also Catholic tradition; Eastern Christian tradition; God; Jesus Christ

Cistercian Order
historical perspective, 33, 204-205, 207
in relation to Merton's work, 97-100, 154
as too active for proper contemplation, 5

Climate of Monastic Prayer, The (Merton), 183-188

Cloud and the Fire, The (Merton), 66

collectivity, social, 101-102, 138, 256-270

community
vs. collectivity, 101-102
contemplative's role in building, 190-191, 256-258, 270-273
and external solitude, 107-108
inner self's relation to, 127-128, 167-168, 196-197
return of solitary to, 47, 55-56, 127, 146-147, 156-158, 257, 268
technology's subversion of, 263-264

compassion, and return of solitary to world, 47, 55-56, 127, 146-147, 156-158, 257, 268

competition, and technology's focus on separateness, 268

Concept of Anxiety, The (Kierkegaard), 192

conceptual knowledge
and active contemplation, 132
and depths of faith, 172-175
and diversion from contemplative attitude, 141-142
limitations in knowledge of self, 93, 121
vs. wisdom, 271-272
Zen way of transcendence, 212-213, 223
See also false self; language

conceptual knowledge of God
as gateway to experiential union with God, 28, 75, 80-81
kataphatic tradition, 11-15, 76, 165-166
limitations of, 11-13, 60, 75-77, 199
as shattered by contemplative experience, 33-34, 78-79

conformity, social, dangers of, 2 57-258

Conjectures of a Guilty Bystander (Merton), 7, 104, 230, 249

consciousness
Cartesian view of, 159, 180n14, 228-230
Christian transformation of, 47, 227
contemplation as heightened, 164-165
contemplative awakening of, 160-161
differentiated, 228-229
levels of, 174-175
Merton's metaphysical model, 231-234
moral, 214-215
and societal transformation, 248
Zen focus on, 212
Zen transformation of, 123-124, 161, 222-224

Constitution on the Church in the Modern World, 127, 262, 269
contemplation
  as discovery, 52-57
  as focal point for Merton's thought, 7-8
  as freedom, 57-62
  gifts of, 1-2
  as interior journey, 3-4
  as return to paradise, 8
  See also active contemplation; infused contemplation
Contemplative Prayer (Merton), 185, 186
creation
  desire and detachment concerning, 71-75, 84n14, 84n17, 94, 121, 125
  as expression of God's love, 74
  See also dualism (duality); original sin; society
creativity, technology's suppression of, 267-268
creatures of this earth, desire and detachment, 71-75, 84n14, 84n17, 94, 121, 125
cultural issues. *See* society

D

darkness
  apophatic tradition, 14-17, 60-62, 121, 211
  as heart of pure contemplative experience, 33-35, 51, 77-80, 134-135, 196, 198-199
  monastic journey into, 191-192
  and purification of self, 136
  reason's role in contemplation, 82
denial, and experience of God, 76-77
dependence on God, 9, 52-53, 95, 148-149, 197, 198
Descartes, René, 159, 180n14, 228-230, 231
desert as metaphor for monastic life, 188-190
Desert Fathers, 188-189, 195, 216

desire
  as distraction from union with God, 72-73, 121, 125
  to know God, 27-28, 38, 96-97
despair as gateway to transformation, 191-192
detachment from creatures of earth, for existential happiness, 71-75, 84n14
devotional practices. *See* active contemplation; liturgy
discernment, 73-74, 82, 97-98, 136
discipline, as necessary to contemplation, 9, 11
discovery, contemplation as, 52-57, 135-136, 166-170, 197-200, 232-233
discrimination, spiritual, 73-74, 82, 97-98, 136
Disputed Questions (Merton), 97-100
distraction. *See* diversion
disunity
  as alienation from true self/God, 7-8, 128-129
  God as separate object of faith, 77-78, 124-125, 159, 162-163, 199, 229-230
  See also dualism (duality)
diversion
  as avoidance of spiritual issues of life, 85n18
  conceptual knowledge as, 141-142
  technology as, 139-140
  tyranny of, 101-104, 106, 125
  See also false self
divinity. *See* God; Jesus Christ; real self
doctrine, religious, Christian vs. Zen, 225-226
doubt, facing of, 173
dread in contemplative experience, 138, 192, 198-202
dualism (duality)
  Cartesian, 159, 180n14, 228-230
  contemplative merging of, 62, 171-172
  and cosmic dance, 176-178
  Merton's, 6, 45, 118

and quasi- vs. pure
   contemplatives, 39
supernatural vs. natural soul
   activities, 158-159, 197, 283-
   285
See also false self; objects;
   original sin

E

Eastern Buddhist, The, 219
Eastern Christian tradition
   Desert Fathers, 188-189, 195, 216
   Greek Fathers, 130, 134-135,
      151n23, 174
Eastern religious tradition
   vs. Christian tradition, 124-125,
      130
   emphasis on unity of
      experience, 118-119
   Merton's attitude, 45-46,
      117-118, 163-164, 209-212
   See also Buddhism
Eckhart, Meister, 15, 16, 135, 215,
   228, 233
egalitarianism of contemplative
   experience, 9, 26-27, 37-38,
   50-51, 281-283
ego. *See* false self
elitism in Merton's view of
   contemplative life, 10, 38-39,
   281-283
Ellul, Jacques, 259, 261-262, 265
empirical self. *See* false self
emptiness, 139, 215-216, 232-233
enlightenment (Zen), 123-125,
   223-225, 239n25, 249
   See also unity
ethics of technology use, 265-266
everyday life, Zen focus on direct
   experience of, 223-224, 239n25
evil, 138-139, 215
existential acceptance, 195, 231-232
existential concreteness in Zen,
   223-224
existential freedom, as necessary
   for contemplation, 60
existentialism, 159, 180n11, 192,
   200-201
existential level of living, 103-104
   See also solitude

experience, direct
   in Christianity and Zen, 226-227,
      235-236
   vs. conceptual knowledge of
      God, 11, 28
   development in Merton's
      writings, 48-50, 155-156
   and Eastern contemplative
      tradition, 211-212
   vs. propositional faith, 173-174
   as source of learning, 281, 285
   Zen focus on everyday, 223-224,
      239n25
   See also apophatic tradition
explanation, contemplation
   experience as beyond, 6,
      160-161
   See also conceptual knowledge;
      language
exterior solitude, Merton's defense
   of, 107-108
external practices, most Christians'
   focus on, 27, 31
external self. *See* false self

F

face of God as experience of divine
   presence, 14
faith
   through darkness of
      contemplation, 34, 77-78
   true vs. false, 103-104, 172-175,
      227-228
fall from paradise, the (Genesis).
   See original sin
false self
   and awakening of inner self,
      135-136, 147, 166-169, 233
   and dread, 201-202
   as illusion, 54-55, 57-59, 119-120,
      228-229
   original sin, 128-129, 130
   perils of solitude, 104-106, 108
   possessions, 95-96
   and transcendence of duality,
      160-161, 215-216
   unmasking of, 34, 62, 191, 231
   worship of diversion, 101-102,
      125
fear, 31, 200-201, 281

freedom
contemplation as, 57-62
and dread, 201
from false self, 147, 167-168
to return to community, 156-157

G

Gaudium et Spes, 127, 262, 269
"General Dance, The" (Merton),
175-179
Genesis myth of the fall. *See*
original sin
Gethsemani, Abbey of Our Lady
of, 90, 211, 278
Gnosticism, 72, 84n15
goalessness in contemplative
experience, 36, 121, 267
God
contemplation as discovery of
true, 52-53, 199-200
as cosmic dance, 176-178
dependence on, 9, 52-53, 95,
148-149, 197
desire for, 27-28, 38, 96-97
as in divine Self, 17, 29, 35, 47,
52, 53-54, 55, 61, 80, 284
grace of, 2, 28-29, 50, 131-132,
136, 196, 217
Holy Spirit, 27, 28, 56, 105-106,
196
immanence vs. transcendence
of, 30
as impressing will directly on
individual, 107
as master to be feared, 31, 281
as present regardless of our
awareness, 4
as residing in emptiness, 139
as separate object of faith, 77-78,
124-125, 159, 162-163, 199,
229-230
as source of happiness, 26
as ultimate destination of
Christian contemplation,
194-195
ultimate mystery of, 11-13,
93-94, 200
Zen as unconcerned with,
221-222

See also conceptual knowledge
of God; Jesus Christ;
obedience to God; original
sin; real self
good works, as insufficient for
unity experience of God,
28-29
grace of God
in inner transformation, 28-29,
131-132, 136
and unsought nature of
contemplation, 2, 50, 131-132
Greek Fathers, 130, 134-135,
151n23, 174
Gregory of Nyssa, Saint, 15, 16
guilt, 137-139, 201

H

happiness, divine source of, 26, 70,
71-75, 84n14
heaven, contemplative role of, 50,
56, 168
helplessness as prerequisite to
union with God, 95, 198
See also dependence on God
hidden contemplatives. *See* quasi-
contemplatives
hidden self. *See* real self
history, contemplatives'
participation in, 252-255
Holy Spirit, 27, 28, 56, 105-106, 196
hope on path of contemplation,
191-192
human nature
Christ's synthesis with divine
nature, 129-130
Merton's view of, 7-8
human relationships. *See*
relationships with others
Huxley, Aldous, 209-210, 261

I

illusion
exterior life as, 3, 95-96, 170-171
false self as, 54-55, 57-59,
119-120, 228-229
infused contemplation
and active contemplation,
131-133, 203-205, 207-208n15

characteristics of, 32-40
as gift of God's grace, 28-29
Greek Fathers' view of, 134
as life-style choice, 38-39
vs. meditation, 62, 80-81, 206
universal call to, 27
See also apophatic tradition;
God; real self
Inner Experience, The (Merton),
113-118, 155
inner landscape of contemplation.
See apophatic tradition; God;
real self
inner self. *See* real self
intellect's role in contemplation,
15, 60-61, 73-75, 77
See also conceptual knowledge
intellectual vs. moral asceticism,
71-74
interior journey, contemplation as,
3-4
See also infused contemplation
interior self. *See* real self
intuition, as tool to apprehend
God, 61, 81, 162
isolation vs. solitude, 55, 127

J

Jesus Christ
as focal point for contemplation,
29-30, 189, 216, 228, 232-233
on Holy Spirit as present in us,
27, 28, 56
redemptive role of, 128-131,
151n23
John of the Cross, Saint, 35-36, 70
judgment, releasing of, 126-127,
222

K

kataphatic vs. apophatic tradition,
11-15, 76, 165-166
See also conceptual knowledge
kenotic experience, 139, 215-216,
232-233, 237, 240n33
kerygma vs. Zen path, 224-225,
240n26
knowledge
subjectivity of self-, 16-17, 121

Zen view of, 214, 224-225
See also conceptual knowledge

L

language
contemplative limitations of, 6,
12-13, 47-48, 161-162, 164-166,
200
as important to Christianity, 226
misuse of Christian, 281
and need for silence, 91-94
paradox as transcendence of, 16,
50, 137
as refuge for Western thought,
229
of Zen, 123, 222-223
La Technique (Ellul), 261-263
lay people
availability of contemplative
experience for, 9, 37-38, 50-51,
281-283
contemplative space in world,
143-145
Lazarus story, 204
liturgy
vs. contemplation, 206
deemphasis in history of
monastic life, 205
as supporter of contemplation,
29-30, 127-128, 133, 203
loneliness and solitude, 89
love
and compassionate return to
world, 47, 55-56, 127, 146-147,
156-158, 257, 268
creative action of, 4
faith as, 77
as originating in God, 74
as path to interior life with God,
15, 28, 31, 33, 36-37, 79,
134-135, 162
as product of contemplation, 6,
168
sanctity as a matter of, 38-39
social imperatives for, 198

M

masked contemplatives. *See* quasi-
contemplatives

materialism, technological
society's worship of, 265-266
meditation
as action of real self, 199
and active contemplation, 29
definitional issues, 193-197
and existentialism, 192
vs. infused contemplation, 62,
80-81, 206
purpose of, 197-200
Merton, Thomas
Asian journey, 234-238
autobiographical current in
work of, 48-50
broadening of perspective,
154-155, 163, 283
on censorship, 98-99
in defense of solitude, 107-108
discovery of social
responsibility, 156-157,
245-249, 255, 261-263
early search for solitude, 89-90
and Eastern religious tradition,
45-46, 117-118, 163-164,
209-212
elitism of, 10, 38-39, 281-283
as generalist, 6-7
on human nature, 7-8
introduction to Huxley, 210
model for consciousness,
231-234
and monastic life, 151n29,
155-156, 211, 278-280
multi-faceted nature of, 277-285
poetry of, 7, 8, 48, 271
respect for Christian tradition,
48, 69, 154-155, 163
and Suzuki, 213-221
synthesizing talent of, 220
and technology, 259
on *The Third Revolution*, 261
"Vision of Louisville," 249-252
writing issues, 4-5, 8, 25-26,
66-67, 113-118
Zen effects on, 9, 196-197,
212-213, 234-238, 249
monastic life
active vs. contemplative, 5, 6, 97,
140-143, 259
balance between solitude and
community, 190-191

and *The Climate of Monastic
Prayer*, 6, 187-188
environment for prayer, 188-193
historical perspective, 202-206
as ideal location for
contemplation, 9-10, 38, 59
meditative experience, 193-202
Merton's experience of, 151n29,
155-156, 211, 278-280
social responsibility inherent in,
246, 251, 253-254
moral dimension
of asceticism, 71-74
consciousness in Zen, 214-215
freedom for contemplation, 60
and ontological sin, 54
of technology use, 265-266
mystery
function of, 264-265
and nature of God, 11-13, 93-94,
200
mysticism, Christian, 67-68, 70, 72,
81-82, 84n15
See also Eastern religious
tradition

N

natural vs. supernatural activities
of soul, 158-159, 197, 283-285
neo-Scholastic approach, 168, 283
"New Consciousness, The"
(Merton), 219
New Seeds of Contemplation
(Merton), 153-160
Nirvana, 223-224, 239n25
"Nirvana" (Merton), 219-220
"Nishida: A Zen Philosopher"
(Merton), 219
No Man Is an Island (Merton), 100
"Notes for a Philosophy of
Solitude" (Merton), 97-100
nothingness
dependence on God, 9, 52-53,
95, 148-149, 197
helplessness, 95, 198
recognition of, 201
See also sin
novitiates, lack of societal support
for, 141-143

O

obedience to God
    Christ's complete, 232-233
    faith as beyond, 173
    and quasi-contemplative life, 29,
        31-32, 132
    in unity experience, 28, 36, 192
objects
    dissolving of, 16-17, 162-163
    inner self relationship to,
        125-126
    self as, 120
    view of God as, 77-78, 124-125,
        159, 162-163, 199, 229-230
    See also false self; subject/object
        dichotomy
original sin
    contemplative redemption in
        Christ, 128-131, 151n23
    darkness in contemplative
        experience, 33-34
    and disunity, 3, 168-169
    and false self, 54-55
    Greek Fathers' view of, 174
    as mythological source of
        alienation, 7-8
    Zen vs. Christian views of,
        214-216
outer landscape of contemplation.
    See society
outer self. *See* false self

P

pacifism of Merton, 247, 262
paradise, contemplation as return
    to, 3-4
paradox, 16, 50, 123, 137, 222-223
passive contemplation. *See* infused
    contemplation
passivity in contemplation, 36
Paul, Saint, 228, 232-233
personalism, Christian, 159-160,
    180n12, 232-233
    See also real self
personality, Christian vs. Zen
    views on, 216-217
philosophy, contemplative
    experience as transcending, 11
pleasing God, 29, 36, 192

See also obedience to God
pneuma. *See* faith
poetry, Merton's, 7, 8, 48, 271
possessions as illusion, 95-96
poverty and contemplation path,
    94-96, 106
prajna (wisdom), 215, 224, 228, 232
prayer
    affective, 29, 32, 205
    historical perspective, 204-205
    Merton's theology of, 148-149
    monastic, 193-194
    See also active contemplation;
        infused contemplation
Prayer as Worship and Experience
    (Merton), 183-184
punishment, Christian
    overemphasis on God's, 31,
        281
pure contemplatives,
    characteristics of, 32-40
    See also infused contemplation
purity of heart
    and appreciation of deeper
        meaning in life, 146
    as Desert Fathers' focus,
        189-190, 195, 216
    vs. emptiness of Zen path, 216
    and path to inner self, 122, 197

Q

quasi-contemplatives
    definitional issues, 31-32, 41n3
    methods for living in the world,
        143-145
    obedience to God, 29, 31-32, 132
    quality of prayer life for, 10
    sanctity of, 39

R

"Rain and the Rhinoceros"
    (Merton), 257-258
real self
    alienation from, 7-8, 128-129
    ancient cultures' respect for, 122,
        140
    characteristics of, 121-122
    and community, 127-128,
        167-168, 196-197

discovery of, 53-55, 135-136, 166-169, 176-179, 197-199, 232-233

and experience of God, 200

God as present in, 17, 29, 35, 47, 52, 53-54, 55, 61, 80, 284

inability to objectify, 16-17

and outer reality, 125-127

as redemption through Christ, 129-131

in solitude, 108

as unique, utterly particular, 93

Zen as path to, 123-125, 194

See also union with God; unity

reason's role in contemplation, 73-75, 77, 78, 81-83, 136

See also conceptual knowledge

redemption, contemplative sources for, 8, 128-131, 151n23

relationships with others

importance of contemplation to, 55-57

and inner self attitudes, 126-127

solitary's refusal to renounce, 105-106, 107-108

See also community; society

religious communities. *See* monastic life

responsibility

personal, 105, 138-139

social, 156-157, 245-249, 251, 253-255, 261-263

reviews of Merton's work, 45-46, 68-69, 175, 220-221

S

samsara, 223-224, 239n25

sanctity

within active contemplation, 30, 32, 133

and intelligence, 71

as a matter of love, 38-39

potential for, 27

satori (enlightenment), 123-125, 223-225, 239n25

Scholastic approaches, 159, 168, 227, 283

Scholasticism and Politics (Maritain), 166

School of the Spirit, The (Merton), 66-67

Second Vatican Council, 127, 262, 269

Seeds of Contemplation (Merton), 43-47, 69, 153

self. *See* false self; real self

self-awareness, 169-170, 228-229, 231

self-discipline, 9, 11

selfishness, 57-59, 62, 167

See also false self

self-sacrifice, 31-32

separateness in Cartesian consciousness, 159, 180n14, 228-230

See also dualism (duality); false self

Seven Storey Moutain, The (Merton), 1-2, 5-6, 246

Silence on Fire (Shannon), 12-13

silence requirement for unity experience, 11, 59, 91-94

Silent Lamp, The (Shannon), 157

simplicity of life-style, 143-145

sin

in darkness of contemplation, 33, 196

vs. guilt, 137-139

recognition of, 148, 201-202

responsibility for, 138-139

See also original sin

society

as collectivity, 101-102, 138, 256-270

contemplative's role in, 105-106, 196-197, 245-256, 261-263

imperatives for love in, 198

return of solitary to, 47, 55-56, 127, 146-147, 156-158, 257, 268

See also community; Western society

solitariness vs. solitude, 101

Solitary Life, The (Merton), 99

solitude

characteristics of true, 96-97, 167

external, 107-108

vs. isolation, 55, 127

Merton's early search for, 89-90

as necessary to contemplation, 9, 36, 59, 81, 156-157

perils of, 104-106, 108
and publication of *Disputed Questions*, 97-100
rejection of diversion, 101-104
and silence, 91-94
vs. social conformity, 258
social witness from, 143-144, 255-256
in urban life, 59-60
See also monastic life
Sower and seed parable, 44
"Study of Zen, The" (Merton), 219
subjectivity, existential, 16-17, 40, 121, 162
subject/object dichotomy, dissolving of, 16-17, 162-163, 172, 199-200, 228-229, 231, 283-284
subjects, inner self's relation to, 119, 126-127
suffering as divine lesson, 36
Sufism, 238n6
Summa Theologiae (Aquinas), 71
Sunday as day of contemplation, 144-145
sunyata, 221-222, 233
superconscious, the, 174, 222
superficiality of life, contemplation as escape from, 2-3
See also false self
supernatural vs. natural activities of soul, 158-159, 197, 283-284
surface Christians, 27, 31
See also false self
Suzuki, Daisetz T., 9, 213-221

T

Tears of the Blind Lions, The (Merton), 8
Technological Society, The (Ellul), 262-263
technology, double-edged sword of, 139-140, 141, 258-270, 272
Temple of Understanding Conference, 235-236, 240n36, 279
Teresa of Avila, Saint, 142-143
Thomas Merton's Dark Path (Shannon), 3, 245, 246

Thoughts in Solitude (Merton), 90-91
transcendence vs. immanence of God, 30
See also unity
"Transcendent Experience" (Merton), 219
Triple Revolution, The, 260-261
true self. *See* real self

U

unbelievers, Merton's views, 67
uncertainty. *See* anxiety (dread); darkness; faith
unconscious, the, 174
unified human person, 119, 141-143
union with God
  conceptual knowledge as gateway to, 28, 75, 80-81
  desire as distraction from, 72-73, 121, 125
  good works as insufficient for, 28-29
  helplessness as prerequisite for, 95, 198
  progress of contemplation toward, 35-36
uniqueness of individual person, 93-94, 124
unity
  Christian and Zen traditions, 118-119, 229, 236, 241n41
  contemplation as recovery of, 8, 216
  contemplative as example to community, 145-147, 156-157
  with humanity, 249, 251-252, 257, 271, 280
  inner self's view of reality as, 126
  and nature of contemplative experience, 10-11
  obedience to God as prerequisite for, 28, 36, 192
  in silence, 11, 59, 91-94
  See also apophatic tradition
unknowing
  and experience of God, 15, 76-77, 79-80, 134-135, 165
  in Zen experience, 222

V

"Vision of Louisville," 249-252
vocal prayer, 29, 32
Void, the (Zen), 221-222
Vow of Conversation, A (Merton),
    277-278

W

Walsh, Daniel, 115-116, 160
Ways and Means (Huxley), 2, 210
Western society
    approach to contemplation,
        158-159, 163
    as collectivity, 101-102, 122,
        139-140
    compartmentalization of life,
        118-119
    ego-driven nature of, 123
    God as object, 77-78, 124-125,
        159, 162-163, 199, 229-230
    separation of theology from
        experience, 227
    See also Christian tradition
What Is Contemplation? (Merton),
    25-26, 113-115
will, human, 73-75, 84n14
wisdom
    vs. conceptual knowledge,
        271-272
    prajna, 215, 228, 232
    as source for building
        community, 270-273
Wisdom of the Desert, The (Merton),
    213-214
withdrawal from the world. *See*
    monastic life; solitude
words. *See* language
workers, removal from meaningful
    production, 259, 267-268
Wu, John C., 97, 219

Y

Yaryan, Willie, 229-230

Z

Zen, etymology of, 239n21
Zen and the Birds of Appetite
    (Merton), 219-221
"Zen in Japanese Art" (Merton),
    220
Zen path
    basic attitudes, 221-222
    and Christian tradition, 194-195,
        213-221, 224-236, 240n26,
        241n41, 255
    and enlightenment, 123-125,
        223-225, 239n25
    origins of, 180n13
    personal effect on Merton, 9,
        196-197, 212-213, 234-238, 249
    Suzuki/Merton dialogue,
        213-221
    as transformation of
        consciousness, 123-124, 161,
        222-224
    unteachability of, 160